WENDELL PHILLIPS

Wendell Phillips

Wendell Phillips

Orator and Agitator

By
LORENZO SEARS

Benjamin Blom
New York

8 - 22 - 68

First published New York 1909
Reissued 1967 by
Benjamin Blom, Inc. New York 10452
L.C.Cat.Card No. 67-13340

TO

RALPH CURTIS RINGWALT, ESQUIRE,

AT WHOSE SUGGESTION THIS BOOK WAS WRITTEN

" Public sentiment is everything. With public sentiment nothing can fail; without it nothing can succeed. Consequently, he who moulds public sentiment goes deeper than he who enacts statutes or pronounces decisions. He makes statutes and decisions possible or impossible to be executed."
—ABRAHAM LINCOLN.

"Agitation is the marshalling of a nation's conscience to mould its laws."
SIR ROBERT PEEL.

"An Agitator's purpose is to throw the gravest questions upon the conscience and intellect of the masses, because they are the ultimate governors in a republic."
—WENDELL PHILLIPS.

PREFACE

WENDELL PHILLIPS was so closely identified with the most important episode of American history in the last century that his life must be considered largely in connection with it and its consequences. Known as the anti-slavery agitation, it assumed as one of its early phases the demand for immediate and unconditional abolition. To this cause Phillips gave his best years as the preacher of a crusade against an institution, at first national and later sectional, which finally came to be regarded as bad anywhere. Agitation of a disputed question was the method, untrammeled speech before the people the means, and superlative eloquence the manner of his warfare. In his later years he became the champion of other causes.

To do him and his work justice, both should be contemplated from the present as the day of an accomplished purpose which was not generally approved in his own time nor correctly estimated. Yet, to be just to his contemporaries, it should be borne in mind that the progress of reforms is slow and the appreciation of them a gradual growth. The difference between him and most men of his generation was in his early apprehension of justice, humanity, and national consistency in a country calling itself free. The interest of his biography gathers around this difference, as well as around the later acceptance and endorsement of his main

purpose by a large part of the nation.   In both periods he
should be accorded a fair presentation of convictions whose
sincerity was equalled by their courageous and uncompromising utterance in the face of sufficient antagonism to
make his persistence heroic.

Aside from his interest to one and another as a reformer,
his oratory is of exceptional value to all who are interested
in the art of public speaking.   Two volumes have been
published, one with his own endorsement, giving all that type
can preserve of some fifty examples of his speeches, lectures,
and addresses.   Besides these there are hundreds more
printed in two weekly journals throughout a period of forty
years, which have been read in order to trace the course of
his thought on national, sectional, and other questions of
importance.   The drift of his comment is given in such
abridgments and extracts as the limits and design of this
book permit, together with examples of his oratory on widely
differing occasions.   To those who desire further acquaintance with entire addresses the volumes mentioned and files
of the *Liberator* and *Anti-Slavery Standard* afford ample
opportunity.

Besides the privilege of listening to him on several occasions
and reading information and comment in contemporary sheets
by friend and foe, the author has found particulars of home
life in the early biographies of Austin and Martyn, to which
have been added reminiscences and letters by some who knew
him well.   Grateful acknowledgments are especially due to
Colonel T. W. Higginson, Messrs. Frank B. Sanborn, Francis
J. Garrison, William I. Bowditch, John P. Reynolds, Jr.,
Edward J. Carpenter, Mrs. Julia G. Blagden, and to others
who have done what they could to add to memorials which

are remarkably few of a man who was oftener before the
people and for a longer period than any other public speaker
of his generation.   L. S.

Providence, R. I.,
   Memorial Day, 1909.

CONTENTS

CONTENTS

PAGE

CHAPTER XIX.   REFLECTIONS ON GOVERNMENT
    POLICY   241

The proclamation by the people — Northern allies of the South —
Negro soldiers — Toussaint l'Ouverture — A temperance lecture —
The state of the country — Hopeful vigilance — The press on abolitionism — Strictures on the Government — English attitude — Sudden gains to the cause — Looking toward reconstruction — Dissolution of Massachusetts Anti-slavery Society — An historic fortnight — Tribute to Lincoln — Work of abolitionists not ended —
Total abolition decreed.

CHAPTER XX.   CONTINUING THE CONTEST   .   . 261

Phillips as an editor — Address to Boston schools — Freedmen's
rights disregarded — Phillips endorsed by Congressmen — Refusal
of nomination to Congress — A lecture trip — Attacks Andrew Johnson — Doubt of Grant — Vital questions — Creating public opinion.

CHAPTER XXI.   RECONSTRUCTION AND OTHER ISSUES   273

On release of Jefferson Davis — Criticism of Grant and Congress —
Motives in criticizing men and parties — Abolition success by defeats
— Religion and social science — Rights of coloured citizens — Negro
suffrage — Labour question discussed — Backward movement —
On Fifteenth Amendment—American Anti-slavery Society disbanded.

CHAPTER XXII.   NEW CAUSES AND OLD   .   .   . 290

Thirty-three years of service continued. — Intemperance taken up —
Christianity and Social Science — Nomination for Governor — Pro-
hibition and Coöperation — Support of General Butler — A coloured
Senator — Favours Republican party — Froude and Phillips on
Ireland — Questions of finance — Tribute to O'Connell — Rescue
of Old South Church — Heroic spirit.

CHAPTER XXIII.   LAST YEARS AND LABOURS   .   . 307

Nomination to Congress again proposed — Eulogy of Garrison —
Religious belief — On liquor trade and Irish question — Oration at
Harvard — Courage to the last — Lecturing on labour and capital
— Address in Old South Church — Illness and death — Honoured
by thousands.

CHAPTER XXIV.   THE SUBSTANCE OF PHILLIPS'S
    ORATORY   318

Value of brief citations — As a lecturer — An exordium — Argumentative discourse —Address expository — Judicial argument—Abolition
speeches — Denunciation — Defensive and aggressive speech —
Eulogy — Academic orations — Dramatic features of his eloquence.

WENDELL PHILLIPS

WENDELL PHILLIPS

I

CHILDHOOD AND SCHOOL YEARS

(1811–1834)

O N MANY accounts it was pleasant and profitable to be
a Boston boy in the early years of the nineteenth
century. Some will say that it is better to be one at the
beginning of the twentieth; but happiness does not necessarily increase with the progress of decades. Advantages of
several kinds are not augmented by steam heat, electric
lights, and gasolene locomotion. Nature and art, thought
and affection have not essentially changed in a hundred years,
and the sources of material prosperity and of intellectual
eminence lie now, as they did then, in natural gifts and
abilities employed in wise ways. Many things, too, that
contribute to a wholesome satisfaction with life were common
a century ago in the Bay City. There were accumulations
of wealth with an unostentatious luxury, and a commercial
life accompanied by intellectual habits, with Long Wharf
on one side and Harvard College on the other, Old South
Church and Faneuil Hall standing between as the symbols of
religion and liberty.

By 1810, 33,000 inhabitants were living on the peninsula
over which William Blackstone had solitary domain when,
in 1630, he invited John Winthrop and associates to come
from Charlestown and taste his spring water, then selling

out to them and removing toward the Narragansett country. But the purchasers throve in their generations, and after one hundred and eighty years' trade in fish and timber, rum and furs, with an occasional cargo of Negroes — under general protest — comfortable fortunes were amassed in many families. Of these the Phillips family was one of the most prosperous.

The Reverend George Phillips, a graduate of Cambridge University and rector of Boxted, Essex, falling into disagreement with some of his parishioners about conformity to the ritual of the national Church, joined Winthrop's company and landed in Salem in June, 1630. For fourteen years he was pastor of the church at Watertown when that village was as large as Boston then was. His son was the minister at Rowley. Then a goldsmith is found in the succession, although a younger brother entered the ministry. Next, two merchants follow, and then a lawyer appears who, by 1809, had risen through minor offices to the dignity of judgeship in the Court of Common Pleas. Two years later his fifth son, Wendell, was born, November 29, 1811, who was to uphold the family name through a good part of the century, but not after the manner of his forefathers. They had filled prominent positions in the standing order of the Puritan Church and State, in commercial affairs, and in social life. He was to distinguish himself and the family name outside these spheres of influence.

Into this inheritance of a good name, ample wealth, and social standing came the child Wendell, who early began to give promise of the man. Those who trace personal qualities and abilities back through a long line of distinguished ancestors can find enough to account for a great deal that is to appear if they look over the records, clerical, legal, military, and civil of the "Phillips Genealogies." There were ministers and deacons, judges and captains, legislators and governors; but they were also the progenitors of the five brothers and three sisters of this eighth child in a family of nine, whose distinction is that Wendell was one of them. And if he was the highly favoured legatee, may it not be truly said that he repaid his inheritances in full and even, according to Shinto doctrine, ennobled his honourable ancestry by retroactive and augmented distinction? In any case, this was sufficient to warrant the above brief summary of ancestral achievement. It is more to the present purpose to note influences that were direct and immediate.[1]

A century ago the family was the first school and parents the earliest teachers. From his father this boy heard wise counsels of self-dependence, and from a Bible-reading mother lessons of steadfastness to righteousness which became principles of conduct in after life. Instead of the amusement by which instruction is now made palatable in kindergartens, sundry boys of that time in the neighbourhood of the Phillips mansion, at the lower corner of Beacon and Walnut Streets, gathered in the garret of Lothrop Motley's home, and, arraying themselves in the cast-off costumes of other days — "cloaks, doublets, and plumed hats, as heroes and bandits, enacted more or less impromptu melodramas." To this

---

[1] The name, Wendell, was the family name of his grandmother, Margaret, daughter of Hon. Jacob Wendell, merchant, and member of the Governor's Council. She became the wife of William Phillips in 1761. Their only son, John, father of Wendell, graduated from Andover and Harvard, became the first public "prosecutor" of the Municipal Court on its establishment in 1800, representative to the General Court in 1803, and Senator for the rest of his life. On the incorporation of the City of Boston in 1822 he was chosen its first Mayor. He died before the close of his term of office in 1823. The children of John and Salley (Walley) Phillips were: 1. Thomas Walley, b. Jan. 16, 1797; d. 1859. 2. Sarah Hurd, b. April 24, 1799; d. 1837. 3. Samuel, b. 1801; d. 1817, a member of the Class of 1820, Harvard. 4. Margaret, b. Nov. 29, 1802. 5. Miriam. 6. John Charles, b. Nov. 15, 1807; d. 1878. 7. George William, b. Jan. 3, 1810; d. 1880. 8. Wendell, b. Nov. 29, 1811; d. Feb. 2, 1884. 9. Grenville Tudor, b. Aug. 14, 1816; d. 1863.

entertainment the lad Phillips added private exercise at home in the direction of his personal bent, arranging chairs for auditors and discoursing to them at a length worthy of his clerical forebears in the Puritan age. When asked if he did not tire of it, he answered, "No; but it is pretty hard on the chairs," an indication that ancestral rigours had softened since Samuel Sewall tried to equal his contemporaries in his single sermon of two and a half hours. Thus the future orator began to educate himself, without a priggish anticipation of his destiny, but simply because it was a natural gift whose exercise was play. Nor, in subsequent years, did time dispel this morning dew of oratorical promise. Even in boyhood, his friend Thomas Appleton said, "Wendell's voice was a very pleasant one to listen to, and his gestures as graceful as could be. He was a fine, manly little fellow, and I was very proud of him as a playmate."

The Boston Latin School, which he entered in his eleventh year, was his first public educator. His father had prepared for college at Andover, where he had been sent to live with an uncle whose predecessors had founded Phillips Academy there and another at Exeter, N. H. This, however, was not a sufficient reason to send the son from home and away from the school which had been one of the features of the city since Ezekiel Cheever from London established it in 1670, having already taught in New Haven, Ipswich, and Charlestown, thirty-two years in all. Cheever was a veteran of fifty-six when all the dignitaries of the town united in calling him to take charge of a hundred and fifty boys, a task in which he won distinction for thirty-eight years, passing off the academic platform at the age of ninety-four, being buried from his schoolhouse where he had trained the most eminent citizens of an entire generation; "a skilful, painful, and faithful schoolmaster," as Cotton Mather said of him in his funeral discourse. After his demise no successor made his place good until Mr. B. A. Gould came in 1816. When young Phillips entered the school Gould had been master six years. Although an English department had been started in 1821, instruction was chiefly in Latin and Greek, which since the revival of learning had formed the basis of a liberal education, and so far as this young pupil was concerned, was admirably adapted to give him that command of language for which he became noted.

His oratorical bent became at once apparent. In a land governed by town meetings and legislatures and educated by pulpit, forum, and platform, the school would be a failure that did not teach boys to declaim. Doubtless it is unnatural to assume the position of great orators even for a few moments, and the sense of incongruity is often the cause of much embarrassment, but much is learned by imitation. At any rate, declamation days do not appear to have been dreaded by the boy Wendell, and it is on record that they were anticipated with pleasure by his companions when he was to speak. A fellow student said: "What first led me to observe him and fixed him in my memory was his elocution; and I soon came to look forward to declamation day with interest, mainly on his account; though many were admirable speakers." Of his appearance it is remarked that he was a finely formed boy, vigorous and tall for his age, and, in connection with his friend Motley, "both ranked high among their fellows on account of their beauty, elegant manners, and social position."

Many who have been schoolboys will recall the
leading declaimer of their platform and the admiration
with which they heard him recite Patrick Henry's "Call
to Arms," or Webster's "Appeal for the Union," or as
a triumphant achievement, Cicero's "Arraignment of
Catiline" in the original Latin. Years afterward they
have asked what became of the juvenile orator and
the great promise of his boyish eloquence. Rarely he
attained distinction; oftener mediocrity or nothing. Not
necessarily, as the career of Phillips showed. The root
of the matter was in him, and his marvellous endowment increased with the years in symmetry, beauty, and
irresistible power.

It was next to inevitable, after five years at the Latin
School, and from his antecedents, that the youth, now
nearly sixteen, should enter Harvard College. In 1827
the Rev. Dr. John T. Kirkland was President, to be suc-
ceeded in two years by the Hon. Josiah Quincy, with whose
son, Edmund, though older than himself, Phillips formed
a friendship which was to last through a lifetime. Lothrop
Motley had returned from the historian Bancroft's Round
Hill School, at Northampton, to enter as the youngest member
of the class, which he would have led had he shown the
diligence in study that afterward made him the historian of
the Dutch Republic. Charles Sumner was in the next
class above, a hermit student taking himself seriously,
and later to be associated with Phillips in a friendly way.
Oliver Wendell Holmes, in the next class, was to be its poet
for thirty years. Of the faculty, Edward T. Channing
was professor of rhetoric and oratory, important studies
to the future orator, and of still greater value under the

direction of an instructor whose fitness for his work through thirty-two years was exceptional and memorable, maintaining, as he did, high standards of purity and elegance in composition and delivery, and also directing the reading and influencing the literary taste of an entire generation of students. George Ticknor was professor of modern languages and belles-lettres, dispensing the treasures which he had gathered in a five years' residence abroad and by acquaintance with leading authors of Europe. Other distinguished scholars occupied chairs in their several departments; and the personal factor was greater in their relations to pupils than is now possible with larger classes. The class of 1831 numbered only sixty-five at graduation, and there had been but one larger class.

It was with such advantages as these, belonging to an earlier time, that a pupil younger than the present average entered college. Although multiplied courses were not then offered to students to their distraction or delight, a good basis was furnished for an education which was to be continued beyond its collegiate beginnings. Four walls were begun, most often for a plain structure at least, but there were not, as now, a dozen outlying blocks placed on which temple columns can never be reared in a single lifetime. Nor was much time wasted on fragments of ornamentation and decoration to the damage of the essential substructure. Neither did some Simeon Stylites build a solitary pillar on whose top he should expound a specialty for the rest of his days. Minds, nevertheless, were as strong and active then as now, and if they ran in fewer channels at once these were likely to be deeper in consequence, with fewer shallows of mental dissipation. The sciences of mind and of ethics, of nature and of human nature, and as the vehicle of conveying thought about these and related themes the continual study of language, constituted the basic education of that day, conducted on a few broad and definite lines. Yet there was a margin for personal aptitudes and preferences. Phillips used to say that his own were for history and mechanics, the latter possibly as a useful diversion.

In history he gave during one year all the time he could spare to the study of the English Revolution of 1640, reading memoirs, speeches, novels, and plays that could illustrate Clarendon and other writers. Another year was devoted to biographies and memoirs of George III.'s reign and the years of our war for independence. Dutch history also had great interest for him as the story of a republic. Among his heroes were Cromwell, Vane, Pym, and Raleigh in England; in America, Jay, Franklin, Samuel Adams, and Eli Whitney. If he could have foreseen his own need of illustrative material in the future he could not have chosen better examples. In literature his favourites were Tacitus and Juvenal, Rochefoucauld, Pascal, Tocqueville, Guizot, and Victor Hugo; in English, Ben Jonson, Jeremy Taylor, Massinger, Milton, Southey, Lamb, Disraeli the elder, and Horace Walpole. Richardson and Scott were his favourite earlier English novelists. It was characteristic of the later advocate of the mentally unappreciated sex that he should consider Elizabeth Barrett Browning the first of modern poets, and Charlotte Brontë and George Eliot profounder writers than Dickens and Thackeray. But this was long after his college days. Taking these together, he read widely outside the academic curriculum. Nor did he neglect its routine, ranking high

in his class, an all-round student with predilections for history
and natural science.[1]

With regard to anticipation of his later distinction as an
orator the gist of testimony is that it manifested itself in
debate rather than orations, as would naturally happen where
these were less frequent than discussion. Still, a classmate
wrote that "there was always the same remarkable power of
eloquence, whether in extempore debate or studied declamation. It was a great treat to hear him declaim as a college
exercise. He was always studying remarkable passages as
an exercise in composition and to secure the most expressive
forms of language."[2] In addition, he took pains to learn by
example from such speakers as Harrison Gray Otis and
Edward Everett, Daniel Webster and Henry Clay, the last
of whom he must have heard somewhere in the North, else
he could not have compared the voices of the two great orators
as he did, saying that Clay's was musical and Webster's full
of strength, his statement argument, and his eloquence sublime — on a great occasion. At other times he thought him
ponderous or even dull. It took a crisis to rouse him —
then he was sublime.[3]

In view of the large and wise use Phillips made of academic
opportunities, matters of minor employment sink into their
proper insignificance. Athletics had not taken their present
conspicuous place among student activities; at least they were

---

[1]Based upon the testimony of his roommate, Rev. John Tappen Pierce, of Illinois.
Mr. Roscoe Conkling Bruce in the Harvard *Illustrated Magazine*, April, 1901, quotes one
of Phillips's college friends as saying that he "sauntered and gently studied; learned easily
and rapidly; was deeply interested in history and chemistry; had a passion for mathe-
matics and attained a standing moderately high; was interested in debating more than
oratory and was the easy master of the college platform."
[2]Rev. Dr. Morrison, sometime editor of the *Unitarian Review*.
[3]F. B. Sanborn's "Recollections of Wendell Phillips" (MS.) in Martyn's "Life," p. 48.
Phillips's admiration for Webster's gifts should be borne in mind later when that statesman's
political course is condemned by him.

not counted among the motives for entering college. Yet there were boats on the Charles, saddles, boxing gloves, and fencing foils — ancient and honourable devices for manly sport; having their values in a rough-and-tumble world in which sudden difficulties sometimes start up to embarrass the unready. In these particulars it is possible that the student of seventy-five years ago may have had an advantage over the abnormally developed specialist of the present time. In any case, it is told of Phillips that as he was known in school as a manly fellow of fine physique, a contrast to some of the prim boys who feared to risk traditional dignity in play, so in college "he was a lover of outdoor sports and helped others to enjoy them, continuing his boating, boxing, fencing, and horse riding, becoming an expert in these manly accomplishments." For the last three he had special fondness.[1]

Socially he belonged to the patrician class, and according to common assent felt his responsibility to maintain the respectability of his birth and breeding. But he had no scorn for democracy if it was not tainted with vulgarity, envy, and bad manners. In the inevitable divisions of college society a small feud was at one time developed, through which he failed of an election to the captaincy of the Harvard Washington Corps, a student from the South being the successful compromise candidate. Nevertheless, though frequent leadership of the aristocracy was forced upon him, he was admired and loved by those who knew him best as an open-hearted, generous, and chivalrous fellow. His own

---

[1]Martyn, on the "united testimony of his classmates," adds, "Life," p. 35: "He was a champion boxer and marksman, fencer, oarsman, and horseman in a day when Boston discouraged athletics; his passion was for horses, and later he was a personal friend of Rarey, the horse tamer." By his own account he sometimes practised shooting at a mark in mature years when on vacations. His diversions belong to a modern age of chivalry, and his spirit in them was agreeable to it.

appreciation of these qualities in Southern students, and the admiration he received from them in turn as their ardent champion, were recalled in later years when he became a strong opponent of their political principles.

To these qualities of mind, body, and disposition it is natural to ask what moral and religious elements were added to complete his early character. Theodore Weld, in his "Eulogy of Wendell Phillips," states that he "had been the subject of a religious revival before entering college," and Martyn asserts that Phillips not long before his death answered a friend's inquiry to the effect that when he was fourteen, after hearing a sermon of Dr. Lyman Beecher's, he consecrated himself to God and his service. In college, Dr. Buckingham, class secretary, wrote:

The excitement of the revival gradually passed off — that is, in a few years. But his conversion for quite a while made a deep impression on his companions, awakening their reverence (the word is not too strong) for this religious boy. I remember well his appearance of deep devoutness in the chapel services. I suppose he needed no conversion from the moral education his mother had given him; but he probably obtained clearer ideas of duty and consecration from the instruction he received and the excitement through which he passed, and became, for the most part, fixed in some ideas of a great, important life. At any rate, his conversion exercised no narrowing influences over him, nor did it make him uninterested in people's welfare in the present life, nor render his theology superior to philanthropy. I have not learned that he ever changed his theological opinions. At one time, in his middle life, he renounced the church as at present constituted or conducted [on account of its position on the slavery question], but kept his practical faith and belief in prayer as well as in works of beneficence.

As fragmentary lines of record and tradition are traced
they point to what may fairly be regarded as an ideal example of academic life, labour, and character. Here
was a young man whose birth and antecedents entailed
obligations to noble conduct. If he was naturally sensible
of his inheritances, he was more heedful of consequent
responsibilities than vain of his environment. If he did
not stoop to efface inborn distinction for the sake of cheap
popularity, he never failed to recognize the essential equality
of man with man, and was always ready with a good word
for the minority. Generations of intelligence and right
living culminated in a noble manhood. His manner was
full of grace, his mind of light, his soul of purity. Revered
by his classmates, he was their recognized leader and
spokesman when a common sentiment was to be voiced.
His conversation was replete with information and thought,
seasoned with humour and spiced with wit. His morality
was unblurred; his religion was based upon the Bible
which lay on his study table and was reverenced as a
mother's gift. Of his special capacity for public speech
he made the most without dwarfing other endowments.
Therefore, if one were to search the records of collegiate
life for an example of well-rounded attainment, for a gentleman, for a scholar who was neither a pedant nor a recluse,
a princely man among his fellows, of vigorous body, right
mind, and wholesome soul, it would be hard to find one
who comes so near a symmetrical assemblage of graces
and excellences as Wendell Phillips of the Harvard Class
of 1831.

The day of graduation divides boyhood from manhood.
To be sure, some continue their education in professional

or graduate schools, which do not appear to be greatly diverse from academic departments in universities; but those who have been in both know the difference, and that college years end on Commencement Day, which, by a singular inversion of meaning ever since the day was set back into the summer from autumn, marks the end instead of the beginning of the academic year. Nothing quite like the college years again comes into the student's life. They remain only as a fading memory, to be revived with less and less distinctness as decreasing numbers return to tell how the world and time are treating them and to renew old companionships for a day.

So, when the graduate went the destined way of his set, to the Harvard Law School, he began the life-work that seemed decreed, the study and practice of the law. The circumstance that the first part of his preparation was in a professional school did not make the learning of legal principles to differ radically from subsequent acquisition in a friend's office in Lowell, or, later, in his own in Boston. He had the eminent jurist, Judge Story, for an instructor, in whose method daily recitation was a prominent feature; and an excellent one it was, making study less a matter of pre-examination stuffing than it is under a system of lectures alone.

In these three years, the law student absorbed the customary amount of legal lore from books, and something more if not better from the profound learning and strong personality of his preceptors. In a school numbering at that time only forty pupils personal relations between the dozen or so students in each class and their instructors was intimate and profitable; and, at the end of three years, knowledge of the rudimentary principles of law should have been correspondingly complete. As might be expected from previous indications, Phillips looked upon statutes and codes as an embodiment and interpretation of human justice, and found in the larger principles of law more satisfying features than in its minute technicalities. It is possible that at this stage of study he sometimes had doubts about his future devotion to professional routine beyond the demands of its inevitable obligations. Indeed, to many of the young men of his neighbourhood and time and since, the law, like teaching, afforded an opportunity to discover if their real calling were waiting in the shadow or perhaps approaching from some unknown quarter. Motley, after two years study in Germany, took to reading law until he could determine what branch of history he would follow. Parkman did the same before he settled down to writing the story of France in America. Ticknor and Longfellow and Lowell combined teaching and writing until they devoted themselves to the more congenial labours of literature alone. It would be difficult to enumerate all those who have found a little law-study the lobby to political activity and success.

At this time, however, Phillips saw nothing beyond the opportunities which spare hours in professional schools afford for marginal pursuits, social, industrial, or special. He did not neglect athletics, although in that day they were not, as now, a "business with assets," which graduates sometimes find more remunerative to pursue than the law, the ministry, or medicine, or especially teaching. Nor did he discontinue his miscellaneous reading, but made it wider and deeper as time, opportunity, and broader vision inclined him to add to treasures already amassed. There was, doubtless, a frequent wavering between these attractive studies and the pages of Coke and Blackstone, although the latter were not neglected. Still, he could not have been unmindful of the part which jury trials take in an advocate's labours, and the difficult and uncertain elements which they precipitate into professional success. He also knew that the lay mind, when it supposes itself an impartial judge of evidence, and sometimes of what the law ought to be, is extremely liable to be insensibly warped by an historical instance which it takes to be parallel or even an anecdote which seems to be illustrative, and is, at least, more easily apprehended than legal abstractions or doubtful testimony. Accordingly, he had good reasons in the midst of professional study to lay in store whatever might be useful in forensic argument or appeal.

Yet he did not find the drudgery of legal study burdensome, nor its details uninteresting. Charles Sumner and Judge Thomas Hopkinson are quoted as testifying to his loyalty to whatever belongs to the profession. As he looked about him, he saw it honoured by illustrious names and crowned with honour from an historic past and with renown from its greater lights. After the three conventional years of instruction and study, he was admitted to the Suffolk Bar with as fair a future before him as could be presented to a young man with everything in his favour except the advantage of a place in his father's office and succession to his practice — made impossible in his case by his father's death just before the son entered college. A partnership had been offered him by his classmate Hopkinson, who had started in Lowell, but he preferred to take his chances in Boston, where he opened an office and entered upon that period of waiting which affords so much time for reading and meditation. This was more and more disturbed by applications to draw a contract or a will or by some case in court. He measured his success by the remark made later, "In those two opening years I paid all my expenses, and few do it now." Friends endorse his statements and add their own to the effect that both in his office and in court his business was increasing and his practice as remunerative as a young lawyer could reasonably expect. The brook is satisfied if it has a fair chance to become a river.

II

THE CAUSE

SO FAR, what had come to the young man of twenty-two was as inevitable as consequent from antecedent. He was walking in the steps his fathers trod, and there was every indication that he would follow the customary lines of social and civil, professional and political activity, with fair prospects of preferment. A moderate radicalism even was not fatal to success in a province which had broken with traditions in government and religion, and independents were generally sure of a respectable following.

But in the early 'thirties a movement was under way which was so unpopular that its promoters might as well have been paroled convicts. To understand its meaning and purpose a few well known conditions may be recalled. They are the key to Wendell Phillips's career.

It is not necessary to detail minutely how human bondage, the old habit of the nations, was fixed upon the new world by the greed of Spaniards, and later by Dutch traders at Jamestown in the year of the Pilgrim landing at Plymouth, until by 1776 some thirty thousand slaves had been landed in the thirteen colonies, and as many more had been born into servitude. The apparent inconsistency with the Declaration of Independence and Equal Rights made at this time was in a fair way of removal when the invention of the cotton gin marvellously

increased the profits of slave labour, smothering the Southern conscience beneath a fleecy cloud, while the North gradually dispensed with a profitless service.   Yet there were those,
both in the North and the South, who did not forget the early
sentiment of the nation's founders against slavery, and who
did not let wholly die the many anti-slavery societies that had
sprung up.   Organized opposition, however, had run low
through Southern antagonism to it, and Northern acquies-
ence grew apace, for commercial and political reasons, until
at the end of the first third of the last century he who spoke
openly against the domestic institution was regarded as a
fanatical disturber of national peace and an enemy of the
Union and a violator of the Constitution.   Upon the passage
of the Missouri Compromise, 1820, the two sections of the
country had tacitly consented to a discreet silence after an
outbreak that was ominous.   This silence was well observed
throughout a hushed decade, save for an unheeded voice here
and there like Lundy's, a peripatetic printer who published
his *Genius of Universal Emancipation*, read chiefly by
Quakers.

Then William Lloyd Garrison, a Massachusetts printer,
who had been associated with Lundy in Baltimore, returned to
Boston and on the 1st of January, 1831, began to issue a little
sheet, nine by fourteen inches, called *The Liberator*, demanding
immediate emancipation of all slaves.   Gradual emancipation had been talked of by some, and colonization in Liberia
had commended itself to Southerners as a good project
for getting free Negroes out of communication with the
enslaved.   Instead of these and similar schemes, this man
in a garret, without a dollar or a single subscriber or a dozen
sympathizers with his undertaking, set up and struck off

with his own hands sheets that were considered incendiary. Like burning flakes borne on the winds they fell in remote Western towns and as far south as the Gulf. Where they lighted other flames were kindled, a few of philanthropy and more of rage. New England for the most part stamped upon the inflammatory paper. In South Carolina a reward of $1,500 was offered for the conviction of any white person circulating it, and the Georgia Legislature promised $5,000 for the arrest and conviction of the publisher. Hostile enactments and threatening letters followed thick and fast in the South and deprecatory appeals in the North. The mails were illegally closed in slave states to the circulation of the *Liberator*, as if it were made of gun cotton. Never was a publication cursed with such maledictions or an editor assured of such a profusion of hemp if he could be drawn southward. An attempt to kidnap him was feared, not without some reason. To all threats, whether reeking with profanity or couched in legal phrases, Garrison replied: " I will not retreat a single inch, and I will be heard. Tell a man whose house is on fire to give a moderate alarm . . .   but urge me not to use moderation in a cause like the present."

Immediate emancipation was, then, the phase which antislavery opinion assumed under his leadership. It has been said that the immediate element was derived from the revival preaching of the time, demanding instantaneous surrender of the heart to God. Be this as it may, the doctrine was turned upon ministers and churches inconveniently when they tried to show the abolitionist how much better gradual emancipation would be, accompanied by deportation to Africa. Foreign missions received a new impulse in that direction, while at home bishops, college presidents, and professors of theology thumbed their Bibles to find sanctions for the patriarchal institution. Meantime the lone editor reiterated his demand in the weekly missive, and in speaking whenever a few dared to listen.

It was the day of organizing societies and holding conventions. Toward the close of the year 1831 fifteen men got together in the office of Samuel E. Sewall, Esq., a descendant of the Colonial judge and diarizer who, 131 years before, wrote the first American anti-slavery tract, "The Selling of Joseph." On the 6th of January, 1832, the New England Anti-Slavery Society was organized by a dozen men, of whom it was said that not more than one or two could have put a hundred dollars into the treasury without bankrupting themselves. Great amusement was afforded by these "nobodies" undertaking to abolish a system recognized by the Constitution, rooted in the interests of half the nation and in the prejudices and fears of the other half; but the little band of so-called fanatics quoted a saying about the slighting of the wise and noble in a certain reform, and with enthusiasm entered upon a task which the least sanguine thought would be accomplished in ten years. With added supporters, agitation spread, until the entire country began to be conscious that a struggle was impending. The new society published tracts, sent out lecturers, and appealed to the churches — generally in vain. The *Emancipator* and the *Evangelist* were established in New York, a signal for the secular and religious press to denounce the movement and malign its supporters. In time came the announcement that on the 1st of August, 1834, Great Britain had emancipated 800,000 slaves in the West Indies. This gave some respectability

to emancipation here, but no great impulse. Instead,
loyalty to the Union, which was in danger from extremists
in the North and South, led by Garrison and Calhoun, and
fear of consequent derangement of business and interruption of prosperity made head against the growing heresy.
Opposition ran so high that in default of available statutes
against unlicensed printing and unaccustomed speech,
mob law appeared to be the only recourse.

It was natural that this should first fall upon the leader
of the abolition movement. His publications had been
taken from Southern post offices and burned — a sort of
lynching by proxy, which was servilely endorsed by public
meetings in the North, apologizing for the aggressive
impertinence of a few fanatics who were getting dangerous
out of all proportion to their number and social importance.
Faneuil Hall had been refused to them, although opened
to their opponents, who addressed the respectability of the
city in August, 1835. On October 21st, a crowd of "gentlemen of property and standing," incited by newspaper
appeals to put down all denouncers of slavery, assailed the
Liberator office, seized Garrison and dragged him through
the streets with half his clothes torn off. Rescued at length
by the police, he was sentenced to jail as a disturber of
the peace, and after another pursuit by the mob was landed
in a cell just vacated by a murderer. Released the next
day, he left the city till the public mind should become
quieted. When it was, the mob, clothed in broadcloth
and its right mind once more, began to suspect that it had
violated the city's traditions of liberty and free speech.

American slavery has thus far been referred to in so
general terms that it may seem to some readers an

insufficient cause for the zealous antagonism it encountered Historical knowledge of its character during the first half of the last century will not need refreshing in many minds; but the majority of the present generation necessarily thinks of African bondage in the South as a thing of the past which had its redeeming features. Now and then, too, Southern writers and speakers present the sunny side of the system as it was in the years before the war — the white side of luxury and ease, with so much of irresponsibility and comfort as fell to the blacks — citing examples of affectionate relationship between master and servant. The Old Mammy especially lingers as a delightful memory of childhood to be handed on in tradition and literature. It was but yesterday that a prominent Southerner raised a storm of prolonged applause when he remarked, in effect, that he had no patience with those who said that the Confederates thought they were right in fighting for slavery; they *knew* they were right. There are indications now and then that the remembrance of the institution is not so abhorrent to all persons that there is no need of recalling some of its features which may show that it was its own reason for its "abolishment," to use Lincoln's word.

In any brief portrayal of its prominent characteristics allowance should be made for the inherited convictions of those whose fathers grew up under its shadow. Although slaveholders were a minority of the white population in the South, they were leaders of opinion and were taught by statesmen, of whom Calhoun was chief, that slavery was both a divinely ordered and humane condition for the Negro. Northern opinion, formed largely by personal narratives of fugitives from bondage, differed from the Southern view.

Travellers, as a rule, confirmed Northern impressions. If "St. Clair"˚ represented the kindlier side, "Legree" stood for inhuman possibilities. It is what can be safely committed under any code that stamps it as good or bad.

To begin with the general conditions of slave existence, apart from exceptional incidents, it is fair to say that they were undesirable. If a compulsory absence of liberty was offset in a measure by an assured subsistence to the Negroes, it may be asked what kind of living was furnished them. Trustworthy accounts and statistics place the cost of food for the plantation hand at from seventeen dollars and fifty cents to twenty dollars per year, or from two and a half to five cents a day — mostly for cornmeal, sometimes with bacon and molasses. Clothing in quality was cheap and coarse; in quantity it grew less with parallels of latitude. Comfortable cabins were not uncommon, but huts that were a mere shelter for the night, foul and wretched, were the rule. There was little time or inclination to clean house after a long day's work. This, on cotton and sugar plantations, was from fifteen to eighteen hours in length, according to the season; the toilers' only stimulus a gang-driver's lash, as admitted by the Southern author of the "Pro-slavery Argument," and corroborated by the general testimony of planters. Nor was the whip discarded at the house among a higher grade of servants as guests often testified. In general, the management of slaves did not greatly differ from that of animals, according to intelligence and tractability. Doubtless their understanding was dull and their tempers provoking, but two hundred and forty years of toil and degradation imposed upon a race was not an eminently exalting or Christianizing process. If the African in rice swamps, cane brakes, and cotton fields was reduced to almost a brute, the genuine religious spirit prevailing in the South in other matters ought to have established something nearer to the ideals of the Society for the Prevention of Cruelty to Animals than the slave codes and their observance in Southern states.

The fact that in return for such food, housing, and treatment as they received, the labour of slaves under duress often netted their owner 35 per cent. annually on his investment does not establish the equity of slaveholding, as it did not improve its conditions so much as might be expected. It was a recommendation for the generally despised overseer if he added to the profits of a large crop by reducing outlays for provisions and clothing to the lowest figures. If the hands deteriorated in consequence, it was counted cheaper to buy a new lot once in seven years and wear out the old. Large profits accordingly went to new investments in land and Negroes, but with high interest on crops often mortgaged in advance and extravagant prices on supplies furnished on long credit. Yet, in spite of wasteful methods, large fortunes could be accumulated when slave labour cost less than ten cents a day. Meantime the increasing price of Negroes with difficulty prevented the revival of the slave trade, and made successful ventures to the Guinea coast as profitable to smugglers as they were disastrous to their living cargoes. If supplies were drawn from slave-breeding states, another kind of misery followed in the breaking up of families, to which was added a fate which the Virginia or Kentucky Negro dreaded as death in his consignment to labour in Gulf states. Worse than threats of flogging was that of selling him farther south.

Soon or late both commonly were made good; the sale because a prime field hand brought from a thousand to fifteen hundred dollars. Local traffic in market towns or by private bargain brought its discomfort in removals to strange surroundings, even if a change of masters happened to be fortunate. If it was not, the terrors of Red River might be added to the loss of comparative happiness on Lake Ponchartrain. The average Negro might not resent being sold with horses and mules, cattle and hogs, but dealers who advertised that "families are never separated" betrayed the better sense of their communities about a not uncommon practice.

However, time adjusts human beings to expected misfortunes, the Negro perhaps sooner than the white man. But there was one disaster that was always lurking along his daily path. His master sometimes called it by the euphemism "correction"; he knew it as flogging. It might be the whipping the youngster got who had run wild and was to be broken into work; no worse than some Northern farmers are said to have given their disobedient sons in the last century or severe schoolmasters their idle pupils. Again it might be a chastisement that disabled the slave for some days; or it was sometimes a scourging that killed him. To be sure, there were laws on some statute books against such crime, but their recorded violation without penalty proves the liability of death to the slave by fiendish torture. Incidentally, the master's temper was exhibited; also the barbarity of a lauded institution. This was no doubt, in some of its aspects, patriarchal and parental; but a backward look through twenty centuries is required to find a code which practically overlooks the murder of a servant, if not of a son or a daughter born of a slave mother.

Instances of burning alive may be passed over on the ground that the practice survived the system, being then and now the work of a mob rather than of a master. The evil that an institution does may live after it, set a bad example, and die slowly. In one respect an old condition is improved, as amalgamation at the South is said to have diminished somewhat since Negroes have become owners of their persons.

In the face of these greater wrongs to a race it seems trivial to mention minor ones, such as the forbidding of instruction to those who may have desired it, and of some other improving privileges. Nor is it necessary to observe at length the reflex influences of slavery upon the morals and manners, the ambitions and disposition, and even the dialect of the ruling oligarchy, fostering arrogance, political dictation, and imperious command, while the majority, the poor whites, subserviently followed, upholding and defending a system that was their bane.

These recoiling evils, however, were not the most apparent ones to reformers. Those which fell directly upon the subject slave, calling out protests from leaders of opinion South and North in the early years of the Republic, appealed to later advocates of emancipation. A few whose eyes had not been blinded by the golden dust of profitable trade, whose vision was as open and clear as their forefathers' had been, believed that the cause of freedom had grown more important with the growth of slavery and its increased rigours. These crimes against human rights they deemed great enough to demand desperate attack. Hence the immediate emancipation phase of anti-slavery.[1]

---

[1]For a fuller account of Southern slavery see Rhodes's "History of the United States," i., chap. iv., with reference to the full sources of information about it.

Before some of the features of this onset are noticed it may be well at the present distance from it to observe the race prejudice which survives and sometimes belittles the contest. It is difficult to define the ideas which mention of the Negro raises in different minds, especially when it is remembered that few persons can contemplate five or ten individuals or objects at once. Hence, a class or a race becomes as confused a picture as a distant crowd, or resolves itself into one specimen after another — usually those best known, good or bad. Opinion of the average black man should be based upon the same observation as in the instance of other races, the white included, namely, of good, bad, and indifferent examples. There are noble and degraded natures in all; but even the Caucasian family has not as a whole reached heights where in matters of sobriety, integrity, patriotism, and good citizenship it can be no pharisee when it says, " God, I thank thee that I am not as this publican" — this black republican. If the complexion of any of the sunburned peoples could be bleached much of race distinction would vanish. According to the recent declaration of biological science the blood of all men is the same, whatever their difference in colour or feature. As St. Paul declared to the men of Athens in A. D. 48, "He hath made of one *blood* all nations of men."[1] It was the human being beneath the Ethiopian's skin which Phillips and his co-philanthropists saw, and which Southern men always recognized more readily than Northern. The bone of contention between the two sections was the natural

---

[1] "I am not aware that Wendell Phillips or William Lloyd Garrison ever claimed that the Negro race was equal in its capacity for improvement to the white race." W. F. Poole, "Anti-slavery Opinions Before 1800," p. 16. This should be borne in mind in view of charges often made against the two agitators as contending for equality of the two races in all respects. Freedom and citizenship were what they demanded for the blacks rather than social commingling.

rights of the coloured man despite his native and imposed limitations and his colour.

In summing up the cause which is the explanation of a life, it may be said that to the Negro it would not have seemed extravagant if General Sherman had coupled slavery with war in his famous and sulphurous metaphor. Doubtless the planter, in the shade of his broad veranda, would have deemed such a lurid comparison over-heated, and textile manufacturers in the North, with ministers and deacons in churches, would have agreed with him. But if they had all been herded under the blazing sun for a long day in a cotton field, working under the stimulus of a driver's lash, they would have discovered a new and vivid illustration of the place of torment. Those who first descried it from afar were called wild fanatics and incendiaries. They simply saw a sufficient reason for unusual protest. The cause of freedom from such a bondage they deemed worthy of labour and sacrifice in the face of opposition and persecution. Time justified their opinion and rewarded their efforts.

III

AN ADVOCATE OF RIGHTS

(1835–1837)

IT HAS been needful to outline the growth of opinion adverse to American slavery up to the year 1835 and to portray its features as a sectional and domestic institution in order to understand anti-slavery sentiment, and what the acceptance of its extremes signified to Wendell Phillips. If he did not fully comprehend their radical character, he could foresee some of the early consequences of his decision. By every token he should have been one of those whom James L. Homer, editor of the *Commercial Gazette*, called "gentlemen of standing and property," constituting a large portion of the Garrison mob. He was sitting in his office, on Court Street, that October day when he heard the tumult and saw a crowd hurrying toward the City Hall. Following it, he became a witness of its riotous acts. He soon met John C. Park, colonel of the Suffolk regiment in which he also was an officer, and said, "Why not call out the guards?" Pointing to the mob, Park replied, "Don't you see that the regiment is in front of you?" The merchants' clerks and other young men of the city militia would not have donned their uniform to shoot their friends for attacking an abolitionist who was imperilling Southern trade, even if the Mayor had statute authority to call out the

military, about which there was doubt and discussion
afterward. Doubtless the young lawyer informed himself
further respecting the suppression of riots. At least such
knowledge would be useful in subsequent years.

It is not possible to say how far Phillips had become
an abolitionist before this outbreak. His friend Weld
thought that his conversion dated from 1831, four years
before. He certainly had not shown great sympathy with
reformatory movements while in college, particularly in
his speech against the formation of a class temperance
society, which he succeded in preventing. He could not
have failed to hear something of the anti-slavery agitation
which followed the publication of the first number of the
Liberator on the New Year's Day of his Senior year; but
college politics and approaching Commencement, to say
nothing of the Gentleman's Club and its aristocratic sentiments, would have more interest for him than the vagaries
of a few uneasy philanthropists. In the Law School, where
the nature and formation of the Constitution was a topic
of study, it is likely that its clauses protecting slavery were
discussed, since Judge Story, as early as 1822, had offered
resolutions favouring colonization in a meeting where
Daniel Webster left the room, saying that "it was a scheme
of slaveholders to get rid of free Negroes." In Phillips's
middle year at the school several books and tracts were
published, one of which came to his attention, Mrs. Childs's
"Appeal in Favour of That Class of Americans Called
Africans."

The first anti-slavery pamphlet, however, he "received
from Ellis Gray Loring, marked with his familiar writing,
the record of his appearance before the Massachusetts

Senate to protest against the attempt to punish meetings like these with the state prison." Loring, a school friend and companion of Emerson, a young lawyer with thriving practice, had espoused the unpopular cause to the sacrifice of fees and social standing; but he never regretted his course nor wavered in his adhesion. At least half of Dr. Channing's anti-slavery reputation belonged to Ellis Gray Loring.[1] Some have dated Phillips's conversion to abolitionism from the day of the Garrison mob. It is more probable that his principal sentiment then was one of indignation at the outrage perpetrated against the right of free speech, which was shared by the best citizens when they came to their senses. Moreover, one of his first public utterances two years later at an abolition meeting where he openly allied himself with the cause was a defence of the ancient right of petition and free discussion. Unrestrained speech was always his main dependence in reformatory efforts.

In the meantime there was another more direct agency in Wendell Phillips's conviction of the merits of the movement. Miss Ann Terry Greene, daughter of Benjamin Greene, a wealthy shipping merchant of Boston, had been left an orphan at an early age, and was living with an uncle and aunt, Mr. and Mrs. Henry G. Chapman, friends of Mr. Garrison, and devoted to his philanthropic purposes. In the early winter of 1836, Miss Greene was to accompany home to Greenfield a cousin of hers, Miss Grew, who had just become the *fiancée* of Mr. Alford, a friend of Phillips and Charles Sumner. These two were invited by the lover to join the stage-coach party in order to divert the other

[1] " Life of William Lloyd Garrison," by his sons, ii., 55.

lady, "giving him a better opportunity for that exclusive devotion which became a part of his new condition." Sumner was the first to promise to go; but the next morning's storm sent him back to bed with the remark that "on such a day he would not go on a stage ride with any woman," a natural observation from a man who did not find a wife for thirty years. But Wendell was more chivalrous than Charles, and found himself assigned by his friend to the girl who had been described as "the cleverest, loveliest, most brilliant young woman, but a rabid abolitionist. Look out or she will talk you into that 'ism, before you suspect what she is about." She herself said that she "talked it all the way to Greenfield and while he was there; that he listened and [afterward in Boston] came again, and that his fate was sealed." In two particulars, as the event proved; for within a year their engagement was announced, and they were married on October 12, 1837. As for the other particular, Phillips used to say over and over, "My wife made an out and out abolitionist of me; and she always preceded me in the adoption of the various causes I have advocated." Yet, to all her zeal in making a new convert may be added a woman's reason for some of it, not concealed from herself it appears; for she confessed: "When I first met Wendell I used to think, 'It can never come to pass; such a being as he could never think of me.' I looked upon it as something strange as a fairy tale. I cannot help thinking how little I have acquired, while Wendell, only two years older, seems to know a world more."

Still, as the story goes, she had the heroism to ask him, when he offered himself, if he was fully persuaded to be the friend of the slave, a question that might have been unsafe to ask of

most of the young men in his circle. She did not have to wait
long for the answer: "My life shall attest the sincerity of my
conversion."[1] An invalid through some defect of nervous
organization, she was compelled to keep her room and much
of the time her bed by reason of weakness and pain. Rarely
to be seen by any except a few intimate friends, she was joyous in disposition, with unfailing good spirits and fond of fun
and stories; in which respect her husband matched her,
so that "hilarity was with them an abiding guest." His
unwearied devotion to his wife, however, was one of the
features of his life which withdrew him from many social and
civic activities. By no means a recluse from choice, or of a
retiring disposition, and always interested in public affairs,
he was more mindful of the enforced solitude of one to whom
his companionship was the almost sole relief, yet who could
rarely accompany him on social occasions, and scarcely ever
hear him speak in public. In every sense he had to be, and
was glad to be, all the world to her, and to acknowledge in
turn that she was the inspirer of his best efforts and a wise
counsellor.

Phillips's first acquaintance among abolitionists was in and
through the Chapman family, when he was a privileged
visitor to Miss Greene, meeting such sympathizers in the
cause as happened in. One day Garrison called when the
suitor was on an errand of his own, and the two men met who
were to be, each in his way, the foremost apostles of freedom
for an oppressed race. Garrison, the elder by six years, the
organizing and executive head, had already been in the work
seven years, lecturing and printing newspapers and tracts for

---

[1] "Ann Phillips," by Mrs. Alvord, quoted by Martyn, p. 86; also "Ann Phillips, A Memorial Sketch," Anon., in library of Harvard University.

the information of any who would read them.   The younger
man just at that time was taking his first lessons; but the
day was not far off when he should be the chief speaker of a
growing sect, as one Paul of Tarsus had been.   But, unlike
the Lycaonians, Bostonians did not say of these two, "The
gods are come down to us in the likeness of men."   They
said things antithetical instead, which were further emphasized all the way from New York to New Orleans.   And each
one of the two returned compliments in his own effective way.

The meeting of these early leaders had interesting features.
The circumstance that one was born poor in everything
belonging to worldly advantages, had educated himself, and
made himself a power aggressive and resistant, and was winning his way despite obstacles that were greater than had
confronted any other American, appealed to a kindred spirit
whom fortune had loaded with every gift; wealth, social position, academic privileges, professional business, and an outlook toward political honours.   If the older man had something to gain and not much to lose, and was gaining something
every week and every year, the younger saw that in this
alliance he, for his part, was throwing to the winds everything
that had made life sweet and honourable, save his faith in
Deity and the supreme object of his affection.   On these
two foundations he must build the superstructure of his life
and labour.   It is possible that to these he added a third, as
he certainly had good reason to, namely, confidence in himself.   Thus armoured, it was fitting that the younger should
receive the accolade of knighthood from the elder by the
hearthstone of his well-beloved.

If, however, he had not been possessed by a chivalrous
spirit, all favouring influences might have been of no

permanent efficacy. Many a man has given good hope and made fair promises of noble endeavour in love's roseate morning whom the dust and heat of the day has turned back to plodding in commonplace ways, or at best in paths that lead to goals of ordinary ambition. Rare spirits only hold fast to ideals that are revealed in better moments and attain supreme results. Without such an idealism Phillips might have been satisfied with the prizes which a legal or political career held out to a man of his inheritance, tastes, and training. But beyond the emoluments of professional and civic success stood the ideal of a republic more than Platonic in its adjustment of rights and privileges among all its inhabitants. To help establish such a state he was ready to surrender personal advantages which are counted great and to labour for this ideal kingdom of righteousness with no thought of self-aggrandisement. There was no possibility of this in the crusade he was joining. Instead, there was the certainty of immediate deprivation with no reasonable prospect of recompense in a lifetime. Such a chivalric idealism explains much of his early career and accounts for some of his later and less successful undertakings. At all times it impelled him beyond the customary beliefs of contemporaries and .nto positions far in advance of them.

The first of these was taken at a meeting of the Massachusetts Anti-slavery Society, held at Lynn on March 26, 1837. Evidently he felt that it was time to make public profession of alliance with the few who had espoused the cause of immediate emancipation. It should be remembered that this announcement antedates by nearly a year his appearance in Faneuil Hall, which is sometimes taken as his entrance into the lists.

There was deliberation enough about this first confession of his purpose to result in a "Resolution" which he took with him or drew up after his arrival.   In either case, there is no sign of unpreparedness in the speech with which he supported it.   This has the marks of a maiden speech in an avowal of consecration to a cause needing the help of all, and, by consequence, having the speaker's sympathy and promise of support.   The report of it three weeks later, doubtless with the orator's sanction, gave as its title, "Special Consecration," and the Resolution read before the speech was as follows:

Resolved, That, having a great work to do, and but comparatively feeble means wherewith to do it, our influence and effort should be devoted mainly to the cause of abolition.

The sentiment is appropriate but general; a broad base for a comprehensive survey of the task before a small but devoted band; and, therefore, the demand upon each and every member of it imperative to do all that he can.   After summing up the difficulties in their path, the weight of public opinion, the prejudice of centuries, the present interest of almost every man in the Union, the passions of one half of it, the indifference of the other, he asked:

And what have we to offer against all this — Interest, counting his dollars; Lust gloating over his gratification; Ambition numbering up his votes; Prejudice rushing forward with closed eyes; Political power, rooted deep as the Union, controlling its policy and movements by slave votes; Love of power, increased by the use of it — all these common to North and South. . . . We are not contending for the liberties of the slave alone.   Free discussion, the right of petition, and freedom for ourselves and posterity.

He then turned to the plea that slavery has been and is dying.

Dead is it? How comes it then, if you but touch it, that it rocks the Union to its centre and base? You say wait and it will die away. Why, then, does it ask for more territory? . . . If our work be not done immediately, it may be that it cannot be done at all. We should come up to this work with our whole hearts because the sin of slavery taints the whole atmosphere, corrupts the life-blood of the nation, and renders all its liberties insecure by destroying the basis on which they rest: because it is a national sin and exposes us to the judgment of heaven. He who sees nothing in the signs of the times, in the state of public sentiment which the discussion of this subject has revealed, that leads him to doubt the duration of our government, must be blind indeed. . . . Slavery is a national sin — and I address New Englanders, who believe that God judges the nations. How long may we linger, when his thunderbolts are already hot over our heads? Every other eye may have been closed to the cruelty and blood which have stained our escutcheon — every other ear may have been deaf to the cry of the oppressed; but the eye which never sleeps has watched the prosperity which grew fat on the tears and toil of the slave, that ear has listened to the sighing of the prisoner, and him who had none to help him — and the arm of Omnipotence may even now be stretched out to avenge. . . . Let no man in the coming year grudge his labour in furthering our petitions. Now is the crisis. Meet it like men. Spare no labour. Waste none on other causes. This work must be done now or not at all. Let others wait. Your interest demands it. Your duty commands it. Do your duty now, and the crisis may never come. The helm of the gallant vessel is for a moment in the hand of the North. If the steersman slumber we are lost. Only wake, only be active, we have passed the breakers, and are safe.

The entire speech, of which the above gives the tenour, could not have occupied over twenty minutes; but the assembly did not fail to discover the promise of an advocate of its purposes and interests with such oratorical gifts as had not hitherto appeared. Nor could it have been insensible to the character and position of the recruit.

Later in the day, it was seen that this declaratory address was not all that he could say upon the subject. At the evening session he offered another resolution as follows:

Resolved, That the exertion of John Quincy Adams and the rest of the Massachusetts delegation, who sustained him in his defence of the citizens' *right of petition*, deserves the deepest gratitude and the warmest admiration of every American.

John Quincy Adams as a factor in the movement against slavery should not be overlooked in the attention which abolitionists necessarily compel. They were not numerous at first, though they soon became so; he stood alone in Congress in the midst of general opposition. He had, at first, not even the full support of abolitionists; for he was not in entire sympathy with their policy. As early as 1820, when he was Secretary of State, he foresaw an irrepressible conflict between slave and free states with the possible dissolution of the Union. Slavery he termed "the great and foul stain upon the nation, and the contemplation of its abolition worthy of the most exalted soul. Never since human sentiments and human conduct were influenced by human speech was there a theme for eloquence like the free side of this question. If but one man could arise with the genius capable of comprehending, and an utterance capable of communicating those eternal truths that belong to this question, to lay bare in all its nakedness that outrage upon the goodness of God, human slavery; now is the time and this is the occasion, upon which such a man would perform the duties of an angel upon earth." This was ten years before the crusade began to be preached. Five years later, when he became President, there was little opportunity to give a practical turn to his sentiments.   It was the decade of hush before a coming storm, for which the South was beginning to draw together, and, especially, to become united in its opposition to him, a league which he took no particular pains to conciliate.   He early committed the unpardonable offence of proposing to send delegates to the Panama Congress where they would meet Haytiens of colour.   The open battle, however, did not begin until after his presidential term was over, and he was sent to Congress as Representative from the Plymouth district.   He was then placed where he could meet all comers in his own way, or their way.   They were glad of the opportunity, and so was he.   They came singly, in squads, and the whole host together.   They retired in the same order, and disorder.   He did not fight for a party, but for a principle.   He loved the joy of battle.   If the conflict flagged he provoked his foes into ungovernable wrath; then he held them up to withering scorn, showed them their blunders, and sent them home humiliated, but hating him with fresh intensity.

These contests were oftenest waged on his side from the firm ground of a fundamental principle of human government — the right of the subject to petition the ruling power, be it King or Congress.   Taking his seat in Congress in December, 1831, he began to present petitions against slavery and the slave trade until the famous "gag rule" was passed to lay all such petitions upon the table without further action. Upon this Mr. Adams renewed his defence of a right older than Norman and Saxon dominion. Opposition from enemies and ill-timed aid of friends did not disconcert him. When the attempt to expel him was made he met it with a speech to which no one wished to reply. Then he pursued his routed adversaries with defiance and contempt, retorts, and taunts.

It was when Mr. Adams was in the thickest of the fight on the right of petition and the threatening question of annexing Texas that Mr. Phillips introduced his resolution of commendation and gratitude and supported it by a second speech at the Lynn meeting.

This speech is denominated as his first in the second series of his collected speeches. It was so placed in the columns of the *Liberator*, but, in an account of the meeting, it is remarked that this resolution was discussed in the evening. Also the Lynn *Record* of March 29, 1837, says:

In the evening Resolutions were debated in the First Methodist Meeting House by Mr. Phillips and others in support of a Resolution in favour of J. Q. Adams. Mr. Phillips spoke with great eloquence and effect. His remarks were entirely extemporaneous.

From this testimony it seems that the other speech, already commented upon, must have been, instead of this, the one which "marked his entrance upon the anti-slavery movement." It should be added that the second series of his speeches was compiled and arranged after his death.

It was a forceful speech of approbation and of admiration for the intrepid defence of *the right of petition* by Mr. Adams

in the face of an enraged opposition delegation from the South
and a subservient one from the North supporting it. Of
"the old man eloquent" he said:

His course during the last session deserves the gratitude of
every American; for in that contest, he was not the representative of any state or party, but the champion of the fundamental principles of the Constitution. The right of petition
we had thought as firmly fixed in the soil of America as the
Saxon race which brought it here. It was the breath of life
during our colonial history, and is recognized on every page
of our history since as the bulwark of civil liberty.
Antiquity and the historical associations of our mother
country had rendered it so sacred that we looked confidently to that for protection and redress when all other
means should fail. . . .

And who does not recollect the thrill of enthusiastic feeling
with which we heard that Adams had thrown himself into the
gap, and was contending, at first single-handed, for the right
of the citizen to petition, no matter what his creed, his colour,
or his party? The effort was the nobler in that he was not a
member of the body of men in whose persons this right had
been invaded. No interest of his or his friends had been
touched. Against our efforts he had all along protested;
but, statesmanlike, he saw the end from the beginning.
When rights were invaded, he was willing to side with any
who rallied to protect them. We hail him as the champion
of free principles. We accord to him the high merit of a pure
attachment to civil liberty which would not permit her to be
attacked, even when she appeared in the garb of a party
which it was his interest, and he felt it to be a duty, to oppose;
of a clear-sighted, far-reaching wisdom, which discovered the
first approach of corruption and snuffed oppression in the
tainted breeze; of a noble disregard to party lines, when to
have adhered to them would have compromised the fundamental principles of our Government.

The main portion of his speech may be regarded as a lawyer's advocacy of a great principle of human rights, and the other part of it as a reformer's insistence that it be allowed to hold in the case of a particular wrong to be presented for consideration and removal. As the morning speech was a declaration of his new allegiance, so the evening remarks may be considered as the announcement of the firm and reasonable ground upon which the conflict was to be waged, namely, the enlightenment of the people, and the exercise of their right to petition the representatives of their will to make the nation what it pretended to be, but was not. There was no fanaticism and no unreasonableness in this initial position. It rested on an inherited right, and on an assertion made by the fathers of the Republic; on the English Constitution and the Declaration of Independence. The Constitution of the United States, and the Union under it were later provisions, to be discussed later in the stress and storm that should be hereafter; but now, fundamental principles of law and liberty were the base upon which the neophyte began to build.

It is not amiss to take the two speeches of that spring day of 1837 as a single symbol of a maturing purpose. Standing side by side on the time-browned pages of a newspaper[1] of seventy-two years ago they have a unity of their own. So appear to us as one the two distant suns which we call the North Star — itself the guide of fugitives from bondage, through free states where they were not freed, to an inclement province where they were no longer slaves, and whence they could not be dragged back to servitude. In these two speeches Phillips had announced the choice that he had deliberately made, to

[1] The *Liberator*.

the great gratification of the little company who attended the Lynn meeting — and to the profound disgust of everybody else, his mother and her family included. To be sure, they heard that Wendell made two eloquent addresses. So much the worse that they were on a subject about which he had better have kept silence, or at least remained non-committal until the tide of opinion had begun to turn. He would have needed to wait only eight months.

During these months he was not conspicuous in the meetings of the Society. His name does not appear on the list of officers. He served on two committees to find a church that would harbour an anti-slavery convention, meeting with ingenious but firm refusals from most of those to whom application was made. Some consistently replied that their churches were for religious purposes only; some that the peace and harmony of their societies would be disturbed; others, like the committee of the Old South Church, "deemed it inexpedient to grant the request." However, the fourth annual meeting of the New England Anti-Slavery Society convened in the Methodist Church on Church Street on Tuesday, May 30th, and in the Park Street Church on Thursday; an event thought worthy of mention as "a significant sign of the times." The Salem Street meeting house was also occupied on two evenings. At these meetings the name of John G. Whittier occurs in a committee on business. There were no less than thirteen public anti-slavery meetings in Boston during the week. No note of Phillips's presence at any of them appears, although it is probable that he was a listener at some. On the Fourth of July, according to the Salem *Register*, in response to an invitation after his speeches at the May meeting he addressed "friends of the cause of

consideration which he paid to these inharmonious coun-
sellors indicates the definite clearness of the call to which
he listened and gave loyal heed. To him the war-trumpet
gave no uncertain sound, and he obeyed its summons
without cavil and without fear.

IV

FREEDOM OF THE PRESS

(1836–1837)

THE position which Phillips took in the first year of his alliance with the anti-slavery movement was upon the broad ground of universal freedom and the ancient English right of petition. His next step was in defence of another general right which had been held sacred since Milton wrote his great argument in the "Areopagitica" for the liberty of unlicensed printing.

The policy of repression which Congress had employed toward petitions was beginning to be directed against the freedom of the press. Andrew Jackson, in his message of December 7, 1835, had made the first adverse presidential allusion to abolitionism, voicing the sentiments which were uttered by state legislatures and Southern newspapers, calling upon the North to silence abolition tongues. Then, attention was turned to the more dangerous work of "incendiary" printing presses, whose pestilent sheets were found in Southern states, with woe to those in whose hands they were found.

In the face of all this, James Gillespie Birney, an Alabama lawyer who had freed his slaves, and had been driven from the bar of the state and other positions of honour, determined to establish an anti-slavery paper in Dan-

ville, Ky. Violence being threatened by a meeting of citizens
he crossed the river to Cincinnati, where no better hospitality awaited him. Then he settled in the Quaker town
of New Richmond, twenty miles up-stream, where in the
summer of 1835 he issued the *Philanthropist*. The following
spring he risked removal to Cincinnati. In three months
his press and types were damaged by a mob, and on the
twenty-first of July a committee was appointed to inform
him that if his paper were not promptly suppressed a mob
would visit him, in which two-thirds of the property holders
of the city would join. A mild but fearless man, he declined
to yield to this demand. On the night of August 1, 1836,
his office was pillaged, and press and types thrown into
the river. The *Philanthropist* passed into the hands
of Dr. Gamaliel Bailey, and twice afterward its press was
demolished.

The next attack upon the freedom of the press occurred
fifteen months later, with more serious result. St. Louis
was the scene of it. In the spring of 1836 a Negro who
had killed an officer arresting him was taken from jail by
a mob, chained to a tree, and burned alive. One Judge
Lawless exculpated the miscreants as moved "by some
mysterious, metaphysical, and almost electric frenzy," and
told the grand jury that the case was beyond the reach
of human law, and therefore transcending their jurisdiction.
The editor of the St. Louis *Observer*, Rev. Elijah Parish
Lovejoy, commented upon the lynching, as editors still
do upon similar incidents, each from his own point of view.
Lovejoy was not a full-fledged abolitionist, but he had a
Northern man's aversion to roasting any animal alive.
This one being nothing but a "nigger," the editor's remarks

were offensive to the people of the Missouri city. Called to account, he displayed inconvenient ideas about the freedom of the press; accordingly, his office was destroyed by a gang of citizens. He removed across and up the river into Alton, in the free state of Illinois, but as soon as his press was landed it was broken to pieces. Certain citizens furnished funds to buy another. In August, 1837, office and press were again destroyed. Another was purchased, broken up, and thrown into the Mississippi. Then, friends rallied and resolved that "the cause of human rights, liberty of speech and the press, demand that the Alton *Observer* be reëstablished with its present editor." A fourth press arrived on November 7th. The Mayor superintended its transfer to a warehouse, and, great excitement prevailing, he appointed a special force to guard it. Seeing no sign of an assault, most of the guard left at nine in the evening, intrusting the care of the press to the editor and a dozen friends. Soon thirty or forty roughs, who had imbibed valour at neighbouring grog-shops, attacked the building with stones and shots. Cries were raised to "Fire the building"; "Burn them out"; "Shoot every abolitionist as he leaves!" The firing was returned and one rioter killed. A torch was applied and as the defenders came out Mr. Lovejoy fell pierced by five bullets. The press was then broken in pieces and thrown into the river.

This act set a thousand other presses humming, a million Americans reading, and many men speaking strong words. But the words which were printed, read, and spoken were by no means the same. In the North there was general unanimity on the freedom of speech and the press, some disagreement about slavery, and more with regard to abolitionism. In the Ohio country there was a strong feeling for freedom of speaking and printing if it did not touch Southern interests. In the South the incident at Alton was regarded as a just retribution upon a meddler, but with apprehension as to what it might do for anti-slavery sentiment. Certainly it did not contribute to the diminution of membership in societies formed to disseminate abolition principles. And, as these were published more and more, controversy grew bitter throughout the nation. In the Northern heavens, sullen clouds were driven by contrary winds; in the Southern sky, heat lightening flashed from the Atlantic to the Mississippi River, and there were mutterings of a threatened storm.

Tidings of the tragedy reached Boston after twelve days, on Sunday forenoon, November 19th — such was the speed with which news travelled in 1837. "The Rev. Mr. Brownson, in the afternoon, preached an impressive sermon on the occurrence"; but most of the ministers did not pronounce upon the subject at once. Early in the week Dr. Channing, at the instigation of Ellis Gray Loring, circulated a petition asking the city government to allow the use of Faneuil Hall for a meeting of citizens in reprobation of the Alton riot. The aldermen declined, "lest the sense of the meeting be taken as the opinion of the city in other places," presumably to the southward. An appeal from this decision to the people was followed by a meeting in the Common Council room, where sundry resolutions were passed, which the city fathers respected enough to grant petitioners permission to hold a meeting on December 8th — "in the daytime, lest if it should he held in the evening Boston might see another mob."

The Huguenot hatred of despotism which Peter Faneuil built into the hall that he gave to the city in 1742 was continued in the town hall which rose from its ashes in 1763; for in the decade before the Revolution, patriots made its walls echo with denunciations of British tyranny. Since then, the old " Cradle of Liberty " had been so unreservedly open to free discussion (except by abolitionists) that in the drift of public opinion a pro-slavery meeting had been held in it on August 21, 1835, in the sixtieth year of American independence. At this meeting the most respectable citizens vied with one another in supporting resolutions deprecating disturbance of the South by Northern agitators, and reaffirming the pro-slavery compromise of 1789; this however, did not satisfy the demand which the South had made for repression of free speech and printing. Penal legislation, with hanging for agitators, was what was desired. The Garrison mob, two months later, was the first result of this meeting. But popular sentiment had been changing slowly since that outbreak, and had received sufficient acceleration by the Alton affair to make a turning point somewhere between the refusal and the granting of the hall. At ten o'clock on the morning of December 8th five thousand people packed the hall to overflowing. The Hon. Jonathan Phillips, as chairman, stated that the meeting was not in favour of any party, but to maintain the spirit of universal freedom, the essential and fundamental principles of civil liberty. After an invocation of the divine blessing by Rev. E. M. P. Wells, Dr. Channing replied to those who thought him out of place in such a meeting as well as to those who had expected him to discuss the tragedy in his pulpit; adding that he preferred to join the citizens of Boston in expressing in a public manner their abhorrence of lawlessness;

and he spoke at length in a similar strain. Resolutions drawn by Dr. Channing, and offered by B. F. Hallett, Esq., were seconded by George S. Hillard in a speech which deplored the increasing frequency of mobs deliberately organized. So far, the meeting appeared to favour law and order. Then the Attorney-General of the state, James Trecothic Austin, from the rear gallery addressed the assembly. After a thrust at the "abstractions" that had been uttered, and a laudation of the Bill of Rights, he declared that this meeting had been convened for an application of these rights to events in the State of Illinois, and to sympathy for the death of an editor there. He sympathized with the people of slave states who lived in constant fear of their lives through danger of slave insurrection. The free state in which the disturbance had occurred was trying to exercise a neighbourly duty of upholding the laws and prejudices of a slave state, and in the process a man was killed and died "as the fool dieth." Liberty of speech and the press were to be used with reference to others' rights. What can we expect than that an abolition press will be destroyed if it is established in a slave state or on its borders? — and so on for two reported columns.

The opposition element in the crowd, reinforced by the indifferent and unreasoning, shifty applauders of every speaker, nearly created a stampede from the hall. The assembly was beginning to resemble that at Ephesus when the city's trade was endangered by a certain reformer — "Some cried one thing and some another: for the assembly was in confusion; and the more part knew not wherefore they had come together."

Phillips, standing with the multitude, for there were no seats, remarked that such assertions ought to be answered;

and someone suggested that he do it, to whom he replied, "I will if you will help me toward the platform." This was the "lecturn" from which Dr. Channing had spoken. The fact that Phillips was in the crowd and not near the chairman has given the impression that his speaking was upon an impulse of the moment. On the contrary, it is more than probable that he had been invited to be one of the speakers, and that it had been arranged that he should follow Mr. Hillard,[1] when Austin broke in from the gallery, and left the hall as soon as he had finished his speech. There was no time for an introduction to the audience, unknown as the young man was to most of it. He introduced himself by saying: "Mr. Chairman: We have met for the freest discussion of these resolutions and the events that gave rise to them." He had struck the American note of fair play, and, despite cries from Austin's following for putting the question, he elicited others of, "Hear him," "Go on," and "No gagging." In a single sentence he had captured the attention of the majority by his presence and personality. He then went on to say:

I hope I shall be permitted to express my surprise at the sentiments of the last speaker — surprise not only at such sentiments from such a man, but at the applause they have received within these walls. A comparison has been drawn between the events of the Revolution and the tragedy at Alton. We have heard it asserted here, in Faneuil Hall, that Great Britain had a right to tax the colonies, and we have heard the mob at Alton, the drunken murderers of Lovejoy, compared to those patriot fathers who threw the tea overboard!

[1] So stated in the *Liberator's* report of the meeting. Yet I have been told that Phillips assured the father of my informant that he did not expect to speak when he entered the hall. Upon which a friend of Mr. Phillips remarked to me, "It might have been an instance of his memory failing him." It is also an example of the contradictions of testimony.

Fellow-citizens, is this Faneuil Hall doctrine? The mob at
Alton were met to wrest from a citizen his just rights — met
to resist the laws. We have been told that our fathers did
the same: and the glorious mantle of Revolutionary precedent has been thrown over the mobs of our day. To make
out their title to such defence, the gentleman says that the
British Parliament had a *right* to tax these Colonies. . . .
Sir, when I heard the gentleman lay down principles which
place the murderers of Alton side by side with Otis and Hancock, with Quincy and Adams, I thought those pictured lips
would have broken into voice to rebuke the recreant American, the slanderer of the dead. Sir, for the sentiments he has
uttered, on soil consecrated by the prayers of Puritans and
the blood of patriots the earth should have yawned and
swallowed him up.

From this point the speech bears less reference to what the
Attorney-General had said, and more to the talk of some in
the community, including editorials and sermons. It is
possible that this would have been the burden of his discourse
if the man in the gallery had not spoken. Expressions like
"The statement which has been made," "It has been asked,"
"Some persons seem to imagine," and similar introductory
sentences appear to preface what he intended to say if he
had spoken according to the announcement that he was
expected to speak and that he was to follow Mr. Hillard.
A note of premeditation is evident in the scoring of Rev.
Hubbard Winslow, pastor of the Bowdoin Street Church, who
had gone out of his way to define republican liberty as "the
liberty to do what the prevailing voice of the brotherhood will
allow and protect."

By such contemporary testimony as can be obtained it
must be concluded that this speech was considered a most
remarkable one in a day when oratory of a high order was

common. Webster, Everett, and Choate, each in his own way, had accustomed the citizens of Boston to deliberative, occasional, and forensic eloquence, generally the result of premeditation and preparation. But, so far as the audience could see, this speech by a new man was impromptu. He had sprung from the throng uncalled, unannounced, and unknown, except by a few. He apparently had no time to consider what he should say in reply to an unexpected harangue which had nearly defeated the purpose of the meeting. One more such would have accomplished this result. It was plain that the young man had turned the wavering assembly back to the original sentiment of the majority, and had recalled the better sense of the multitude to the vital issue that had been imperilled in Illinois, and had now been nearly abandoned in Massachusetts. He had headed off an inglorious stampede from independence to subserviency, from liberty of speech and of printing to the gag-law and censorship of the press. To do this in the way it was done was more than to charm an audience for an hour with periods which voice its concurrent beliefs. It was an exceptional triumph of oratory under adverse conditions, and it will stand among the very few instances when the speaking man, and his personality behind his words, have together been stronger than the collective mind of a multitude.[1]

Recognition of the extraordinary achievement was spontaneous and unstinted. But it was not unqualified; for with great praise for the wonderful performance, material enough

[1] "Phillips was already a favourite public speaker before Sumner had given any promise of future distinction as an orator." Pierce's "Life of Sumner," i., 155. But in ii., 7 the author remarks that Phillips "began his career as an orator in his reply to Austin." Sumner began his in a Fourth of July address on "The True Grandeur of Nations," ten years later, 1845. *Ib.*, ii., 384.

was at hand for the detraction with which people love to interlard their commendation, and show how well balanced their own judgments are. Therefore, after the vociferous applause was over, and the favourable comments of the departing crowd had been uttered, and glowing reports of it given at many dinner tables, and soberer mention made in one newspaper after another, notes of regret followed quick and often that the young lawyer should have sacrificed such talents and prospects to the unpopular cause which lay back of the one which he had defended so well, but upon which (abolitionism) all the speakers had been pledged not to touch. Doubtless, too, there were some who said that he could never do so well again, and that with "one-speech Hamilton" he would earn his reputation by a single effort, but never add to it afterward.

As the biographic imagination is sometimes charged with extravagance in its interpretation of events long past, it may be well to note how contemporaries viewed the occurrence. First, the resolutions were carried with unexpected unanimity — "after the whirlwind of applause had died away," one says. It was better than this. A Mr. Bond followed Mr. Phillips in a speech long enough and ordinary enough to allow the enthusiasm of the audience to cool; accordingly, conviction must have been produced sufficiently abiding to secure a vote of "unexpected unanimity"; although the parenthetical clause — "a considerable number not voting at all" — indicates that conservative Boston had its doubts on the subject of unlicensed printing, as the forefathers had in the days of the Cambridge press which gave them so much trouble despite its appointed censors. Mr. Garrison's paper said that "Mr. Phillips replied with great effect," and

includes him among those who made "admirable speeches."
But Mr. Garrison did not think that the object of the meeting
went far enough in not insisting upon discussion of the
slavery question. The same paper quotes from the *Daily
Advocate's* correspondent a most enthusiastic description of
"the torrent of eloquence of irresistible force, which was
cheered from every quarter of the hall and echoed and
reëchoed through its arches when he sat down." The
Westminster Review of December, 1838, in an article by
Harriet Martineau, observed:

The crisis to which this meeting brought the fate of the
abolitionists hung at last for the space of three minutes
upon the lips of one very young speaker, who was heard
only because of his rank. It came to the turn of a hair
whether the atrocious mob-speech of the Attorney-General
should be acted upon, or whether liberty of speech and
the press should prevail. Happily the eloquence of young
Mr. Phillips secured the victory.[1]

Similar testimony to his impromptu address occurred in
other publications. It was chiefly remarkable for the power
to adapt readily to the demands of an occasion the conclusions
at which the speaker had arrived by meditation. They were
to him what their "commonplaces" were to the old Roman
orators, but of more vital consequence. This is the best
explanation of his immediate power. It was what he saw
imperilled that gave force to the skill of his deliberate speech.
The man was behind the orator. And beyond the man was
the principle of freedom to discuss any proposition, not
excluding the inscription on the bell that swung over Indepen-

---

[1] This speech was ranked by George William Curtis with Patrick Henry's farewell oration
at Williamsburg and with Lincoln's at Gettysburg.

dence Hall, to "proclaim liberty to all the inhabitants of the land."

But after all contemporary testimony has been taken there remains an uncounted factor which is as volatile and powerful as an ethereal force of nature. This may be called the dramatic element which sometimes attends effective speech. Evolved from the occasion, the speaker, and the audience it becomes pervasive like a spirit of the air and of the storm, and its doings cannot be accounted for by the principles of common experience. There was nothing intentionally dramatic in this sudden appearance upon the stage of a young man comparatively unknown, but many occurrences have had a dramatic ending that was unexpected. One event that made this speech scenic was the immediate turning of the prevailing sentiment away from its direction on account of a few words calmly spoken by a young attorney who happened to have the rarest power given to man — the control of other men's minds. This can best be measured by comparing it with physical prowess. A trained fighter of marvellous strength might oppose the fore-front of a mob with temporary effect in a hand-to-hand encounter, but would certainly be overwhelmed by numbers in their growing anger. Yet here was a man who in a dozen quiet sentences stilled the stormy impulses of five thousand, turned prejudice to favour, and led the forces which inspire action and direct away from one purpose to another and different determination. There have been frequent instances where the previous disposition of a multitude has been augmented and hurried into precipitate acts by inspiring appeals; but there have been so few examples of reversing the current of resolve that Shakespeare made his great orator's triumph to lie in turning

the people's hatred of Cæsar into fury against his patriotic
assassins. He thought it dramatically necessary to accomplish this by deliberate and progressive play upon the hearts of
the populace, urging on and holding back their resentment in
prolonged discourse. In a single paragraph, addressed to
nothing beyond the audience's sense of a comparison of their
forefathers' resistance to taxation by mobbing tea ships to the
Alton destruction of a printing press with the murder of its
owner, this man brought about a change of opinion in the
face of deep-seated prejudice which was more dramatic in its
suddenness among a throng of intelligent and educated people
than the hounding on to vengeance of a Roman rabble. It
was a dramatic end to Demosthenes's speech when the
assembly cried out, "Up, let us march against Philip," but
they hated him before the orator fanned their animosity into
flames. This man turned the assent of the throng to the
words of his predecessor into repudiation of them, with loud
acclaim of his branding the recreant American as a slanderer
of the dead. It was a masterly stroke of oratory — the
precursor of many such feats — unpremeditated, bold,
efficacious. The immediate recognition it won was another
feature of its scenic character, voiced in the tumultuous
applause that followed, and in the approval of shouted
agreement with the speaker's sentiments. Citizens went out
into the winter noon knowing that whatever their opinions
had been or still were, they had witnessed a dramatic act in
the old Hall of Patriots such as could not be reproduced on a
theatrical stage; for the protagonist had set a thousand minds
in a new direction and recalled thousands more from
momentary deviation back to the principles of free speech
and personal liberty for which their forefathers had

contended. They felt also that an orator of great promise had sprung up in the city, and many asked who he was. An aristocrat of twenty-six years, who had left his law office and the courts, abandoned great prospects, and lost his friends and general favour, all for the visionary cause of universal liberty in the land — another factor in a career that promised to be dramatic in the future.

V

LABOURS AFIELD

(1838–1839)

A S THE South feared, abolitionism was greatly helped
by the Alton murder and the comments upon it by
Northern speakers and writers. The British, who had
shaken themselves clear of slaveholding in their colonies,
were now free to denounce it here. Accordingly, anti-
slavery societies multiplied. Eight hundred of them had
been formed before 1837, and at the rate of one every day
during the two previous years. In Ohio, alone, there were
three hundred, one with a membership of four thousand.
But, relatively to the entire population, the abolitionists were
few. In Massachusetts even, there were more than a
hundred towns where there was no anti-slavery society,
and Boston itself, where the first one was started six years
before, was by no means converted to its purposes or convinced of its usefulness. No immediate results followed the
Faneuil Hall meeting, since its speakers had been restricted
to reaffirming the ancient right of free speech, without open
reference to slavery, the remote cause of assembling. The
time had not arrived when the city would open the " Cradle
of Liberty " to speakers who carried the doctrine of Adams
and Otis and Hancock beyond the white race limit.

Phillips himself, with his knowledge of men and the hour, knew that something more than a single address was needed to bring many persons to a new view of an old condition of things. If, too, he remembered that the occasion, rightly improved, is a large contributor to oratorical success, he could hardly hope for another so propitious to occur in the near future. However, he improved an opportunity that soon presented itself to supplement his Faneuil Hall speech with an address on Forefathers' Day, December 22, 1837, at a meeting in Marlborough Chapel commemorative of Lovejoy. In this he reviewed unfavourable comments that had been made on the murdered man's defence of his rights, chiefly by non-resistant abolitionists, some of the clergy, and pro-slavery advocates. He argued as a lawyer, that the Alton editor stood upon his constitutional rights; that he was one of the force enrolled by the Mayor to sustain the laws; cited the precedent of the men who were assembled to protect the library of Harvard College at the time of the Mount Benedict mob; asserted that Lovejoy's paper was not an abolition sheet; that only three out of fifteen or twenty in the building were abolitionists; that they took arms, not to vindicate slaves' rights, but their own; that the rioters fired first; that the ministerial profession confers no right to neglect the duties of a citizen, and forfeits no right to protection; that Lovejoy fled from place to place and suffered thrice patiently; that insulted law called for justification. In closing he touched upon the cause of it all:

With what an answer has he furnished us to the oft repeated question, What has the North to do with slavery? Point to the grave of Lovejoy and utter no word. The tree of slavery may be planted in Southern soil, but its cold and blighting shadow, its death-distilling branches, are mildewing all our free institutions. " Nothing to do with it," when it can chill the free speech of Faneuil Hall and make us forget that freedom of speech was our fathers' guiding star over the ocean ?

I have one word to add, which shows our immediate duty and our city's responsibility. It is said the rioters at Alton were heard encouraging each other by reference to old Boston. Alas, my native city, art thou indeed so fallen ? To be praised by praiseworthy men, was once pronounced the highest honour. To what depth of degradation must she have fallen, whose time honoured name has become the motto and war-cry of a mob!

Marlborough Chapel had been built for a rallying place of the agitators, and although Phillips's defence of Lovejoy and his liberty to speak and print was as restrained and logical as a legal argument need be, there were no restraints of speech promised. Hence his malediction of the evil influence of slavery at the close of this address, and his lament over Boston's example on the mob of 1835.

It became evident to his associates that they had gained something more than an enthusiastic philanthropist when, on January 26, 1838, he made a still more argumentative plea before a committee of the Massachusetts Legislature on the unconstitutionality of annexing Texas to the Union. He could argue a question of national importance before the legislators of a state whose influence was a power throughout the North and West. He referred the committee to a consideration of the nature of the Constitution as established by the people of the United States for the entire nation, and not for one state or section only, tracing the growth of this view through the several declaration compacts. He discussed at length the question which had been considered by the framers of the Constitution regarding the admission of new states from territories beyond the limits of the Union fixed by the treaty of 1783. Then he took up the matter of acquiring territory by conquest or treaty, and asked if in the exercise of the treaty-making power the Government could be totally regardless of all other provisions of the Constitution. His citation of the opinions of jurists, statesmen, and of legislative acts shows what attention he had given to the issue which was becoming of alarming importance; as was indicated by this closing paragraph of an hour's argument:

Sir, Jefferson, when performing what he confessed was an unconstitutional act, remarks, "I confide in the *good sense* of our country to correct the evil, *when it shall produce ill effects.*" I submit to this committee whether this time has not arrived.

To ally ourselves with Texas, is to hoist the banner of the Republic over a slaveship, and become partners in the voyage. "To uphold slavery in a new country," said Daniel Webster, in 1819, "what is it but to encourage that rapacity, fraud, and violence, against which we have so long pointed the denunciations of our penal code? What is it but to tarnish the proud fame of our country? What is it but to throw suspicion on its good faith, and render questionable all humanity and the liberties of mankind?"

Incidentally it may be noted here that Phillips perfectly understood the value of quoting authorities having weight with his hearers; and none could be of more value, in addition to that of early statesmen, than Daniel Webster's. His opinions of twenty years before were more serviceable to the speaker than those of a later date. Doubtless there were members of the legislative committee who regretted that so promising an advocate and interpreter of the Constitution as Phillips had shown himself should espouse a view of its powers and limitations that would be sure to affect unfavourably the trade and manufactures of New England by opposing the Southern scheme of annexing Texas.

Detail work incidental to his new alliance soon began. In three months he was appointed one of a delegation from Boston to an anti-slavery convention in New York. In June he was reported as one of the "interested and animated debaters among those who usually attend our meetings." On July 4th he delivered the address of the day in Lynn; August 30th he was present at a convention in Worcester; on September 21st he attended a peace meeting in Marlborough Chapel, at which he opposed a resolution in favour of the doctrine and practice of non-resistance, which was becoming a disturbing question in abolition circles, and of which more would be heard later. At Worcester, in October, as chairman of a committee, he reported resolutions "to vote for no man who was not opposed to slavery, and to keep out of all political party affiliations," another tendency which was to become a further cause of dissension in years to come. These were his principal appearances during the first complete year in abolition ranks. He had attended other meetings and served on committees and discussed measures of minor importance. It was of more consequence that he closed the year 1838 by forming a city anti-slavery society on Christmas Day in Boston, and was chosen its first president. For a recruit and a young man his record ought to have been eminently satisfactory to his co-workers. There is no evidence, however, that they were inclined to make a leader of him, or that he aspired to leadership. That position was occupied by Mr. Garrison, and the younger man would not have wished to disturb him. Moreover, there were other things to be done besides the speaking in which he excelled. Even his oratory had to be in the line of information and instruction as much as in eloquent persuasion.

The year 1839 opened with an opportunity to the orator almost as favourable as that of his first appearance before a representative city audience. On January 24th the public opinion of Boston had advanced so far as to permit Faneuil Hall to be opered for a meeting in favour of abolishing slavery in the District of Columbia. This measure had been broached ten years before by Lundy, who urged petitioning Congress — a suggestion that was taken up by Garrison in Bennington, Vermont, three months later, resulting in a petition, bearing over twenty-three thousand names, being sent to Congress in January, 1829. It was received and referred to a committee, which brought in such an adverse report that Congress considered no legislation for abolishing slavery at the Capitol until the South seceded, thirty-two years afterward. Southern men saw in this proposal to free slaves in the District of Columbia the beginning of emancipation throughout the South; but Northern people considered that they had rights enough in the District to warrant them in asking that a sectional evil be removed from national ground. Accordingly they kept on memorializing Congress for an entire generation. Still, it had taken Boston a third of this period to endorse the movement sufficiently to allow its Liberty Hall to be used for a discussion of the subject. At length the doors were unbarred and Wendell Phillips, one of a dozen speakers, offered the following resolution:

Resolved, That whether the members of Congress sustain freedom of speech in the Capitol or not—Massachusetts and Faneuil Hall are never gagged.

It was a declaration for the present and the future rather than of what had been true during the last decade. Then he said:

Two things we have certainly done; we have opened these doors, and we have pictured that man's features [John Quincy Adams's] on these walls, not to honour him as the ex-President of the United States, but as *the man* who alone has dared, on the floor of Congress, to maintain that slaves have a right to petition. It is fitting that we should meet here. We have united to finish what our fathers left unfinished when they declared that all men are born free and equal. . . . The patriot as well as the abolitionist is concerned in the struggle. When we first commenced the contest for the rights of the coloured man, we supposed that all our own rights were safe. The right of petition was a right which our fathers brought over with them. It is of English, not of American, origin. But we have learned another lesson: we have found that in order to establish the rights of the slave, we must first establish our own.

He then touched upon other rights that were endangered:

It is said that our efforts will dissolve the Union. . . . We may preserve the form of the Union, but it will be value-less, if bought at such a cost [of free speech]. There is no Union at this moment for any man in this hall that will sustain our own rights. He cannot set his foot in Virginia. . . . It was the boast of ancient Rome that she had thrown over her citizens the shield of her own powerful protection. No matter in what remote or barbarous land he might be found, as a Roman citizen he was sure of protection. Not so with Massachusetts; her citizens are seized in sister states and sold into slavery; a Senator of

the United States threatens wholesale hanging, while her
Webster is dumb and her Fletcher is gagged.

Webster had held that the Constitution was a compact
between the states, and that the North must accept it with
the unfortunate permission of slavery and let it alone.
Phillips continued:

How did Massachusetts understand the compact? That
we were to be *free* under the Union as we were free before.
If the thoughts and suppositions of the parties, and not
their words, are to settle the nature of compacts, let Massachusetts speak, as well as Virginia.   Let her tell the thoughts
of her Heaths and her Sedgwicks, her Quincys, and her
Otises, and other leaders of the revolution.[1]

Alluding to the meeting that had been held for the
defence of slavery in Faneuil Hall in 1835:

That meeting spoke for oppression, and it ought to
have been silenced, as it was, in forgetfulness and disgrace. They said they were seeking to prevent the
dissolution of the Union. Love the Union as we may,
and cherish it as we do, equally with the loudest of our
opposers—we say, perish the Union if we must abandon the slave. God has so bound us to the slave that
we cannot abandon him. We are embarked in the
same vessel, and must be saved or perish together. So
let it be our firm determination this day that we will live
or die with the slave.

If there had been any uncertainty about Phillips's
position, it was dispelled by this speech. The Constitution
and the Union had been the two pillars on which the

---

[1] With regard to the opinions of eminent Virginians those of Washington are well stated
in Lodge's " Life of Washington," pp. 105-108; of Henry in Tyler's " Life," p. 388; of Jefferson in his " Works," as indicated by indexes.

prosperity and the existence of the Nation rested; and no state had furnished so eloquent an advocate of this axiomatic doctrine as Massachusetts. Whatever Calhoun had threatened or Clay deplored, Daniel Webster had stood by the Constitution, as a compact indivisible. Philanthropic persons might be carried away by their pity for bondmen, but to assail the entire Constitution for an unfortunate article, without which it would not have been adopted, and to split the Union in two because one section of it would not abolish an inherited wrong, was demanding more than Boston would make haste to admit fifty years after the compact was made. It had been wise in permitting free speech. Abolition speeches, a dozen of them, had been made; but it is probable that more followers would have been secured by a refusal of the hall. Even Phillips lacked the spur of opposition, and apparently added nothing to the fame he had won. Possibly it was difficult to be enthusiastic under conditions revealed by a reporter's note — "When it is considered that the reporter was taking notes in a room without fire or seats, and that the thermometer was below zero, that his paper was full, and all the pencils he could borrow used up, he humbly asks to be forgiven for the remainder of the remarks" — made after the sixth speaker had finished.

Phillips did not fail to discover that the success of the cause must be accomplished by hard work, with its petty details; by information, instruction, and exhortation from humble platforms and before audiences of dozens and twenties. If he "enlisted for the war" he would have to forget the distinction won in the first encounter, and descend to the commonplace task of recruiting, organizing, and drilling, with now and then an address at a general muster of officers. But this was what many a blue-and-gold hero had done in the beginning of his career; besides, it is demanded by any new movement, and old ones, too, for that matter. For this sort of work he found abundant opportunity as general agent of the Massachusetts society, an office to which he was appointed early in 1839. His duties were similar to those of a state missionary—to organize stations wherever there were schoolhouses. Meetings were to be held in churches, halls, and vestries, when they could be had; committees appointed and lecturers assigned. To him it was a new and strange undertaking, not without its disagreeable features, as all itinerants know. The welcome offered by country villages was often doubtful and sometimes dangerous; the hospitality of the faithful was equally dangerous in respect to diet and lodging. Nevertheless, Phillips braved things that were perilous and persons who were far from congenial, going up and down the state among the hundred towns where no societies had been established, and in which old prejudices had to be overcome and a new sentiment created. The measure of his devotion to the cause he had espoused is best estimated by the disagreeable conditions of such an undertaking to a man of his tastes and way of life. Jonathan Edwards among the Stockbridge Indians was not much more out of place. Even he had his own roof and his own table for refuge when night came — and the presidency of Princeton was his early reward, though brief.

Phillips's reward — he received no pecuniary compensa-

tion — was in the slow growth of opinion among what is
often the flighty element in communities — people who are
ready for any new 'ism; frothy folk who mark the farthest
advance of some chance wave up the beach before the
general tide arrives. They are the uncomfortable accom-
paniment of far-sighted pioneers and reformers, light-
headed enthusiasts who flank a stately procession and
detract somewhat from its dignity, as do small boys on the
sidewalks from the splendour of military reviews. Moreover, those who recall Lowell's essay on Thoreau will
remember that the beginning of the second third of the
last century teemed with eccentricities of all sorts. In
the revolt from a Puritanism that had served its purpose,
there was a sense of freedom which cropped out in queer
directions:

Every form of intellectual and physical dyspepsia brought
forth its gospel. Wild-eyed enthusiasts rushed from all
sides, each eager to thrust under the bird that chalk egg
from which a new and fairer creation was to be hatched
in due time. Presartorial simplicity, plainness of speech,
even swearing, disuse of money (unless earned by other
people) — all had their evangelists. Communities were
established where everything was to be common but common
sense. All stood ready at a moment's notice to reform
everything but themselves.

It was this long-haired, hare-brained minority in communities that was always in the front seats when any apostle
of new thought appeared, and often to his discomfiture.
They did not help any cause to which they gave their effu-
sive assent. The wise speaker spoke over their heads,
addressing more deliberate thinkers of retiring mien.

This head-foremost element Lowell termed "the whistle and trailing fuse of the shell." But having depicted the humorous side of that period of ferment, he adds: "But there was a very solid and serious kernel, full of the most deadly explosiveness. Thoughtful men divined it, but the generality suspected nothing."

One by one these "thoughtful men" saw the force of what Phillips had to say about the entailed inconsistency between the Declaration of Independence and the Constitution; between a free republic and a slave-holding Union. They asked, "What can we do?" He answered, "Band yourselves together, agitate, discuss, read, petition, write your representatives, and *vote*. By and by your ballots will settle every question and right every wrong." Separation was the extremest measure and disunion the greatest disaster that had occurred to statesmen. And yet, was it pure rhetoric, or a statesman's prophetic vision, that made Webster speak in January, 1830, of "the broken and dishonoured fragments of a once glorious Union; of states dissevered, discordant, belligerent; of a land rent with civil feuds, or drenched it may be with fraternal blood"? No such vision was possible to the pioneer abolitionists. Indeed, so contrary to the thought of civil strife was Garrison, that his non-resistant doctrine was one of the germs of later disagreement in the camp. Votes were the ultimate appeal; and he himself would not even vote. But he would always agitate; and agitation was the business of the general agent, Wendell Phillips. As a consequence, societies sprang up here and there in his circuit of the states. They were so many centres of information and proselyting. Their influence rippled out to other towns, and these joined in county associations, to be represented in state conventions. The man was beginning to fulfil his mission.[1]

---

[1] The assistance which the leaders received from many devoted associates, which both Garrison and Phillips were always forward to acknowledge, should not be passed over without mention. Their names and labours cannot be recounted at length within the limits of this sketch, but it is mere justice to say that they have been generously remembered in the " Life of W. L. Garrison," by his children.

VI

IN EUROPE

(1839–1841)

A LITTLE later Phillips's work was interrupted. Mrs. Phillips's health, never the best, declined so rapidly, that her puzzled physicians advised a European trip. It is possible that they thought a temporary absence from the arena of that early contest might be beneficial to the woman who was waiting and watching at home while her husband was working in the field. Neither of them was willing to desert the cause for a day; but the doctors, backed by the Phillips family — who hoped that he might be "cured of his fanaticism" — hastened the departure. The two delayed only long enough to attend the annual meeting of the New England Anti-slavery Society, held in Boston May 30, 1839.

Extracts from a letter addressed to Mr. Phillips on his departure by the Massachusetts society indicate the esteem in which he and his work were held at the time and what, in a measure, he had accomplished.

We feel that in a worldly sense few have made larger sacrifices upon the altar of humanity than yourself. Descended from a highly respectable lineage, connected with an elevated class in society, possessed of rare abilities which qualified you to reach and to fill high and respectable offices in the gift of the nation, in the springtime of manhood when the love of popular applause, rather than of doing good, generally inflames the youthful mind, you turned your back upon the blandishments of a seductive world, repudiated all hope of political preferment and legal eminence, made yourself of no reputation for the benefit of the perishing bondman, and became the associate of those who, for seeking the abolition of slavery by moral and religious instrumentalities, are up to this hour subject to popular odium, to violent treatment, to personal insult. You buckled on the abolition armour when there were blows to take as well as to give, and from that hour to the present we have ever found you in the front rank of the conflict, reckless of all consequences growing out of a faithful adherence to principle, and giving *yourself* as a freewill offering to the sacred cause of human liberty. In the most difficult and trying periods your vision has been clear, your faith unfaltering, your course unswerving from the strict line of duty. . . . We shall regard your absence as a real loss to the board, to the society we represent, and to the great anti-slavery organization in the land — a loss which cannot be made up. As the general agent of the society for the last five months your labours have been arduous, indefatigable, and in a high degree successful. For those labours you have refused to accept even a slight compensation. . . .

We bid you an affectionate farewell. We trust that your amiable partner (whose generous donations to our cause have greatly helped to advance it) will be fully restored to health, and that you both will be safely returned to us through the mercy and goodness of God.

To this personal commendation was added a summary of the growth and condition of abolitionism for the information of British friends. A brief abstract may serve to show its status at the close of the first decade of the organization:

Ten years ago there was only one advocate of immediate emancipation; now hundreds of thousands are in league
for it. In 1829, not an anti-slavery society, of a genuine
stamp, was in existence; in 1839 there are nearly two thousand. Then, scarcely a newspaper open to discussion;
now multitudes, and pamphlets are issued by the million.
No lectures then; now, they cannot be estimated, with con-
ferences, associations, and societies. Seven hundred thousand
persons have memorialized Congress. Ten times as many
slaves find their way to Canada as in 1829. The revolution
in public sentiment has even been more extraordinary.

With such commendation and credentials Mr. and
Mrs. Phillips sailed from New York in the packet *Welling-
ton*, on June 6, 1839, and arrived in London in July, whence
they proceeded by slow stages through Paris and Lyons
to Italy, intending to pass the winter in Rome. In January
they were writing home about a city which was familiar
to fewer Americans in those days than in these — about
the Palace of the Cæsars and the Pantheon, Trajan's Pillar
and the Colosseum, Titus's Baths and Nero's Golden
House, St. Peter's and the Vatican. Amidst all this came
the news of what interested them more — that a world's
anti-slavery convention had been called to meet in
London the following June, and that they had been
appointed delegates with a number of other men "and
women." The last two words look natural and inoffensive
in the commission, but they contained an element of intestine
commotion that produced immediate ferment, and came
near bursting asunder the compact body which had just
completed so triumphantly the tenth year of its existence.
To be sure, little rumblings had been heard, and some

dissent between brethren of individualistic temperament; but the need of unity in the common cause had hushed discordant voices. Women worked with men, as in the days when their grandmothers loaded muskets for the grandfathers to fire. They also did a share of the talking, and letter-writing to the newspapers, and were enrolled with the men on committees and delegations. From 1835, American women, aside from their natural sympathies for human suffering, had been inspired by the example of English women who had laboured for immediate emancipation of slaves in the West Indies.[1]

The efforts of the English, however, had resulted mainly in petitions to Parliament. In this country the "woman question" crept into the anti-slavery cause at the convention which formed the American Anti-slavery Society in 1833. It met with opposition and, in 1840, caused a division in anti-slavery ranks, resulting in the New Organization, which lived thirteen years, sadly crippling the general cause.

If there was a marked difference of opinion on the woman question in this country, there was practically none in England. When the mixed delegation reached London they found that the committee on credentials declined to admit women delegates to seats on the floor. They were welcome to the galleries. "It was not according to British custom," was the substance of the reply to American remonstrance. When the Convention assembled Phillips moved that the list of delegates be decided upon, and opened the discussion of female representation. The call, he urged,

---

[1] They also had an example nearer home, not so well known, in the petitions by Virginia women to the House of Delegates, after the Southampton insurrection of 1831, "to devise a method for the abolition of slavery."

embraced the friends of abolition everywhere. The Massachusetts and American societies had admitted women to a share in their deliberations. Their delegates had, under the call, the right to a place in the Convention. [Cries of "No," "No."] Professor Adam, of Harvard, declared that if women had no right there he had none, since his credentials were from the same society. Dr. John Bowring, afterward Sir John Bowring, M. P., endorsed these views.

William H. Ashurst, a London lawyer, and George Thompson, who had lectured in America, and for fifteen years had been a labourer in the cause of emancipation in England, and here by invitation of the abolitionists, took sides with Mr. Phillips; but the other speakers voiced the general English conviction and custom. The fact that one of these entreated the Convention to be calm, suggests that it was getting excited over the question. Another delegate, Rev. Nathaniel Colver, asserted that a large portion of the American abolitionists thought as the English did on this subject. Rev. Elon Galusha, also a delegate from America, confirmed this statement. James G. Birney said that the question had led to a split in the American Society and to the forming of a new organization from which women would be excluded; and he ventured to add that those who favoured woman's rights advocated certain heresies about government.

To this Phillips replied with a denial, and the stormy debate of several hours was closed by an overwhelming vote to exclude female delegates. Their chief advocate, Wendell Phillips, responded with good nature to George Thompson's "hope that we shall proceed with one heart and one mind," by saying, "All we asked was an expression of opinion, and, having obtained it, we shall now act with the utmost cordiality." It was said, however, that certain women of the company did not agree to his assurance that they would "sit with as much interest behind the bar as if the original proposition had been carried." It was to this meeting that Phillips went with the admonition from his beloved Ann: "No shilly-shallying, Wendell."[1]

It cannot be denied that this World's Convention was disappointing. It turned out to be little more than a conference with, and under the control of, the British and Foreign Anti-slavery Society; which distinguished itself mainly by emphasizing English, and, largely, American sentiment on the place of woman in public assemblies. A protest against its action, drawn up by Professor Adam, signed by several American delegates and presented to the Convention, was laid on the table and ordered not to be printed among the proceedings. In a meeting of the British society held directly after the adjournment of the Convention, the protesting Americans, Phillips among the rest, were not invited to speak. Instead, Birney and Stanton were assigned parts, and Remond, a coloured man, stepped forward of his own accord, and was repeatedly cheered by the audience. Garrison, who had arrived late at the Convention, took his seat in the gallery, which he could not be induced to leave, thus making his silent protest against the rejection of his female co-workers. On this account, he was not included among the Exeter Hall speakers. He would have been likely to say things on the rising issue not agreeable

---

[1] In an undated letter to Colonel T. W. Higginson Phillips wrote: "The old world is not ready for our question (woman), but *acts without thinking*, generally, on the rule of admitting both sexes." Higginson MS.

to English ears.   And it is safe to say, that before the vast
London audience Phillips might have had the second great
opportunity of his life; that he would have dropped the
minor question and left it where the Convention had buried
it in its British grave; and that on the greater issue of emancipation, on which English and American opinion was then
and there a unit, he would have delivered an address that
would have given him international fame. He must
have foreseen the likelihood of such an opportunity, for
which he would not be unprepared.   If he also foresaw the
loss of it through his championship of women who were helping in the abolition movement, this sacrifice must be added
to the others he had made for the cause.   But it could not
but be doubly great in not being allowed to speak for it in the
world's metropolis.   No note of personal complaint or disappointment escaped him in his letter to the public at home
about all that had taken place, which he closed by saying:
"Circumstances, we think, make it our duty to remain on
this side the water another winter.   .   .   .   You will believe
us when we say, we had rather be with you, and enjoy the
privilege of sharing your labours."

An invitation to address the first annual meeting of the
British India Society in Freemason's Hall, July 6th, did not
afford him an opportunity equal to the one of which he was
deprived.   The probable damage to cotton raising in the
South from British competition in India was a theme only
indirectly inspiring.   This scheme might possibly make
slave labour in America unprofitable through penny-a-day
tillage by the Ganges, but there was a lurking suspicion that
even free labour might be unrequited.   The speaker did
well with a topic which meant more for British prosperity,

rivalling American, than for emancipation; but he must
have felt hampered by the twofold nature of his subject.
His best statement was: "Deliver America from the incubus
of slavery, and her beautiful prairies will beat the banks of
the Ganges; and Yankee skill in the fruitful valleys of the
South will beat England and British India in any market in
the world." But it was not the speech that he would have
made in Exeter Hall.

In a few weeks Mr. and Mrs. Phillips turned their faces
toward the Continent again, notwithstanding the solicitations
of English friends urging a longer stay. Medicinal springs
in Bavaria were tried to little purpose, but the travellers lost
nothing by the way in their leisurely progress from place to
place through Germany, Switzerland, and Northern Italy.
In October they were in Milan, and settled in Florence by
November; thence to Leghorn for sea breezes in midwinter,
and afterward to Naples and Rome in the spring, whence they
journeyed to Paris in the early summer, and to London once
more after almost a year's absence. What all this was
to them can best be summarized by a letter to the *Liberator*
of May 28, 1841, from which the following paragraphs are
taken with necessary condensation:

'T is a melancholy tour: and I do not understand how
any one can return from it without being, in Coleridge's
phrase, a sadder and a wiser man. Every reflecting mind
must be struck, at home, with the many social evils which
prevail around; but the most careless eye cannot avoid seeing
the painful contrasts which sadden one here at every step,
— wealth and poverty, refinement and barbarism, cultivation and debasement. .   .   . There is much to admire in
the democratic method of Catholic worship. The beggar in
rags, the peasant in his soiled and labour-stained homespun,

kneel on the broad marble, side by side with fashion and rank, seemingly unconscious of any difference between himself and his fellow worshippers. . . . Italy, however, is truly the land " where every prospect pleases, and only man is vile." All Europe is, indeed, the treasure house of rich memories. Mayence, the mother of printing and free trade, Amalfi, with her Pandects, the fountain of law — her compass of commerce — her Masaniello of popular freedom; Naples, with her galaxy of genius; Rome, whose name is at once a history and a description, will ever be the Meccas of the mind. But all the fascinations of art, all the luxuries of modern civilization are no balance to the misery which bad laws and bad religion alike entail on the bulk of the people. For even when she marries a matchless sky to the Bay of Naples, the impression is saddened by the presence of degraded and suffering humanity. . . .

I am glad to have had the opportunity of holding up the cause calmly before my mind, of being able to look back upon the course we have taken; and having done so, I am convinced more and more of the claims it has upon each one of us; and I hope to be permitted to return to my place, prepared to urge its claims with more earnestness, and to stand fearlessly by it without a doubt of its success. . . .

When Paul's appeal unto Cæsar brought him into this Bay of Naples he stood a prisoner of a despised race in the presence of the pomp and luxury of the Roman people. Even amid their ruins I could not but realize how strong the faith of the apostle to believe that the message he bore would triumph alike over their power and their religion. Struggling against priest and people, may we cherish a like faith.

After a fortnight's stay in London and the vicinity, Mr. and Mrs. Phillips celebrated the Fourth of July, 1841, by embarking from Liverpool on a steamer — at that time regarded as hazardous as some other ways of observing the anniversary of our independence. In thirteen days, on July 17th, the *Caledonia* reached Boston, and, in the papers of the 23d the Massachusetts Anti-slavery Society's officers announced a social meeting to welcome Wendell and Anne G. Phillips and three others, two of whom, the Chapmans, had recently returned from Hayti. This reception took place in Chardon Street Chapel in the afternoon of August 2d, at which Garrison, Phillips, and others, made speeches of welcome and reply.

The principal object of their two years' stay abroad had not been accomplished; Mrs. Phillips's health was little improved. However, they brought home a store of memories, as only they can who have the antecedent knowledge around which treasures of history and art may cluster. To Mr. Phillips such a pilgrimage was what similar travels have been to many whose education has been begun by the texts and preliminary chapters of university courses, but finished only with the completed years of life. This second stage of it, taken as a matter of course by his English contemporaries, was of more value to him, as it was to some of his associates here, by reason of the difficulty and rarity of the tour in his day. All lovers of Longfellow, for instance, will recall what he brought out of Europe for America, and gave back to the Old World with the interest which talent pays. And no one can read the speeches of Wendell Phillips from this date without observing their enrichment by spoils from the old empires beyond the sea.

For the remainder of the summer the two stayed with Madam Phillips in her commodious house at Nahant. The wife wrote to an English friend:

The village of Nahant is about a mile from our house; there Dame Fashion struts about three months in summer, but we have the blessing of being out of her way, doing as we please. . . . We are considered as heretics and almost infidels, but we pursue the even tenor of our way undisturbed. Sometimes Wendell goes off abolitionizing for two or three days, but I remain on the ground.

In the autumn they took possession of a small house, No. 26 Essex Street, which Mrs. Phillips had inherited from her father. It was in a neighbourhood to which the names of Garrison, Jackson, Chapman, and Loring gave an abolition complexion; and in the social ostracism of the company such association was congenial, or at least all that was left them. In this new domicile Phillips found opportunities to use his mechanical skill, from planing a door to sawing soapstone; but by Thanksgiving Day he was at leisure to describe the feast to an English woman, historically, religiously, and gastronomically:

To worship where their fathers knelt, and gather sons and grandsons under the old roof-tree, to — shall I break the picture? — cram as much turkey and plum pudding as possible; a sort of compromise by Puritan love of good eating for denying itself that "wicked papistrie," Christmas. . . . Ann gets tired out every day trying to oversee "keeping house," as we Americans call it when two persons take more rooms than they need, buy double the things they want, hire two or three others, just, for all the world, for the whole five to devote themselves to keeping the house in order. I long for the time when there'll be no need of sweeping and dusting, and when eating will be forgotten.

Of herself the wife writes:

She laughs considerably, continues in health in the same naughty way, strolls out a few steps occasionally, calling it a walk; the rest of the time, from bed to sofa, from sofa to rocking-chair, reads the *Standard* and *Liberator*,

sees no company and makes no calls, looks forward to
spring and birds. . . . Wendell speaks whenever he
can leave me, and for his sake I sometimes wish I were
myself again, but I dare say it is all right as it is. What
anti-slavery news I get, I get second hand.

This might be taken as the daily record of a life which
was to be prolonged through forty-four weary years more
of increasing invalidism, outlasting the life of her husband
by two years and two months. Yet, in suffering and enforced seclusion, her joyous disposition, unfailing spirits,
and keen sense of humour kept the house from being
gloomy to her constant companion and the few friends
who could be admitted to its needful privacy.[1] Neither
was there any diminution of interest in the cause, nor of

---

[1]Without children, Mr. and Mrs. Phillips adopted, in 1851, Phœbe Garnaut, only
child of an estimable friend of Welsh birth who had married a native of France and come
to Boston, where her husband soon died. From her thirteenth year the girl "was a bright
and loving companion to Mrs. Phillips until her marriage to Mr. George H. Smalley took
her to another city and finally to London." Mr. Phillips's namesakes, Wendell Phillips
Garrison and Wendell Phillips Blagden, were the constant recipients of affectionate remembrance, several expressions of which in unpublished letters reveal the fondness of both Mr.
and Mrs. Phillips for children, in the latter amounting to a devotion to her little nephew
that was almost pathetic. And in the letters which the husband wrote "for Ann and Wendell
Phillips" the charm and tenderness of his affections are revealed. In a proportionate degree
this was true of his regard for any who had been or were his friends. One of the letters
on the occasion of the baptism of a grandnephew and namesake, Wendell Phillips Blagden,
must stand alone as an example of many:

"MY DEAR NIECE: How near did you ever come to scolding Sam? I 've no doubt he has
sometimes richly deserved it, for that 's a way our family has. *I* have come as near getting
all I deserved of late, as I ever did, for not writing you. But I could n't. Did you ever hear
of the swearing Worcester County man, famous for the poetry, eloquence, and pathos of his
oaths? Well, one day the folks saw that the tailboard of his cart had fallen down as he drove
up hill and all his potatoes were dropping out. They ran along in the fields, behind the
wall, to hear how he 'd swear when he first saw his mishap. Finally, glancing back, he saw
the vegetables scattered along the hillside behind him. Alighting, his arms dropped nerve-
lessly by his side as he said quietly: 'I feel wholly unequal to the occasion!'

"Now, that 's just my case. You see, Ann was so elated, overcome, and delighted with
'her baby,' as she called him — found out such eulogies on his beauty, manliness, weight,
and general perfection, showed him to all comers and rated their sense according to the
extent to which they went crazy over the photo — that I gave up being secretary to the family.
But she won't let me off — insists that I shall expose myself in the vain attempt to daguerreo-
type her ecstasy.

"Seriously, I have not seen her so charmed and thoroughly delighted for years as when
she opened the box and saw the photograph. I thank you most sincerely for many happy
hours in that weary room where she lies in patient helplessness. She never parts with the

material aid which her competence enabled her to render; nor was ever less the inspiration she afforded the knightly man who, with solicitude for her hourly comfort, fared forth into a world of strife to return often from scenes of insult and peril, with hopeful answer to the old, old question, " Watchman, what of the night?" — "The morning cometh."

---

picture, keeps it near her and expatiates to everybody. I cannot say that I blame her *very much* (!) or that she has not good cause. He *is* a noble fellow in spite of his name, and I don't believe that even that will ever keep him down.

"I have n't been out of the house but once of an evening for months, but I believe if Ann had not been so wholly helpless that she would have insisted on my coming on to the christening. Indeed, she began to debate how it could be done. But assuming for once(!!) a pretence of authority, I crushed that madness out before it came to a head.

"With all serious and hearty earnestness we congratulate you on your beautiful boy and wish him all the good, sweet things, all the grand, useful purposes and powers that will fulfil your aspirations. God bless him life-long.
"Love to you and yours
"ANN AND WENDELL PHILLIPS."
— *Blagden MSS.*

VII

ON THE PLATFORM

(1842)

THE pursuits which had been interrupted by two years' absence in Europe were now taken up once more. To a young and active man with a liberal education and recognized abilities, a mere existence, even with a competence, could not be satisfying. His legal profession counted for little with this one, on account of certain scruples about practising under a government whose Constitution contained articles against which he protested. For authorship he believed that he had no aptitude; the use of a pen was distasteful to him, as his letters indicate, and even in the preparation of addresses he usually discarded it.

In mental processes of composition, whether in blocking out general lines of discourse, or in the arrangement of paragraphs and the construction of sentences so carefully that they might seem, like Everett's, to have been written and memorized — for this head-work he had no superior. Nor was it a matter of slow and painful preparation altogether and always. No man was readier with a quick reply to an unexpected interruption to the course of his argument. Rejoinders had the same unhesitating flow of thoughts and pertinent words as if they had been foreseen in the privacy of his study. Not often a prisoner there for more than a day or two, not bound to desk and inkstand, he acquired the habit of composing whenever and wherever his mind was in a working mood. This was as likely to be on the platform as in the quiet of his home. His thinking was clear, therefore his statements were plain; his sense of proportion and emphasis keen, therefore he wasted nothing on irrelevancies, and gave the grace of symmetry and the force of pungency to his discourse. For such a mind and such a man, there was, in his time, an admirable arena — the lecture platform.

It was an outgrowth of the lyceum or debating society, as this, in turn, was the product of the disputatious, information loving, and literary disposition of a people who had practised freedom of speech and of thought, within certain limits, for two hundred years. There was hardly a village schoolhouse in New England that had not its winter evening debates; and in the larger towns and cities these were diversified by lectures from such celebrities as could be afforded. In cities, courses of lectures were often maintained apart from debating clubs, or at least from their performances.

As early as 1830 the lyceum lecture was fairly started as an educational factor among a people thirsting for knowledge, and also relishing its presentation in oral and literary form. This appetite had been inherited from forefathers whose chief intellectual entertainment had been Sunday sermons two or three hours long, and Thursday lectures in which a more secular complexion was admissible, especially in times of political excitement. To a large extent these pulpit performances took the place of present-day books and newspapers — Sunday papers included.

So, in the thirties and forties, did the popular lecture. On the topic of the evening the attentive listener absorbed knowledge which the speaker had been storing up during weeks of study or years of experience. Sometimes the hearer got an uplift through a moral or eloquent appeal, especially if the lecturer had a purpose, a cause, or a reform to promote. Such speakers, if they had graces of oratory, found many opportunities to promulgate views which otherwise might have gone begging for a hearing. Doubtful doctrines escaped from sources regarded with apprehension by staid communities who were proof against heresy but not against oratory. If eloquence once got the better of orthodoxy it was apt to be called back for another hearing winter after winter. Emerson was particularly liable to recall, as the elders were not always sure that they understood exactly what he said, and the surer youngsters were always willing to risk hearing the same again.

First and last, for about forty years, the lyceum lecture was a great and entertaining educator. Successive lectures were anticipated with eager expectation and listened to with as much pleasure and more profit than the modern play. The best speakers of the generation were in constant demand, and every man who had a gift for popular exposition found a place on the lists of agencies known as "lecture bureaus," with which associations and committees arranged for intellectual supplies according to their pecuniary ability. Among the greater lights and earlier was Edward Everett, who could not be had for ordinary occasions, but whose eulogy on Washington may be regarded as preëminently the first in rank of its class and the most widely heard. It was welcome all over the land, with its purpose of making

Mount Vernon a national possession, to which it contributed over fifty-three thousand dollars, two thousand more being added by the author of it. Rufus Choate illustrated American history by addresses somewhat above the taste of the average audience, but not above the intelligence of the best. Horace Mann delivered a volume of lectures on Education, and Ralph Waldo Emerson two volumes on a variety of themes, which appeared in print afterward as essays. Rev. Drs. Bellows and Chapin, clergymen of New York, were speakers who carried audiences along the lines of their topics almost by bodily force, as also did Henry Ward Beecher by an immense magnetic power, coupled with humour and a sympathetic delivery. George William Curtis's literary addresses, and particularly those on the relations of education to citizenship, were always of the highest class, drifting into advocacy of universal freedom as the war years approached. All together these distinguished men, and others almost their equals, with some specialists in science, art, and travels, made the lecture period one of great value and renown. Like the oratorical age, of which it was both the product and in part the creator, it passed away with the reactions that followed the Civil War, having served a purpose which neither pulpit nor press could accomplish with their then limited sectarian, or party, ministries.

Upon this instruction from the platform Phillips had entered as early as 1836; at first, with subjects from the domain of natural science, according to his intellectual bent. In 1838, he produced a lecture on the "Lost Arts," which was destined to be delivered hundreds of times; probably the most popular discourse of any kind that belonged to the lecture age; of which he said in the opening paragraph: "This lecture belongs to that first phase of the lyceum system, before it undertook to meddle with political duties or dangerous ethics; when it was a merely academic institution, trying to win busy men back to books, teaching a little science, or repeating some tale of foreign travel, or painting some great representative character, the symbol of his age. I think I can claim a purpose beyond a moment's amusement in this glance at early civilization." His purpose in this lecture was to show that the customary mood of self-veneration and conceit which impels us to take off our hats to ourselves — like Coleridge's German whenever he spoke of himself — may be rebuked by observing some things in which the ancients surpassed us.

His enumeration of these and comments upon them under the heads of glass, medals, colours, fabrics, masonry, and the mechanical devices employed in pyramid building and obelisk raising was doubtless interesting to the people of a former generation and limited cultivation; but a large share of the lecture's attractiveness must be attributed to the colloquial ease and dignified grace with which the speaker discoursed of seven wonders that perished with antiquity. There was no opportunity for reformatory eloquence, although he did introduce allusions to the "irrepressible Negro" and the American politician, comparing the latter to the Damascus blade "which could be put into a scabbard like a corkscrew, and bent every way without breaking." Whatever may be the value of this lecture as reading matter — and it is still not without interest — the persistent demand for it through many years determines its worth as a spoken address, as delivered by its author to the hundreds of thousands who heard it. It was never written out by him, but by a reporter, and presented to him by friends with the words: "We have not done it for your sake, Mr. Phillips, but for posterity." Such was the contemporary estimate; and such, it may be remarked, is often the difference between the effect produced by the living voice and magnetic presence, and that by cold type and the lapse of years. It is possible that the lecturer himself often wondered why it was so popular. Since it was, however, he had his own use for it in the direction of a larger purpose. He made it an advance agent in doubtful territory, which might secure for him a second invitation to speak, when it would be safer to introduce something on his chosen theme of abolition.

An instance of this preparatory method occurred the winter after his return from abroad, when he was invited to deliver a lecture in old Concord on "Street Life in Europe." He kept fairly well to his subject, giving slavery a few thrusts by the way. The effect of them was to obtain for him an invitation to speak on slavery the next winter. But a respectable minority, as the time approached, pronouncing his allusions, "vile, pernicious, and abominable," urged that he be asked to speak on some other subject. The majority voted otherwise, and, encouraged by the ruling sentiment, he was particularly severe upon Church and State. At the next meeting of the lyceum his lecture and himself were the subjects of denunciation by two of the village squires, who called him an "audacious stripling" who had proclaimed "monstrous doctrines"; and while they complimented his eloquence they warned the young

against its insidious charm. The orator had been notified
by his friends of what was likely to happen at this meeting,
and as it was an open one he would have an opportunity
to reply. Asking permission to do so, he said, in part:

I agree with the last speaker that this is a serious subject;
had it been otherwise I should not devote my life to it.
"Stripling" as I am, I but echo the voice of the ages, of
our venerable forefathers, of statesmen, poets, philosophers.
The gentleman has painted the dangers to life, liberty,
and happiness that would be the consequence of doing
right. These dangers now exist by law at the South.
Liberty may be bought at too dear a price; if I cannot
have it except by sin, I reject it. But I cannot so blaspheme
God as to doubt my safety in obeying Him. The sanctions
of English law are with me; but if I tread the dust of law
beneath my feet and enter the Holy of Holies, what do I
find written there? "Thou shalt not deliver unto his master
the servant who is escaped to thee; he shall dwell with you,
even among you." I throw myself, then, on the bosom
of Infinite Wisdom. Even the heathen will tell you, "Let
justice be done though the heavens fall"; and the old reformer answered when warned against the danger of going
to Rome, "It is *not* necessary that I should live; it *is* necessary
that I go to Rome." But now our pulpits are silent —
who ever heard this subject presented until it was done
by silly women and striplings? The first speaker accused
me of ambition; let me tell him that ambition chooses a
smoother path to fame. And to you, my young friends,
who have been cautioned against exciting topics and advised
to fold your hands in selfish ease, I would say, Not so;
throw yourselves upon the altar of some noble cause. To
rise in the morning only to eat and drink, and gather gold
— that is a life not worth living. Enthusiasm is the life
of the soul.

This incident may be taken as an example of the channels

which were open, or sometimes closed, to the agitator, and of the methods he employed to disseminate doctrines whose character is indicated by the above remarks. His spirit is also exhibited by them — fearless, confident of the ground on which he stood, and of the ultimate verdict of the North when it should come to its better sense, and get the better of its commercial greed.

He embraced the lecture system as giving him an opportunity to reach the people of almost every town and city in his own and other states year after year for nearly an entire generation before the main purpose of his life was accomplished — from 1836 to 1866, and for eighteen years more, during which he advocated other causes. When it is remembered that the audience in each place was made up of persons from all the church congregations, and of many who belonged to none; of citizens from all political parties or no party; of old and young, male and female, it will be admitted that no preacher or association of preachers, no newspaper of a single class, nor all of a single party or creed together, could reach so many thinking people the country over as the lyceum lecturer. He might not have the general assent to his propositions that the preacher expects; nor the unquestioning absorption of his statements that the editor's type favours; but if he had the art of persuasion, itself resting on personal conviction, he would have the opportunity on many platforms of making ten converts where the denomination's pulpit and the party's newspaper made one. These, in the main, confirmed and fortified the beliefs of the faithful; the other reached those who strayed for an hour from their customary haunts and were listening to unfamiliar ideas and views of which they had never heard, unless as heretical. If the lecturer had the magician's skill, as Phillips had, to make black white, and convince in the face of rooted prejudice, at least while he was speaking, the chances of unsettling old opinions were multiplied. He might not eradicate them at once; but the roots were loosened and the soil that had been settling around them for generations was shaken as if in the line of an earthquake. Sometimes men felt that the everlasting foundations of things, especially of the Nation, were being broken up, or at least assailed, and they cried out at the sacrilege and hurled epithets at the speaker.

Enough has been seen of the trend of Phillips's opinions and their expression to indicate the use he would soon make of the platform. More and more the anti-slavery cause was engaging his attention, and any favourable occasion was likely to call him out.

The first of these after his return from Europe was afforded by the reception of an appeal from seventy thousand Irishmen to their countrymen in America, urging them to identify themselves with the abolition movement. Aside from containing the names of Father Mathew and Daniel O'Connell, the chief distinction of the memorial was its size. Even this could not have surprised one who knows how easy it is to obtain signatures recommending philanthropy three thousand miles away. The Irish ignorance of conditions surrounding their countrymen in America was more astonishing. Perhaps they could not understand in Ireland what it was to be a Democrat here in the 'forties; and how the party stood on the slavery question. But, whoever set the snowball rolling, the voluminous petition was here, and the abolitionists determined to make the most of it

at the annual meeting of the Massachusetts Society in Faneuil
Hall on January 28, 1842.   Two or three speakers discovered
enough Irish blood in their descent to commend them to
as many of their five thousand cousins in the city as happened to be present; but Wendell Phillips could not fall
back upon a Celtic pedigree.   Acquaintance with O'Connell
and admiration for him as the leading agitator of the day
was the conciliatory note of his address, together with
reference to Emmet and Curran and Grattan.   Referring to
the devoted earnestness and untiring zeal with which Ireland
had carried on for so many years the struggle for her freedom,
and to the men who lost no faith in the cause, he spoke
of the generous isle and the valour of its heroes and statesmen, of the catholicity of a church which allowed men
of colour in St. Peter's at Rome and beneath the portals
of the Propaganda College, with none to sneer at their
complexion or repulse them from society, and cited the
protests of a long line of Popes denouncing the sin of making
merchandise of men.   He spoke of Ireland as a land of
agitators from whom we may learn a lesson in the battle
for human rights, and of the welcome that American
abolitionists received in Dublin (of which O'Connell was
then mayor).   His appeal was to the love of liberty which
every Irishman brings to this country, exhorting him to
cast no vote without asking if the hand to which he intrusts
political power will use it for the slave.

Will you ever return to his master the slave who once
sets foot on the soil of Massachusetts ? [No, no!]   Will
you ever raise to office or power the man who will not pledge
his utmost effort against slavery ? [No, no, no!]   Then
may we not hope still for freedom ?   Thanks to those noble

men who battle in her cause the world over. The ocean of their philanthropy knows no shore; humanity knows no country; and I am proud here in Faneuil Hall, fit place to receive their message, to learn of O'Connell's fidelity to freedom and of Father Mathew's love for the real interests of man.

The entire speech was an early manifestation of Phillips's breadth of sympathy, notwithstanding an intensity of feeling which sometimes incurred the charge of narrowness. To be sure, his immediate concern was to win Irish sympathy and coöperation; but he asked nothing for bondmen here that he was not willing to give to the oppressed in Ireland. This feature of his philanthropy, which appeared at the outset of his struggle for human rights, reappeared from time to time in his advocacy of other causes than that of the slave.

O'Connell made handsome return by pronouncing this speech "the most classic short one in the English language," and added, "I resign the crown. This young American is without an equal." But his immigrant countrymen here, after roaring their applause, went out and read what their newspaper had to say on the other side of the question and accepted the counsel of a New York archbishop. Thenceforward, as before, they voted the straight Democratic ticket, and hated their black labour competitors for the next twenty years. After the war broke out they made amends.

So far, Phillips's advocacy of the anti-slavery cause had contemplated prior and fundamental issues, as the right of petition, a free press, and unhampered discussion. A more direct defence was now to be made, marking his entrance upon a hand to hand strife with the slave power, to be continued until that power fell.

George Latimer, a fugitive slave from Norfolk, Virginia, had been pursued to Boston and arrested on a nominal charge of theft. As a runaway, his case was referred to the United States Circuit Court, coming under Article IV., Section 2, of the Constitution: "No person held to service or labour in one state, under the laws thereof, escaping into another, shall, in consequence of any law or regulation therein, be discharged from such service or labour; but shall be delivered up on claim of the party to whom such service or labour may be due."[1]

There was no reason to suppose that Judge Story could reverse the plain intent of this article as agreed to by the several states and by the decisions of the Federal Court in those states. But there was a growing opinion among the citizens of Northern states that this part of the compact was a violation of the rights of man, and of a higher law of humanity which had been gradually coming into recognition century by century since the beginning of the Christian Era. An open meeting of citizens was called, for the expression of their opinion on the subject of returning fugitive slaves, and, incidentally, of the agreement by which it must inevitably be done. Faneuil Hall was the place; the time, nine o'clock Sunday evening, October 30th. The abolition leaders took charge of the meeting and appointed speakers; but such a rabble took possession of the hall as made the turbulent crowd at the Lovejoy meeting five years before to be remembered as a Sunday-

---

[1] For a discussion of the introduction of this article into the Constitution see G. T. Curtis's "History of the Constitution," ii., 449.

school in comparison. It did not look as if Boston was
being rapidly converted to abolition doctrine and practice.
Speeches were delivered in sections and fragments, as the
speakers could get a chance between hisses and howls,
cat-calls and cursing. Respectable citizens had attended
church that day; it was too late for the usual evening meetings,
and the godless element who had been under customary
Sabbath restraint were having a meeting after their own
hearts to uphold the Constitution and the laws of the land
with respect to slaves and slaveholders. Taken together,
it could not have been a fair representation of the average
sentiment of the city, unless that upon the platform be
regarded as a counterweight. But the intelligence, humanity,
and justice displayed there under difficulties got a better
and wider hearing next day in the press, whose tone was,
that whatever might be the opinions of speakers who could
obtain Faneuil Hall, they had a right to be heard without
interference from a mob of which the city ought to be
ashamed.

So much has been said of the character of this riotous
assembly as prefatory to a speech by Mr. Phillips, which
has not always been considered in connection with these
exasperating provocations.

Fellow-citizens, I will ask your attention but a single
moment. I wish only to bear testimony in favour of liberty.
[Uproar.] No generous man will try to drown my voice
when I plead the cause of one not allowed to speak for
himself. . . . The swarming thousands before me,
the creators of public sentiment, bolt and bar that poor
man's dungeon to-night. [Great uproar.] I know I am
addressing the white slaves of the North. [Hisses and
shouts.] Shake your chains; you have not the courage to

break them. This old hall cannot rock as it used to with the spirit of liberty. It is chained down by the iron links of the United States Constitution. [Hisses and uproar.] Many of you, I doubt not, regret to have this man given up, but you cannot help it. There stands the bloody clause in the Constitution — you cannot fret the seal off the bond. The fault is in allowing such a Constitution to live an hour. . . . When I look upon these crowded thousands, and see them trample on their consciences and the rights of their fellow-men at the bidding of a piece of parchment, I say my *curse* be on the Constitution of these United States. [Hisses and shouts.] . . . Shall our taxes pay men to hunt slaves? Shall we build jails to keep them? [Uproar.] If a Southerner comes here to get his lost horse, he must prove title before a jury of twelve men. If he comes to catch a slave, he need only to prove title to any Justice of the Peace whom he can make his accomplice. I record here my testimony against this pollution of our native city. The man in the free state who helps hunt slaves is no better than a bloodhound. The attorney is baser still. But any judge who should grant a certificate would be the basest of all:

> "And in the lowest deep, a lower deep,
>   Still threatening to devour him, opens wide."

Of course, many were shocked at this outburst against the Constitution — a sacred compact, and the embodiment of the Nation's law. To denounce it on account of a sentence or two about property in slaves, and its protection, was to make a small part greater than the whole. Moreover, to let the discussion of it alone was a most necessary condition of commercial prosperity. To malign the precious document was to revile the wisdom of statesmen and patriots, and to pronounce a curse upon it was deemed next to cursing Deity. Apparently, to Mr. Phillips and his co-workers, the Constitution was a compromise with a part of the Nation, which had determined to maintain and perpetuate a great wrong, at first generally admitted to be an evil element in the body politic, but later a profitable factor in trade. Yet one who should disturb the foundations of government and commerce for a sentiment about an institution which had its beneficent features — such a one was a fanatic, if not a traitor, in the eyes of the mixed multitude.[1]

It was remarkable, therefore, that anything came of this turbulent meeting beyond rescuing the fugitive Latimer by the payment of four hundred dollars to his pursuer. But this precedent was not likely to discourage other slaveholders from similar pursuit, besides making Boston a market for light-footed slaves. Consequently a "convention of freemen" was held November 19th, and a petition drawn up, praying the Legislature to "forbid all persons holding office under the laws of the State of Massachusetts from aiding in the arrest or detention of persons claimed as fugitives from slavery; to forbid the use of jails or other public property, for their detention; and to prepare amendments to the Federal Constitution that should forever separate the people of the state from all connection with slavery." This Personal Liberty Act was passed March 24, 1843.[2]

In the speech which he made it is to be observed that Phillips's indignation at the slave hunt under the Constitution was intensified by the mob's noisy defence of the arrest. With the Lovejoy meeting in mind, he must have felt that

---

[1] "The Constitution, a bundle of compromises, all needful." — Roosevelt's "Life of Gouverneur Morris," p. 122.

[2] Later, the Legislature passed resolutions addressed to Congress recommending an amendment to the Constitution whereby the "three-fifths representation for slaves" should be abolished. These resolves were presented to Congress by John Quincy Adams, December 21, 1843.

his commanding power over an audience was to be severely tested. Defeat threatened him for a while in this second encounter with the masses. He won by interrupted onsets and sheer persistence. Another feature also of this speech is noteworthy — that he took no pains to conciliate the crowd. Instead, he employed a method of attack which became common with him, namely, to launch his unwelcome theses in their most repellent terms at the outset, stirring up the ire of opponents and making the situation as difficult for himself as possible. This, then, became the joy of battle, and to convince and silence his adversaries all the greater triumph. In time, those who were familiar with his tactics learned to accept his startling assertions unmoved, and to wait for the proofs, real or apparent, which were sure to follow.

Once more: it was no ordinary feat of oratory to stem the tumultuous tide that surged up from the rabble. Great praise is often accorded speakers when a sympathetic audience listens breathlessly to eloquent periods, as did the distinguished assembly to Webster's second reply to Hayne, or the hushed multitude to Lincoln's encomium of the slain at Gettysburg. But there was no sympathy or interest or reverence in the senseless crowd in Faneuil Hall that Sunday night when a young orator of thirty-three first maddened and then held in check a many-headed monster called an audience by courtesy. He met in the early years of his career the worst trial and severest test of a speaker. If he had shown the white feather or conducted a graceful retreat, he would have betrayed the secret of their possible success to every mob that should follow. It was a critical juncture, a thousand against one.

For the one to prove himself superior to the thousand was not only a personal triumph, but a victory for the only art by which one man can baffle a raging multitude.

The sharpness of Phillips's invective set people to thinking, as it certainly did to talking. A new view of the Compact had been published, and one and another inquired if there was a particle of truth or reason in it. It took many years to convince the majority that there was. The last clause in the above resolutions, to "forever separate the people of the state from all connection with slavery," may be regarded as the first note of dissolving the union between free and slave states that had been formulated in the North.[1] Disunion had been in the hearts of one extremist and another, in the North as well as in the South; it had been spoken by one neighbour to another, advocated in the freedom of anti-slavery gatherings, and printed among other extravagances in the journals of the coterie. At last it had appeared in the scarcely less responsible utterance of a small public meeting, attempting to formulate the resulting opinion of the Latimer incident. It was a stake driven to show how far extreme sentiment had moved forward on the flood of excitement. The general public regarded it with abhorrence, and as the wild dream of malcontents, revolutionists, and fanatics.

But what was the disunion they advocated, and how did it differ from that which was afterward effected by the South? Holding with the fathers of the Nation that slavery was an evil to be extirpated and a wrong inconsistent with

---

[1] Unless the conditional prophecy of the ninth resolution of the "Irish Address" meeting, drawn up by Garrison, be taken as precedent: "If the South be madly bent upon perpetuating her atrocious slave system . . . the American Union will be dissolved in form as it is now in fact." — "William Lloyd Garrison," Garrisons, iii., 46.

the character of a republic, they saw but two ways of dealing with it — by amending the pro-slavery provisions of the Constitution, as provided by the instrument itself; or, in case this should be impossible through Southern refusal, by withdrawal of the North in order to have no further responsibility and complicity in slaveholding. The latter was the only possible escape from a share in wrong-doing. Moreover, so long as union between the two sections stood, the North was powerless to touch slavery where it existed; nor would it ever have been abolished had not the South, by seceding, dissolved the bond and made it possible for Lincoln to reach slavery in territory abandoned by states, and Congress to make emancipation universal. But even if the North had withdrawn first, it would have had the justification of its purpose to clear itself from sharing in a crime against humanity; while the South seceded through fear of losing its share in the immediate advantages and profits of that wrong. In the final event the North avoided separation, and the abolitionists saw their desire accomplished in an unlooked-for way.

Meantime, disunion feeling was continually breaking out in the South over large areas. It was Southern policy to keep the Constitution inviolate, since it was the ægis of their interests. So far, they seem to have had the reasonable side of the conflict. If this Compact was sacred and practically unalterable, as it had come to be considered in distinction from the early views of its framers,[1] its defenders were loyal to the Union. But if a clause in it of doubtful justice and humanity should be attacked and repealed,

[1] As late as 1812, separation was a question of expediency merely. — Lodge's "Life of Webster," pp. 176, 177.

they would go for disunion. Moreover, if the Constitution
and the later enactments under it could not be made to
cover new territory for the extension of slavery, the threat
of disunion was immediately heard. "Texas or Disunion"
was a South Carolina toast on the Fourth of July, 1844,
and a convention of slaveholding states was demanded
by South Carolina and Alabama in order "to count the cost
and value of the Federal Union." Their loyalty to the
Union was conditioned upon the integrity of an elastic
Constitution which should be made to cover a growing evil,
whose germ the makers of that Constitution deplored,
but admitted in 1789, for the sake of unity. At this time,
the points of agreement between the North and South
were, among the producing and trading classes, that slavery
was commercially profitable; among conscientious and
reflecting people, that it was unjust, inhuman, and corrupting;
among extremists in both sections, that it was hastening
separation and dissolution of the Union. This last radical
view was terrifying to conservatives, who were beginning
to accept the possibility of such disaster. Schemes were
invented to save the Union with slavery and without it;
but those without it were stifled on presentation to Congress.
Let alone, the Constitution and Union and slavery would
save themselves; but, by 1843, on the introduction of the
recommendation from the State of Massachusetts, that the
three-fifths representation for slaves be abolished, there
was a feeling that disagreement had got beyond a
band of radicals. The war had been carried into
Africa, and was likely to be congressional and national,
as well as personal and sectional. In accordance with
this forward movement some abolitionists thought that it

was time to make the cause a political one and win by
legislation of their own, eventually, what they had been
asking others to legislate for them.

Against this policy of allying abolition with politics the
two principal leaders threw the weight of their influence.
Phillips had surrendered his legal practice because he
would not stand sworn to support a Constitution which
protected slave hunters. Later, he had given up voting
under the civic system until it should be reorganized free
from any taint of association with injustice. Starting the
discussion in anti-slavery circles, he published in 1844 an
argument entitled, "Can Abolitionists Vote or Take Office
Under the United States Constitution?" The negative
of this question was unanimously endorsed by the American
Anti-slavery Society in the same year by a resolution,
written by Phillips: "*Resolved*, That secession from the
present United States Constitution is the duty of every
abolitionist; since no one can take office under the United
States Constitution without violating his anti-slavery
principles, and rendering himself an abettor of the slaveholder in his sin." It is not necessary to detail divisions
of Reuben for which there were great searchings of heart. It
was a question of ways and means with some; of conscience
with others. Garrison and Phillips kept the high ground
of educating the popular mind and heart up to voting
for reforming men and measures, without setting them
any example at the polls, except that of so great an abhorrence of present conditions that they would not exercise
rights of franchise conferred by these. This was consistent with their position as pioneers and road breakers.
Their place was far in advance of the host. If they some-

times struck an impossible trail and blazed the wrong trees, it was what other surveyors had done. With a dark forest before them, it is remarkable that they ran their line so close to what afterward became the Nation's way through the wilderness. Their conscience was their compass; and if they did not allow for variations, their purpose was polar.

It was at this time that Phillips directed his attention to an influence which was obstructing the abolition movement. Five or six years before, as has been observed, the clergy of Massachusetts and Connecticut had demurred against the intrusion into their churches and parishes of zealots in a cause about whose merits there was much difference of opinion, and pastoral appeals to the congregations had been issued to dissuade them from encouraging such intruders. These addresses drew down strong words of condemnation from the abolition press, whose editors in turn were stigmatized as infidel and blasphemous — Garrison being charged with saying that every day was a Sabbath, and every man a minister. It was no trifling matter to antagonize the clerical element in New England during the last century; and the men who were having hard work to get a peaceable hearing for a philanthropic cause felt that the class from which they should have received their chief support had turned against them. When, therefore, Phillips offered his resolution at a meeting in New York about the opposition of a pro-slavery church and priesthood, it was in recognition of their identity with the most respectable element in communities and its opinion, sanctioned by religious beliefs or associated with them. He himself had lost none of his early faith, which was of the orthodox Calvanistic type, although he had not become a member of a church or parish society. These organizations represented the religion and morality of the upper and middle classes, and their views on the slavery question would be reënforced by religious and ecclesiastical authority. Whoever should speak of this lightly or adversely needed to have weighty reasons for his animadversion. He would be expected to defend with uncommon arguments such a resolution as this, offered in a New York convention:

Resolved, That anti-slavery is only to be advanced by trampling under foot the political and ecclesiastical links which bind slavery to the institutions of this country.

After remarking on the progress that the cause had made and that there was room for still more, Phillips said that the pulpit teachings of the country did more toward the preservation of slavery than statesmen and politicians in a Nation that is called Christian. The Constitution and the Church are in the way of emancipation. The framers of the Constitution had no idea that it could be used for the protection of slavery, which they thought had received its death-blow by the prohibition of the slave trade. And as for the Union, we have no right to sacrifice the liberties of one class to the fears of another. Of the entire speech a passer-by, John Neal, editor of *Brother Jonathan*, dropping in, wrote for his paper:

Having very little interest in the subject under discussion, we were meditating an escape to the street, when a gentleman with light hair and a countenance remarkable for its intellectual expression took the platform. He had scarcely opened his lips, when we were wide awake, and listening to a burst of eloquence perfectly startling. The man was faultless in his elocution, graceful in his action, and his argument was sustained with a language vivid and full of that generous power of feeling which is the life and soul of true oratory. His voice broke a little before he closed, but the speech was every way worthy of the best orator of any Nation.

VIII

RECOGNITION AND LEADERSHIP

(1843)

PHILLIPS was now recognized as one of the principal champions of abolitionism. As such he was chosen to draw up a respectful address to be presented to President Tyler, a slaveholder, on the occasion of his visit to Boston in June, 1843, when Bunker Hill monument was dedicated.

This protest reminded the Chief Magistrate that he had subscribed to the Declaration of Independence and had sworn to support the Constitution, whose design was to secure the blessings of liberty to the people, and that he was to join in commemorating the services of those who had bled and died in the cause of human liberty. Therefore he was asked to acknowledge the rights of man by breaking the chains of his own slaves, an example which would go far toward the emancipation of three millions of American people, and render his name illustrious to the latest posterity. As might have been expected, this appeal received no consideration, but it served to advertise the abolition movement in papers which published the address.

Further recognition had been accorded Phillips in his appointment as General Agent of the Massachusetts Society, entailing the practical work of lecturing here and there, introducing abolition doctrines in places where they had not been published, and organizing clubs and societies. Occasionally he wrote an open letter or pamphlet which might be used as a tract for thoughtful people to read and discuss; notably one on the binding nature of oaths to support the Constitution so long as one held office, practised law, or even voted; the alternative being to surrender these rights rather than endorse the document by which they were conferred. This abnegation of privilege, he held, would give abolitionists a stronger hold on the community. A little later he sent out another argument entitled, "The Constitution a Pro-slavery Contract; or, Selections from the Madison Papers."

Fifty years passed under this Constitution show us slaves trebling in numbers; slaveholders monopolizing the offices, dictating the policy of the Government to the support of slavery, trampling on the rights of free states and making the courts of the country their tools. We demand that every honest man join the outcry — "No Union with Slavery."

This was one of the advanced pronouncements of disunion at the North to match threats in the South by a party which wielded a wider influence than the radicals of New England, because led by men prominent in national politics, respected and followed at home, feared and obeyed in Congress, and in the North by the majority of citizens. Southern threats of dissolution were met by servile deprecation and compromises. Suggestions of disunion by abolitionists encountered malediction and persecution. Calhoun and Yancey were regarded as men who had a grievance; Garrison and Phillips as fanatics and disturbers of the peace. Reviling disunionists of its own section, the North encouraged the South to make demands which eventually dissevered the Nation.

At the same time anti-slavery sentiment was gaining ground in Northern states. It was helped on by the reception which the Legislature of South Carolina gave to Hon. Samuel Hoar, whom the State of Massachusetts had sent to test in the United States courts the constitutionality of a law by which coloured sailors were imprisoned while in the port of Charleston. The Governor was called upon to expel the Massachusetts envoy from the state; an act in which a hotel keeper took the initiative, and an escort completed, protecting Mr. Hoar from threatened violence. Officially, Massachusetts did not at once demur, but separation from offensive states received an impulse in the North. It was an opportunity which Phillips seized, presenting resolutions at a meeting of the Massachusetts Society, recommending that the Governor of the state demand of the President of the Union that Mr. Hoar be sustained by the Federal Government in his constitutional right of residence in the port of Charleston. If this were refused, Massachusetts, on all principles of national law, would become sovereign and independent.

This interstate discourtesy rankled in Massachusetts memories, and for a while dampened zeal to propitiate slaveholding interests; but profits of trade soon healed wounded pride, and the affair might have been forgotten if abolitionists had let it die. It was one of the freaks of political fortune that Phillips should incidentally become the champion of an official who would not have returned the compliment, and who is reported to have remarked, forty years later, that though he could not attend the agitator's funeral he approved of it. So slow did prejudice die in the last century.

On the arrival of a second address from Ireland, in November, 1843, Phillips once more appealed to the countrymen of O'Connell in behalf of the enslaved. He quoted the bull of Pope Gregory XVI. in 1839 against slavery and the slave trade, which he had seen affixed to the door of St. Peter's the winter he was in Rome, and then asked where the sect could be found that had so condemned slavery as the Catholics, proposed three cheers for the abolitionist, Pope Gregory XVI., and showed the inconsistency of a pro-slavery Irish immigrant from an oppressed land riveting the chain from which he had just freed his own neck. He should have no prejudice against the Negro. Thanks were due O'Connell for rallying sixty thousand Irishmen at home and for bidding his countrymen this side of the Atlantic to stand by the cause of human rights.

The vice-president of the Repeal Association venturing to remark that there was a difference between being a foe to slavery and an open abolitionist, and another following in similar strain, Phillips showed his readiness in rejoinder in a reply which elicited applause, laughter, and cheers. If he had conciliated the Irish element in the hall, he did not spare the two speakers who had attempted to divert the sentiment of the meeting from its natural course. It cannot be condensed with justice to the orator. Only the last of it can be given:

Sir, our chairman asked if a slaveholder could help repeal, if a tyrant could aid liberty. Some answered, Yes. I want their names. I want a responsible person to say here that repeal overrides humanity; that the slaveholder of Carolina is a worthy second to O'Connell at the Corn Exchange. Give me a name and I promise to send it to Dublin; and if the satire with which its wearer is scathed does not make all that was poured on the unlucky

Brougham milk and water in comparison, I do not know Daniel O'Connell.

Phillips's admiration for the eloquent advocate of freedom for the oppressed of his native island won little beyond a noisy response from Irish citizens of America. They had made sure of their own freedom and franchise. What need of liberty, competitive labour, and franchise for another race, especially if belonging to another political party? The difference between emancipation in Dublin and Charleston was as wide as the Atlantic ocean in the mind of the immigrant.

IX

PROTESTS AGAINST POLITICS

(1844)

UP TO 1840 the anti-slavery movement had preserved an apparent unity among its many-minded supporters. Other questions, however, at length intruded themselves, such as woman's rights, non-resistance, and participation in government, which finally split the fraternity into two bands — the Old and the New Organizations. One of these adhered to the original methods of moral suasion; the other began to court alliance with the Church and the world in order to use both for its benign purposes and thus to hasten the day of their fulfilment. Out of this sprung the germ of a political party, having the removal of slavery as its chief object. Incidentally, its growth was favoured by an increasing opposition to the extension of slavery in the Southwest, manifested in the ranks of both the Whig and Democratic parties. As early as 1840, despite New England protests, the seceded faction had been committed to political warfare, and 7,000 votes were cast for Birney, its candidate, in the Harrison campaign. Four years later this number was increased to 69,000 by voters who called themselves the Third Party, which afterward became the Liberty Party, then Free Soil, at length to be absorbed into the Republican host after sixteen years.

Mention of this divergent action is needed to make clear the position of a primitive abolitionist like Phillips. He held to the necessity of convincing one person and another, one community and then another, of a national crime. When conviction should become general he believed that it would find its own mode of expression, either through existing parties or a new one. To form one earlier was to make abolitionism the butt of more ridicule than if it kept solely to its instructive and persuasive methods. These had produced some results, but not sufficient to warrant political organization of a few thousand voters. It was playing politics before coming of age.

In this position Mr. Phillips was consistent with that ground which was taken by the reformers at the start — to keep clear of all political entanglements. They were at least freed from suspicion of coveting the delights of leadership and the rewards of office-holding, while possessing entire freedom of action when occasion demanded independence of all hindering alliances. Such an emergency was approaching.

The disunion sentiment North and South was augmented by the threatened annexation of Texas. Slaveholders saw new states in the broad belt of fresh territory stretching westward, blooming with prosperity and wealth in limitless cotton fields, and insuring the balance of power in Congress. If they could not have this, there was room enough for a Southern republic of their own. Calhoun spoke for them when he discovered that they were already a minority in the House and evenly balanced in the Senate.

Sir, the day that the balance between the two sections of the country is destroyed is a day that will not be far removed from political revolution, anarchy, civil war, and widespread

disaster. The balance of this system is in the slaveholding
states. They are the conservative portion, and, with due
balance on their part, may uphold this glorious Union of ours.
But if this policy [of excluding slavery from the new territory
wrung from Mexico] should be carried out, woe, I say, to this
Union.

In Massachusetts an anti-annexation convention of
delegates from its ten congressional districts had been held
on the 29th and 30th of January, 1845, in Boston. Its
members were of the highest standing in their respective
neighbourhoods.

A committee "to correspond with such committees as
might be appointed in other states" was appointed, as in
Revolution days, and an Address to the People of the United
States was adopted setting forth the moral, political, and
social objections against annexation. The prevailing tone
of discussion was moderate, but Calhoun's threats[1] had their
counterpart in President Allen's remark that, "rather than
have Texas annexed, he was for a dissolution." Garrison
would have the state look upon the Union as dissolved "if
the infamous plan should be consummated, and proceed to
form a new government for herself and such of the free states
as will aid her in carrying out the great purposes of our fathers
in behalf of civil liberty." The Address itself, however, called
for nothing stronger than hostility and denunciation. The
next day, Phillips presented his view of the subject in a
resolution to the effect that the annexation of Texas was
unconstitutional and in itself a dissolution of the Union, the
last of a long series of aggressions and usurpations on the part

---

[1]Calhoun said in the Senate in 1837: "There is but one question that can dissolve the
Union and that is involved with slavery." — McMaster's "History of the American People,"
vi., 478. On agreement of the North to let it alone. — *Ibid*, p. 178.

of the South, making it the duty of Northern states to organize a new National Government.

As usual, the pioneer was in advance of the main army;
but that it was following at a respectful distance is seen by
the resolves of the anti-annexation meeting, as well as by act
of the Massachusetts Legislature February 3, 1845, in a long
protest against the treatment of Mr. Hoar by South Carolina
addressed to state governors throughout the country two
years after the indignity was suffered. However, nothing
more desperate than retaliation is suggested, with emphasis
upon the virtue of patience.

To the ever-recurring question, "Why not marshal yourselves into a political party?" he replied that radical reforms
could never be carried on by political organizations, since the
politician must conceal half his principles to carry forward
the other half and is always looking back over his shoulder
to see how many are following. The reformer's object is
duty, not success. He can wait. The two consistent men
in the country, Calhoun and Garrison, no party could bear.
Parties delight in trimmers.

The entire speech, made in New York in May, marked the
steadfastness with which Phillips adhered to the principles
of the original abolition movement as opposed to political
schemes and to ecclesiastical alliances when they were not
whole-hearted in their opposition to the sin of the nation.
Concession and compromise he believed prolonged the evil
and put off the day of its eradication. The remedy must
kill the roots of a cancerous disease, else it would reappear.
Anything except total abolition and emancipation was merely
surface healing and salving over a sore whose cause was in
the blood of the body politic. The medicine to cleanse it

was costly; a part of the states had given up their slaves before the surrender should become greater. For those states that had kept them and profited by them the sacrifice would be proportionately greater, but ought to be made. It is doubtful if at this time he foresaw the magnitude of the loss not only of slaves in the South but of lives, South and North, when the disease was finally removed by the knife.

To the charge that he was fomenting serious dissension must be opposed the optimistic view which he took of the peaceable methods advocated and pursued by himself and his associates. He used the weapons of persuasion and conviction only, without threat or bluster. His arguments made for peaceable withdrawal from complicity with the South in slaveholding, but there was no advocacy of retaliation for intrusion into Northern territory and trespass upon the rights of coloured men who had acquired citizenship. The natural privilege of self-defence was as far as he went in advising them about a possible emergency, and flight was always safer. If he stirred up strife it was first the struggle that he made men have with their own consciences, which finally grew to be a discord between the consciences of two sections of the land, without entire unanimity in either one. Each always had its sympathizers, open or secret, in the territory of the other, embittering the main contention by secondary dissent, alienating neighbours and dividing households.

X

NORTHERN ALARM

(1845–1849)

DANIEL WEBSTER had attacked Phillips and his co-workers for their disturbance of the general contentment which prevailed, saying: "You that prate of disunion, do you not know that disunion is revolution?" To which Phillips replied: "Yes, we know it, and we are for a revolution in the character of the American Constitution and a change of the face of society in the South from mediæval to modern conditions, and from love of lucre in the North to a sense of political honour." This and much more was the tone of his remark at a meeting of the citizens of Massachusetts, without distinction of party, to protest against the annexation of Texas. Hon. Charles Francis Adams presided; the historian and secretary of the state, John G. Palfrey, Charles Sumner, George S. Hillard, Rev. William H. Channing, Wendell Phillips, and others, spoke on resolutions which protested against perpetuating slavery in the new state. A single paragraph from sixteen is cited to show the drift of Phillips's remarks, and as containing an allusion to an implement which has recently attracted much attention to John Bunyan and the "Pilgrim's Progress." His employment of the figure is exact.

We have seen the allegory of the muck rake of Bunyan made a reality by men of our own times, who suffer the temptation of the sticks and straws beneath their feet to divert their eyes from the freeman's crown that hangs above their heads. We have seen men spellbound by the mean magic of place and gain, even while over the mirror of the present steals the giant shadow of coming despotism. . . . No partial efforts can save us now. The slave power is, and always has been, mighty in the land. It has scattered to the winds the mightiest parties — it has laid low the fairest reputations, it has thrown down the bulwarks of Saxon liberty covered with the hoar of innumerable ages, and now it looks on this last triumph as a checkmate. God grant that it may overleap itself, and that this effort to rally all honest men to the conflict may be crowned with complete success.

It did overleap itself six weeks later when Texas was admitted with slavery and the prospect of a war with Mexico. A new party sprung up in the North to check Southern aggression. Abolitionists, however, saw no reason for joining it, since it did not demand immediate emancipation. Other men might combine and vote for political safeguards; these few who had begun the long warfare on humanitarian lines were going to hold their course straight on, though it should lead them through fens and over mountains, as it had done and was doing every year. Other surveyors might squint and consult about circuitous ways that were feasible and grades that were easy; these men, like Nicholas, had drawn a straight line for their road to Moscow and nothing could deflect them from it. Sometimes outsiders were drawn in to work with them, as on the occasion when the abolitionists held a meeting in Faneuil Hall, September 24, 1846, to protest against the return to New Orleans of a slave

stowaway who had reached Boston, and escaping from the
ship, was recaptured by city officials and put in irons on a
Massachusetts vessel bound South.

John Quincy Adams had by this time become enough of an
abolitionist to preside, and Dr. Samuel G. Howe, the philanthropist, stated the object of the meeting, John A. Andrew
presenting resolutions, and Charles Sumner supporting them.
The road breakers were getting into good society, or else it
was itself in bad company, according as the rest of the city
divided its opinions.

Phillips's view of the affair that had called the citizens
together is of more interest here.   A full report of it is lacking,
but an editorial note observed that "the speech of Wendell
Phillips revealed the advanced state of public opinion on this
great and fundamental principle of withdrawal from slaveholders."   It was the only way that then seemed possible to
haters of human bondage, and all the more possible in that
its supporters likewise were ready to withdraw.   Upon the
issue which made for this separation and was stirring all the
North, the war with Mexico, he declared his sentiments in an
address on December 29, 1846, in Faneuil Hall.   After
remarking upon the small beginnings of the movement, its
unexpected success, the necessity of strong measures in
Church and State, the timidity of the Constitution framers
in dealing with the crime of the colonies, the inefficiency of
compromises, the failure of the Church, and the resort to
political methods which avail little, he comes to the political
war with a neighbouring republic and asks:

War for what? Poor Mexico! We want her territory;
we want it for slavery. The parties say, "The President
made it, and must support it."   I say that in politics there is

no root which reaches deep enough to grapple with slavery.
As for the Church, we believe that in it lies the only power to
which we can appeal for strength deep seated enough to
grapple with slavery—the deep, vital idea of *duty*. We must
speak strongly, because the crisis demands plain talking. Let
the Church of our times deal with the slavery of our day as she
anciently dealt with national sins when she came across them.

Early in 1847 Calhoun summed up the political status
of the North as follows: "1. Abolitionists —about 5 per
cent. of the voting population. 2. Sober people, willing to
see slavery abolished, but not by overthrowing the Constitution — 70 per cent. 3. Highly respectable people who
sympathize with the South — 5 per cent. 4. The remainder
— 20 per cent. — who care less for principles than for the
spoils. Yet the abolitionists hold the balance of power from
the nearly equal division of Democrats and Whigs. Hence
the danger to the South should any party unite with the
abolitionists."

As a companion piece to this outlook may be presented
the remarks of Phillips on January 26, 1848. Forty
thousand women of Scotland had addressed the women of
America in the customary manner of a ponderous roll of
signatures to a written appeal. It elicited from him the
tribute he was always glad to give to the assistance women
were rendering to the cause, adding that "from a woman's
lips the Old World first heard the doctrine and learned the
lesson of immediate emancipation. Ah! that little word
immediate. What an amount of meaning it has, and how
potent to show the real character of a man's opposition to an
evil which he is combating!"

The little band which Calhoun had reckoned as 5 per cent.
of the voting force of the North was not to be identified with

the Liberty Party by Phillips nor with any voting contingent.
He was bent on keeping genuine reform limited to the most
difficult methods and to those people only who would hold
to the original policy, even if its triumph should be a generation distant.   Therefore, he clung to his maxim that, "With
God one is a majority."   Numbers meant a letting down
of a high standard.   To keep this he would wait a lifetime.
Any other victory was not worth winning.   The handful of
fighters for it were nearer 1 per cent. of the country's voters
than 5; nor would they vote at all.   Their power was that
of a single idea, slowly spreading, gradually growing — the
little sapling that by and by should split the rock.   A hint of
how this would be done is contained in this very speech, showing that to its author had not yet occurred the way in which
it would come about at last almost twenty years later.   In
fact, no one of that day believed that slavery could be
abolished and the Union saved.

The question had been raised here and there as to what
the North would do in the event of a servile insurrection.
It was one that was generally evaded as unpleasant to discuss or even contemplate.   Phillips evidently had no
disposition to interfere with any race that should make
a desperate rising for its deliverance from despotic bondage.
He feared that it might come.   If it should, he wanted
the North to stand still — to give it no encouragement,
but also to have no part in sending its men to help desolate
the hovel of the slave.

That the abolitionists were taking in earnest the matter
of disunion appears from Phillips's remarks before the committee on disunion petitions which were coming before
the Legislature.   The morning papers had suggested

that any attention paid to these petitions was a waste of time which is paid for by the public. After intimating that it would be well for the press to touch with a reverent hand anything that relates to the *right of petition*, just as the grave had closed over Adams, amidst testimonies of national respect but once before equalled on this side the ocean, he proceeded to say that these tributes were paid on account of his defence and practice of this right of the few and the humblest to be heard by the Government. Then he turned to his topic, disunion.

It is not a rare word in our national history. Disappointed ambition has often, for a moment, longed for separate confederacies, in which there should be more presidential chairs than one. And sometimes even a state, thwarted in its favourite purpose, has threatened to shoot madly from its sphere. But the abolitionists are the only men who have ever calmly, soberly, and from their mature conviction, proclaimed at the outset their purpose to seek the dissolution of this American Union; and this from no bitterness of personal or party disappointment, but solely at the bidding of principle and from a sense of duty. These petitions are called revolutionary. They are intended to be. We hope they are akin to the measures and principles of our 1776. Wise lawyers doubt whether a state can constitutionally secede from the Union. We do not propose this as a constitutional measure. The right of a people to alter their form of government has never been denied here. It is upon that right we stand. The right of each generation to govern itself.

The year of the great hegira to California, 1849, was full of ferment. Its determination to be free had clouded Southern expectations of the Pacific coast, while Northern subserviency to slaveholding interests was growing slack. Agitation of the engrossing question was invading state legislatures and becoming persistent in Congress. Calhoun wrote a long address for his colleagues to send to their constituents, setting forth the difficulty of catching fugitives in free states and charging the North with bad faith in declining to support pro-slavery articles of the Constitution, and Garrison chimed in with the statement that if the North could not keep its part of the compact it should withdraw. Middle states papers thereupon deplored the secession which extremists of both sections threatened, and moderate journals on both sides joined in conciliatory propositions. For his own coterie Phillips wrote in the *Liberty Bell*, under the caption, "Everything Helps Us": "Success is no test of the merit of an individual and defeat no argument against him. An enterprise, enclosing a right principle, always triumphs. It meets with nothing but victories. It passes itself into the bosom of its seeming conqueror and silently it becomes its vassal. . . . It may yet come to pass that it will be given out as a subject for themes at Harvard, 'Which did the most, Garrison or Calhoun, for the downfall of American slavery?'"

At this time he pronounced the Free Soil movement the result of anti-slavery agitation carried into politics; half-hearted as yet, and therefore constituting no reason for modifying advanced views which insisted on the right of petition, and even revolution, when the Constitution antagonizes public opinion, ranging itself with the law of God. But political parties, supporting the Constitution, could do nothing against its provisions for slavery; only

fanaticism, so called, could work effectively for emancipation, and therefore abolitionists do not join political parties.
Christianity might, if it would, equalize and renovate
society and be a pioneer of humanity for a sixth part of the
population now in bondage.

There is no misunderstanding what Phillips's position
was at this time. It is easier to understand now, however,
than in 1849. Even then it was seen to be consistent, but
with what was regarded as treason or next to it. In simple
terms, he considered that a noxious weed had overrun the
land. Its baleful bloom and poisonous fruit were in the
South; its roots ran in Northern soil, above which once it
thrived moderately but not profitably. Some said, Keep
it where it is; others, Let it run into fresh fields; others still,
Remove it gently and gradually, by emancipation, trans-
planting slaves to Africa, after their purchase from owners.
The thoroughbred abolitionist said to the slaveholder,
Uproot it now. Free your slaves to-day. You have no
property rights in them that you are not stealing. Give
up your stolen goods.

The strangest thing of all is that these ultra-reformers
kept their faith in an unconditional surrender strong enough
to labour on without any sign of gain in the South. Their
view, by no means general in the North, must possess an
entire half the country before such a sacrifice could be
thought of. Even then every inherited belief and every
present interest was against it. Full payment for slaves
would not have provided with certainty for future cultivation of crops. Moreover, instead of emancipation sentiments
growing in the South, they were diminishing through Northern
increase of them and of agitation. Slaveholders were rising

up in wrath and combining for resistance to aggression, uttering threats of secession with more probability of carrying them out than the little band of disunionists at the North could show. In the face of all this, Phillips, now President of the New England Society, could say at its annual meeting of 1849: "We shall do it yet. The times have changed. We have changed the tone of public sentiment, or, rather, events have changed it for us. Massachusetts is an asylum for the flying bondman, to some extent. Put that down to our credit."

The third of August, a day of fasting for prevailing cholera appointed by President Taylor, Phillips, in a long speech at Worcester, was inclined to consider as a day of humiliation for the national sin of slavery, with which abolitionists had nothing to do, since they had spent their lives in protesting against it. Instead, it should be a day of feasting to celebrate the freeing of nearly a million slaves in the West Indies, the first effort of the English people to effect a national change by moral means. Discussing the difference between their methods and our own, British statesmen and American, he observed that no man worth remembering failed to record his protest against the crime, citing Burke, Pitt, Brougham, Romilly, O'Connell, and Wilberforce. The social prejudice against colour was not powerful as it is here, even in the North where we are the jailors and constables of the institution, as Channing said. He wanted legislative rebellion against this bondage to the South. The Constitution and Union are fetters to us and weapons to our foes. To the stock objection of danger in freeing American slaves, he brought the example of eight hundred thousand West Indian blacks and their peaceable conduct when they might have wiped out their white masters, who were only one-tenth of their number. The experiment was successful if there was one of them left alive, if anarchy did not reign. Not only was the freedman quiet, but just as much was raised and exported, if that must be counted as an element of success. "Do not hesitate to follow the English example. Educate the slumbering conscience. We are still a noble people. Show them their duty to get rid of slavery and they will spring to the work with the energy of a people waking new and fresh to their duties. You have it in your power to stir up your statesmen, and to call out their talent to do your work."

Ralph Waldo Emerson's appearance at this meeting and his philosophical view of the general subject of American slavery are both interesting and instructive. He rejoiced in the march of events and the progress of the great universal human genius which turns even our vices to the general benefit. He regarded the planters of the South as barbarous people in the process of improvement, not accountable like those whose eyes have been opened to the best Christianity. Enervated by their climate, demoralized by their habits, still they are as innocent in their slaveholding as we in our Northern vices. But as man rises in civilization the institution will become discreditable, and perish, as the old institutions which have gone before it.

An echo to the sentiment of this meeting came back from the West Indies soon after in resolutions adopted here and there on the same anniversary, proposed and passed by the very planters who had resisted the purchased

emancipation of their slaves and had denounced the abolitionists of England. They also broadly suggested to other
"countries in close commercial relations with Great Britain"
that they imitate their example of emancipation. In two
weeks after the Worcester celebration Phillips addressed
a long letter to James Haughton, of Dublin, Ireland,
on the inconsistency of Father Mathew's silence about
slavery when in America — a greater evil than intemperance
— a silence all the more observable in view of his prominence
in the Irish Address of 1842, when he said that "no one
could be neutral"! In seeking to save his influence he
has lost the confidence of reformers. Every Northern
Doughface sees the great Teetotaller belittled to his own
level. He has got so humbly upon his knees before the
slave power that our editors cannot get low enough to be
level with him. Silence from such a visitor is most significant support; and he quoted Howard's fearless denunciation
in Vienna of the prisons of Austria, despite the warning
that his words would be reported to the Emperor, adding,
"God grant the world another Howard, and may he visit
these states."

Phillips had now been connected with the anti-slavery
movement some fifteen years. Beginning with the advocacy of rights which were to be secured as preliminary to
the abolition of slavery — the rights of free discussion, of
a free press, and of petition to law-making bodies — he had
gone on to assert the natural rights and to condemn the
wrongs of the enslaved, and to attack the articles of the
Constitution under which these wrongs were possible. He
had presented appeals from Great Britain, and pointed to
the peaceful emancipation of its slaves in the West Indies.

He had called on the South to imitate this act, and had denounced the North for its apathy and complicity in a national crime. Despite all, he saw the intention of the South to extend slaveholding into new territory; but as a hopeful sign he observed in the North a growing opposition to such extension. To threats of disunion in slave states he was ready to oppose the withdrawal of free states, declaring that separation was better than a union which endorsed human bondage.

In these years he had devoted himself entirely to public discussion of this disturbing question, and others of less consequence, before representative audiences that received him and his proposals with varying degrees of disapproval. He had never failed to gain attention by the charm of his eloquence, and usually conquered opposition before he ceased speaking. Many had been made to think soberly of a national inconsistency, and the promise of a harvest in the far future from a diligent sowing of wholesome truth was fair. At the age of forty, he was in the midst of a movement which was spreading from a little band of enthusiasts to an increasing number in every Northern state. Its voting power commended it to political consideration, and the voters themselves saw the value of united action. Although Phillips himself discountenanced political alliances, he knew that ballots would eventually win. Meantime it was his business to educate voters wherever they would hear him. As an orator he had learned by long practice to do what the old style of speakers could not do so well as he in the free-lance methods which he followed. He was armed at all points and ready for every attack. He had discovered the cost of maintaining unpopular doctrines, but this had given him the loftiness of a reformer. Standing alone, or with a pitiable minority, and leaning upon none, he gained the strength of the independent, and trusted to the power of right when once accepted by an instructed people. He had need of all his faith and hope and courage as the first half of the century closed.

XI

PACIFICATION AND AGITATION

(1850-1851)

THE middle of the century marked the end of the first
period of anti-slavery strife. Its results were seen in
a wide-spread conviction that slavery ought not to be
extended beyond its limits at the time; but this opinion was
not efficient enough to prevent the annexation of Texas.
This advantage gained, the supporters of the institution were
willing to join with upholders of the Union in bringing about
a second "era of good feeling"; and the leaders of the two
sections, Webster and Calhoun, both addressed themselves
to the question, How can the Union be preserved? Calhoun had given his solution of the problem in the Senate on
March 4th — the South to have more territory, her runaway
slaves to be returned by Northern assistance, all agitation of
the disturbing question to be stopped, and the "equilibrium"
restored to slave states — that is, the balance of power.

Three days after, Webster pronounced his famous Seventh
of March Speech, otherwise, his political death chant. If it
had been as positive and uncompromising for his half of the
nation as was Calhoun's for his, doubtless the Union which
he counted dear above all else might have been endangered.
His opponent's threat of secession was ringing in his ears, and
he went more than half way with apologies and concessions

to a disgruntled South for the sake of peace and the Union as it had thus far been maintained. It is not necessary to charge that he was bidding for the presidency. Let it stand that a united country was the end and aim of all his political life, and that he actually represented the views and interests of a large and respectable constituency, who hastened to send him testimonials of their accord. Nevertheless, he soon found that he had struck a note to which the general Northern feeling did not respond, and that he had won nothing from the South. All that had been secured was temporary quiet. Men went back to their farms and merchandise and there was a clearing sky. It looked as if the abolition question were to be laid aside for the want of such a leader as Daniel Webster might have been, and in his failure to seize a passing opportunity. Many were glad that he did not ally himself with abolition, while losing their pride in him for his lack of courage, or for prizing the Union and Constitution above national righteousness and good repute among the nations. The few radicals meanwhile lowered not an inch their banner on which was emblazoned, "No Union with Slaveholders."

Within a fortnight after its delivery Phillips had written a review of Webster's speech almost as long, which showed that on occasion he could handle the pen to some purpose, distasteful as this method of address was to him, as compared with public speech. At the outset he defines his own position as a disunionist, not from any love for separate confederacies, or as ignorant of the thousand evils that spring from neighbouring and quarrelsome states; but he would get rid of this Union because experience had shown it to be, in its character and construction, an insurmountable obstacle to the *harmony* of the nation. He would substitute for it one that would insure harmony of all the races and all the states. With this view, he says, Mr. Webster has no sympathy. "He has nothing to propose on the removal of the disturbing element. A true friend of the Union would seize this moment to propose some grand and comprehensive plan of abolition, instead of shutting his eyes to the future, not daring to look impending danger in the face. No man can tell by his three hours' speech whether he loves slavery or hates it. His argument is that we are pledged by the Constitution and acts of Congress to let slavery alone, and to let it spread in the new Texan states, five of them, that may be admitted by a gross breach of the Constitution." This is considered at length; also Mr. Webster's surrender of the Wilmot Proviso, quoting his former pronouncements, and observing his recent change. The alleged impossibility of slavery in Californian territory is discussed, with the admission of justice in Southern complaints against the North, indicating another sudden change of front. His chief offence, however, is the baseness of endorsing slave-hunting in free states. "Villain is not too harsh a name for a man who is ready to return fugitive slaves. It is a poor excuse that he squared his morality by the statute book of his time. Great men refuse to be confined by a country's fashion. He could see clearly enough when he was looking at Kossuth and not at a Negro. He also volunteers to support other thoughtless and cruel regulations; to surrender any person claimed as a slave, according to the atrocious provisions of Mr. Mason's bill; he is non-committal in his reference to the imprisonment of Northern coloured seamen in Southern ports; resents instructions from his constituents; passes over tamely and

pusillanimously the unconstitutional acquisition of so much
Southern territory since 1803; is silent on the subject of mis-
chievous compromises, and suddenly favourable to a scheme
of colonization which he formerly regarded as a slaveholder's
trick." To Webster's question, "What is to remain American?" Phillips replies: "In our opinion, whatever clings to
the great American idea of taking pains to reënact, and practise, so plain a law of God as that *all men are created equal.*"

In this condensation of eight newspaper columns nothing
more than the stakes on the plain can be noted, showing the
general direction of comment and criticism. In his reprobation of the great statesman's last effort Phillips spoke for the
extremists, as Whittier did in his verse entitled —"Ichabod"
— whose glory had departed. But both these condemnatory
utterances echoed a feeling which the North and South had
in common, that the chief Senator of the free states had
truckled to the slave power to save the Union intact. On
the street it was called "the best bid that had been made for
the Presidency." Instead, it might have been remarked that
he was one of the three political leaders who were too great to
occupy the presidential office, according to the standards and
requirements of the mid-century.

In the same week that this review of Webster's speech was
published a meeting was held in Faneuil Hall of "citizens of
Boston and vicinity who have read with surprise, alarm, and
deep regret the speech of Hon. Daniel Webster in the
United States Senate."[1]

At this meeting, Phillips supplemented his strictures in
print by a speech in which he arraigned the Senator who had

[1]For Mr. Webster's final position among his Northern friends, see Lodge's "Life" in
chapter on the "Seventh of March Speech," p. 301, first edition.

struck a false note that jarred upon the general sentiment of the free states. He likened this course to an impossible desertion of Sam Adams to the British or a defection by John Hancock. "Grant his premise; it is the cause of liberty on the one hand and of tyranny on the other. He gave aid and comfort to the enemy and tended to make slavery perpetual. His present doctrine is inconsistent with his past; is apostate to his pledges. Surrendering one of his constituents to the terms of Mason's bill, he surrenders him to slavery. The defender of the Constitution forgets its guaranty of trial by jury, which Southerners tell us is inconsistent with slavery. He accuses Northern legislators and apologizes for Southern; and changes his speech for readers in each section." Such are a few points in an hour's discussion of which the following is one of the closing paragraphs:

If he has so little knowledge of the moral sense of New England as to think that he can stand up in the face of this community after he has pledged himself to be a slave-hunter, let him learn to respect the intelligence of New England, which knows at least when it is betrayed. Let him learn that we have been too good disciples not to carry out his lessons into deeds; that we mean to stand by the principles of the ordinance of 1787; that where the South clings to the right to carry their slaves into the territory of the West, just there we will be vigilant.

Press comments upon Webster's speech varied according to interests represented; but the general condemnatory character of them in his own state was heightened by his Revere House remarks to friends assembled to welcome him on his return from Congress. His exhortation to Massachusetts to overcome her prejudices and support recent enactments sunk him still lower in the opinion of his opponents. He had turned his back upon the North and was facing South, as they thought. He thought, it is to be charitably presumed, that he was boxing the compass to save the Ship of State.

At the May meeting of the American Anti-slavery Society in New York, in 1850, Phillips and other speakers with great difficulty were able to get a hearing, the famous Rynders mob taking possession of the hall and dividing attention with the delegates. The chief interest of this meeting now is in a letter of sympathy to Garrison written by Whittier, and the appointment of Lowell on the executive committee for the ensuing year. Literature was coming to the help of reform. Subsequently, a meeting was held in Plymouth Church, Brooklyn, since there was danger of interruption at the advertised hall. Rev. Henry Ward Beecher took the responsibility of opening his church and called the meeting to order, saying that it was in his blood and in his bones to stand up for free speech. He then introduced Wendell Phillips, who continued the discussion of this right and also that of severe speech when the occasion demands it.

From Luther down, the charge against every reformer has been that his tongue is too rough. Be it so. Rough instruments are used for rough work. To lift up our voice against slavery has been called blasphemy and infidelity. I say this — that with forty thousand pulpits, seven hundred thousand slaves have grown into three millions, and that statutes so bloody have been enacted under their teaching that those of Draco are light in comparison. While in the old country every great man desires to place on record his sentiments in favour of liberty and progress, Websters can be bought up here faster than nature can make them. An

American's logic is as clear as the sun upon every subject in the world except one. If it relates to a white man, it is lucid and bright; but the moment you touch on a black man, it veers about like the needle of a compass when it comes near a mass of iron. Would to God that one night would sweat out all the black from the skins of slaves, and then there would be no difficulty about the question. You love the American banner. But every sixth man under its stars and stripes is a slave, with whose blood its folds are stained. With regard to the fugitive slave, the turning point on which so much hinges at present, I would say, Constitution or no Constitution, God has given us a conscience superior to all law, and whenever a slave touches our free soil, let him be free beyond the reach of a tyrant. A mighty question is now involved in this, namely, whether an immoral Constitution ought to be obeyed; but I have not time to discuss it now. Remember that the Bible is heavier than the statute book.

Mr. Beecher, at the close of this lecture of an hour and a half, thanked the assembly — not for being gentlemanly — but for conceding the right of liberty of speech, which had been denied in New York.[1]

In Boston, a few weeks later, the New England Convention was not treated so well. During day and evening sessions endeavours were made repeatedly to disturb, insult, and break them up. Seven newspapers of the city joined in ridiculing the whole affair with scurrility and caricature. It looked like a reversion to the original type of opposition twenty years before. The explanation is found in the tense-strung condition of public feeling. Sentiment was getting more evenly divided and more generally aroused. The recent encroachments of the Slave Power, its exactions

---

[1] Of the audience it was recorded by a correspondent of the *Hartford Republican* that they hissed at first, then partly cheered — but the last three-quarters of an hour was one storm of deafening cheers. This was the usual conduct of Phillips's audiences for thirty years.

in Congress and demands upon the North were making abolitionists and free-soilers every day. On the other side, conservatives and business men were conceding everything to save the Union and Southern trade. Strife in Northern cities was greater than it could be in Southern; yet harmony in them also was by no means entire.

The points which Phillips emphasized in his speech at the Boston meeting were, at first, in answer to the old charge of abuse and denunciation made against abolitionists, saying, in substance, that words are made for us; if abusive, the fault lies in deserving them; the abuse in applying them unfairly or unkindly. To arrest the attention of the masses the plainest speech must be used. If you dislike our words, show us that they are not true. The best thing for an honest man is to speak that which comes uppermost. Why is it that no daily press in New York, Boston, or New England reports us with the slightest fidelity, but always interlards its sketch of our meetings with abuse in order to make it palatable? "Tray, Blanche, and Sweetheart all bark at us." The littlest press is of importance to us, just as Daniel Webster's speech is of importance to us. When anti-slavery articles are really wanted, depend upon it, the Respectable Daily will furnish them; as when the hand touches eleven on the dial the Websters and Winthrops will make their great anti-slavery speeches. Mr. Webster says that the Constitution orders the return of fugitive slaves. So say we; and that is the reason why we hate the Constitution. Let posterity be our judge. Harvard College once trampled on Dr. Follen for his anti-slavery principles. Ten years later how anxiously did the college attempt to explain away the ugly fact!

The rest of the speech is devoted to Webster and his unhappy retainers in Boston. He judges him by his former pronouncements and by his highest law — the Constitution. "The Northern side of his memory is paralyzed," as Beecher says.

On the 18th of September the climax of slaveholding encroachment was reached by the enactment of the Fugitive Slave Bill. It had already passed the Senate, and now received in the House 109 yeas to 75 nays. In a modified form it was already a part of the Constitution, but not very effective. To make it more efficient, additional provisions now required the appointment of slave-catching commissioners and assistants in the states and territories, who, upon the claim of any master or his agent, should seize a fugitive, his own testimony not to be allowed. Persons hindering the execution of the law were to be fined $500 and imprisoned six months; for causing an escape, $1,000; an officer permitting an escape was to be held for the value of the slave; and for default of duty, in his capture, a fine of $1,000 recoverable by law was imposed. For a slave returned, his fee was to be $10; and $5 in any case.

The temper with which this law was received in free states is indicated by one of the resolutions passed the next day at a meeting in Salem, Ohio, a state which, with Massachusetts and New York, had been in the front rank of opposition to the Slave Power for twenty years. In substance it urged the principle of death to kidnappers for the defence of personal rights and liberties. Massachusetts spoke in more measured language in resolutions adopted at a mass meeting in Faneuil Hall on the 14th of October, Josiah Quincy presiding. Their substance was, that our moral sense revolts against the law; which we denounce as contradictory to the Declaration of Independence; that we cannot believe any citizen of this city will take part in returning a fugitive; and that we ought to demand *instant repeal* of the law.

At this meeting the appearance of Wendell Phillips is mentioned, as might be expected, "who spoke for about an hour in his usually clear, forcible, and eloquent style."

To the question of danger under the Fugitive Slave Law to numerous coloured folk living in Boston, and as to what they had best do, he said that he was unprepared to reply. He could not talk of violence. "In this law the bulwarks of liberty are all broken, and it is a base libel to call it a constitutional law. We must trample it under our feet. It expects and provides for disobedience; God forbid that it should be disappointed. By peaceful resistance we must interrupt the slaveholders and say that the fugitive who has breathed Massachusetts air shall never go back. Many have been here from twelve to twenty years, and we are not going to people Southern plantations with men born in Massachusetts. Disobey this law until the courts rule it unconstitutional."

Coloured citizens, however, were not divested of their fears, and from Boston, as from the Northern cities and states, there was a general exodus to Canada, adding to the twenty thousand negroes already living in the Dominion. Meantime arrests were multiplying, often of blacks who had acquired citizenship and were getting their living in New York, Philadelphia, and Western cities. They were not allowed to say why they should not be surrendered to any claimant on the flimsiest of demands.

In Boston an instance occurred five months after the passage of the act, February, 1851, when one Shadrach was haled before the Commissioner. At his citation before the court, a crowd of coloured persons attended and managed to get him so mixed with them that all at once he could not be identified, and was suddenly passed out and hurried off in a "black cloud," which a white one could not overtake this side the Canada line.

Great outcry against Massachusetts was made by the South for this open violation of the Compromise of 1850 and for the disturbance of the era of good feeling which was to follow it. This was partly restored by a different issue in the next arrest. Thomas Sims, a slave who left Georgia on Washington's birthday, 1851, had been in Boston a month when he was taken and lodged in the court-house on the evening of April 3d and brought before Commissioner Curtis the next day; Charles Sumner, Richard H. Dana, Jr., and Samuel E. Sewall appearing for the prisoner. After the hearing of his pursuer's testimony that he was the slave of one James Potter, and after further legal proceedings, he was remanded, to be escorted under a military guard of some three hundred, led by the Mayor, to the brig *Acorn*, bound for Savannah. Boston had begun to redeem her reputation at the South. The city press congratulated citizens that the affair had terminated in such a way as to deserve credit from Southerners and to discourage abolitionists. But they were not silenced.

On the day following the arrest of Sims Phillips addressed a great public meeting on the Common, and another in Tremont Temple three days later, and still another four days afterward in Washington Hall on the day of rendition. The burden of his speeches was the subserviency of Boston with all its traditions of liberty to pro-slavery enactments for fear of alienating Southern trade. The seizure and return of slaves in the streets of a free city had roused the liberty-loving spirit of the middle class, but cotton and commerce were too important factors to be overlooked in State Street. Moreover, to side with abolitionists would have been an ignoble way of asserting the old doctrine of liberty. But there was no lack of its presentation by Phillips and others, not only on this immediate occasion, but in the following January and on the succeeding April anniversary of Sims's rendition. The speeches on these two occasions were placed by Phillips's consent early in the first volume of his addresses. They are followed by a notable one on the Philosophy of the Abolition Movement, which may be considered as an exposition of his attitude on the question which was then agitating the entire nation.

The Fugitive Slave Law was now doing its worst, not without opposition in some places, and causing the flight of about ten thousand Negroes from their homes in free states to the Dominion of Canada. Few besides abolitionists were more greatly stirred by this sudden migration than they would have been by the flight of geese to Northern lakes. Egypt generally was glad at their departing, especially the common labourers in the field and in the simpler trades. They made wages higher for the new immigrant by their absence. A greater indignity was needed to stir greater numbers in the North. It was to be perpetrated shortly.

Meantime there was an occasion to provoke remark

from Phillips in the coming of Kossuth to enlist the sympathy of Americans for his native Hungary, oppressed by Austria, which was marked in his speeches by no discrimination between different sections and no word for the enslaved. The inconsistency of such silence did not escape the leaders of emancipation. Phillips arraigned the Hungarian on the 27th of December, 1851, in an address of great length and power in which he applied the principles of liberty, justice, and humanity, for which Kossuth pleaded, to a race that he had avoided mentioning. In this speech are seen his milder methods of dealing with a person whose chief desire, like his own, was for freedom, but whose partial advocacy was repellent to one who never did anything by halves. It was a criticism rather than a diatribe, based upon the consistency and whole-heartedness which he had a right to expect, but which, by the way, would have been fatal to Kossuth's hopes of general assistance if he had preached deliverance to the captive in the United States. But Phillips spared no man who was politic in his qualified devotion to a principle; and when he offered resolutions a month later at the annual meeting of the New England Society he condemned Kossuth's course in praising American statesmen indiscriminately, and in endorsing the Mexican War and the Fugitive Slave Bill, as falsehood to his high professions and treason to the cause of human rights, injurious to his nation and fatal to his own fame. This time he forsook the calmness of his first speech, and even of his customary discourse, and for once became violent in manner as well as denunciatory in his address.[1]

---

[1] An open letter to Kossuth by Garrison printed (in part) in the *Liberator*, and in full in a pamphlet of sixty pages, contrasted the Hungarian's subserviency to slavery with the attitude of some other notable foreigners, and recounted the atrocities of the system about which he had chosen to be silent. See "Life of Garrison," iii., 351.

XII

DARKNESS AND DAYBREAK

(1852–1853)

THE force with which abolitionists had chiefly to contend
in the mid-century years of truce between the North
and South was represented by Daniel Webster, the advocate
of quiet by compromise. Consequently, this man who had
been the pride of the Whigs and of New England became a
target for Phillips on account of his recent unfriendly attitude
toward the growing anti-slavery sentiment, and because he
represented the non-interference policy of commercial and
political interests, which had made haste to endorse his
conciliatory position. It was the latest stand taken by
wealthy and influential neighbours. In dealing with Webster,
Phillips was addressing them also, and combating the
power that belongs to vested interests and social preëminence.
Besides, Webster had condescended to cast a slur upon
the abolition movement, calling it a "rub-a-dub agitation,
whose only result was a little noise." Phillips retorted
by saying:

He knew better. He knew better the times in which he
lives. . . . Any name, however illustrious, which links
itself to abuses is sure to be overwhelmed by the impetuous
current of that society which is potent to clear its own channel.
Thanks to the printing press, men now do their own thinking

and statesmen have ceased to be either the leaders or the clogs of society.

"The Revere House statesman," as he calls his latest opponent, he then proceeds to dissect and compare with the Webster that once was, and his statesmanship in 1852 with what it ought to be.

Let the statesman take care lest this "morbid philanthropy" beat all his dead institutions to dust. He is but a feather's weight in the balance against the average of public sentiment on the subject of slavery. I believe in the twenty millions — not that live now, necessarily—to arrange this question which priests and politicians have sought to keep out of sight. When the nation sees that the interests of a class only are subserved by human bondage, then the change will come.

With such sentiments did Phillips stem the quiet but strong current that was setting against the cause in 1852 with greater effect than the noisy mobs of a score of years before. With philosophy based upon historic movements, and illustrated by English and French examples in particular, did he brace the energies and buoy up the hopes of his associates in New England and wherever their weekly sheets, the *Liberator* and the *Standard*, bore the reports of his addresses or the articles he sometimes penned as a contributory or an associate editor. But they were especially favoured who heard his voice and saw his presence, although they could not account for his marvellous power. It was not in what Webster had called the sum of eloquence — "godlike action," nor in the organ tones of a voice like his own — sometimes, his contemporaries said, clothing nonsense with thunder. It was the conversation of one with a hundred or a thousand, so quiet, so direct, so clear, that each hearer felt himself addressed, and often forgot the multitude around him until some tumultuous response told him that a thousand hearts had been struck like his own. Had the orator been in the ranks of either of the two great parties his fame would have been still greater in all the Nation. But the inspiration of a humane cause would have been lacking in politics, which took little account of it at that time.

The speech from which a few lines have been taken was made on January 28, 1852, and was followed by another on the 30th in which he attacked the other great obstacle that for twenty years had stood in the way of freedom — important commercial interests, otherwise Southern trade.

Property has been regarded as the great element the Government is to stand by and protect — the mills of Lawrence, the ships of Boston, the mines of Pennsylvania. If placing one dollar on the top of another be the chief end of man, be it so. Dr. Johnson said of a certain Scotsman that if he saw a dollar on the other side of hell, he would make a spring for it at the risk of falling in. The Yankee character seems too near that. Massachusetts representatives have always looked to the Southern Cross; not to the North Star. They never looked to the state that sent them. They are beginning to look toward Faneuil Hall; not like Webster, to the " October sun of the Old Dominion." In this hall has been the rebuke of the City Government and of the commercial interest whose servant it stooped to be.

Three months later, on the first anniversary of Sims's rendition, he struck a new note of desperation at the working of the Fugitive Slave Law. A great defeat had befallen the cause of abolition. For the moment his sadness might have been mistaken for despair.

The delusion cannot be kept up that fugitives can be pro-

tected in Massachusetts.   Therefore tell them to fly — or to
arm themselves.   I am willing to wait for the abolition of
slavery; it must proceed slowly.   But the return of a fugitive
is a different thing.   If circumstances prevent flight, there is
a course left if you have the courage to face it.   I do not
advise it.   I can only tell what I would do in your case.   The
appeal to a Massachusetts jury for a man's right to liberty
and self-protection might not be in vain.   It is the launch-
ing of a new measure in our enterprise; but I know of no
pledge against it.   No, I am not a non-resistant.   I have
no defence except I make it.   If I do, who will cast the
first stone ?

Although Phillips had never committed himself to the
non-resistant tenet of Garrison, this open suggestion of self-
defence shows to what extremities the progress of pro-slavery
legislation had brought the sons of liberty.   And yet for a
white citizen of the North to shoot a Southerner who was
forcibly dragging him to a tobacco, cotton, or rice field for a
lifetime of unpaid labour and its accompaniments, if it had
been possible, would have been justified by the entire Nation.
A black citizen somehow was not the same sort of a citizen,
and if he had escaped from bondage he was simply property,
like a strayed mule — in Southern eyes and national law.
Abolitionists did not see it so; therefore they were political
and social outlanders.   Even among themselves there were
grades of outlandishness.   The non-resistant extremist ought
to have satisfied the slave-catcher in making his kidnapping
easy by not resisting him.   Phillips proposed to make it as
dangerous in the instance of the black as the white; but this
was an unpopular view in Charleston and Richmond; also
in Boston and New York in the middle of the last century.

In the last week of 1852 Phillips wrote a two-column

obituary of Daniel Webster, who died on the 24th of October. Its tenor may be gathered from scattering sentences.

We are sometimes blamed for our judgments of men whose general characters are good. The examples of bad men are of little importance. It is the faults of popular idols that are dangerous. It does not concern us here whether he was a great man. As a whole his life was a failure — he failed to impress any great or original idea upon his times — has stood on both sides of most national questions — talked against slavery up to 1850 without stirring one heart against it, and then supported the fatal compromise. In simple intellect no American has ever equalled him, but he contented himself with saying common things uncommonly well. He never piloted the people into broader and deeper life. He made great speeches. He may live in print; Washington, Jefferson, Hamilton, Garrison, will live, print or no print. Had he led the van of American ideas he would have been tenfold more than the President he wished to be. He was fated to live long enough to see all the plans of his manhood become obsolete ideas, except just those he had abandoned. His latest and ablest argument was the duty and rightfulness of slave catching! He is mourned in ceiled houses and in the marts of trade. Fugitives thank God they have one enemy the less. Grant all his merits. The friendless and the hunted cannot help rejoicing at his death!

Phillips answered the objections to radicalism in his annual review of the cause's progress in January, 1853, which was the dark hour before day. His note is defensive and boldly explanatory of adhesion to the abolitionist position and purposes when the legislation of the country had ranged itself in battle array against them. On their own platforms new converts were offering advice which lacked the wisdom of experience, and showing a zeal that was without knowledge.

To these he gave the counsel and instruction of a veteran. Then he pictured the institution of bondage, as it existed, in colours that were as clear and strong as those of an Egyptian charnel house. It was no doubt the reverse side of the Gobelin tapestry, whose fair front was most often kept before visitors and authors from the North, but the ragged side could be seen by any who cared or dared to find it, or read its frequent disclosures in Southern papers.

We are charged with denunciation when declaring the enormity of making merchandise of men — of separating families — selling daughters to prostitution — forcing unrequited toil — making torture possible, if not common, and death a thing to be welcomed. Prove to me that harsh rebuke, indignant denunciation, scathing sarcasm, and pitiless ridicule are unjustifiable, any weapon which ever broke up the crust of prejudice, roused a slumbering conscience, shamed a proud sinner. Our aim is to alter public opinion — to induce every one to aid in the abolition of slavery. We do not *play* politics: anti-slavery is no half-jest with us. We speak of the dead as of the living. We are now out-talked, out-voted. But our words bide their time.

He then reviewed the literature of the movement from Lundy and Adams to Sumner's last speech and "Uncle Tom's Cabin," and vindicated the original methods, which time had justified by what had been accomplished despite opposition and ceaseless criticism. "If there was no great revolution or reformation apparent, no other course could have accomplished these ends. If they had been defeated in Congress, the creators of Congress had been enlightened." A ground-fire had been smouldering and spreading which needed only a breeze to make it blaze. And the wind was rising in the West.

Soon after, Phillips, speaking in New York, saw no hope of a Union without slavery, and no deliverance except through the demolition and rebuilding of it or a separation of the North and South. Therefore Henry Ward Beecher exhibited the greater faith a few minutes later when he said:

I do not believe that the half of these United States will always stand as slaveholding. By all the victories of Christianity in the past I am inspired with hope for the future; and I have faith in a public sentiment which in spite of recreant clergymen, apostate statesmen, venal politicians, and trafficking shopmen, shall fall upon this vast and unmitigated abomination and utterly crush it. I would rather see Christianity destroy it in seventy-five years than Mammon in fifty and do that which legislation could not do, and which the commerce of the country could not do.

It is not strange that neither the despondent man nor the hopeful one saw how the event was to be brought about within the next decade. It was a year of discouragement and gloom. In Congress there were not over ten out of three hundred who would oppose the extension of slavery, and fewer still who would attack it in its strongholds. President Fillmore could congratulate the Nation that agitation was subsiding and a general acquiescence in measures of peace prevailed.

Amidst this mutual reassurance and congratulation there was a little cloud arising seaward. From the Society of Friends in New England a humble request appeared in Congress in May, 1852, asking for the repeal of the Fugitive Slave Law. Presented by Senator Sumner, it was attacked by Senators from Mississippi and Georgia as threatening the dissolution of the Union, if its purpose were carried out in the repeal of that law.

It was near the close of the session before Sumner could get an opportunity to defend his celebrated thesis that "slavery is sectional and freedom national; and that the Fugitive Slave Act lacks that essential support in the public conscience of the states where it is to be enforced which is the life of all law, and without which any law must become a dead letter."

He closed his argument from legal and historical points of view with a letter from Washington about the return of a fugitive, saying in effect, that he would yield the point rather than create any disturbance or uneasy sensations in the minds of well-disposed citizens. In this four hours of his first elaborate speech in the Senate, Sumner won great praise as uttering an emphatic protest against the notion that the compromise act was a final settlement of agitation about slavery. The mutterings against the Fugitive Slave Law and the resistance to its execution in the North had at length found a voice in Congress to repeat and reënforce the sentiments which abolitionists had been disseminating among the people for over thirty years. To be sure, the measure advocated received but four votes; but the silence had been broken, the lid had been lifted, and the kettle was found ready to boil over. The dreaded agitation was not subsiding after all. Sumner had only to move an amendment to an appropriation bill intended to pay the expenses of slave hunters, and the cauldron was full of toil and trouble.

To Phillips the renewal of strife in Congress contained the promise of a larger interest in the question at issue, which would become national instead of local. Yet he did not give up his claim that the reappearance of congressional antagonism, interrupted since John Quincy Adams's day, was due to Northern sentiment implanted by himself and his associates. Not over sanguine about political assistance from half a dozen legislators, he did not fail to discover the dawn-streaks of a new day in which anti-slavery opinion would grow stronger with the law makers. This would have its reflex influence with the people who got their politics from Congress rather than a lecture plat-form. But he kept his faith in this agency and hoped more from state action than from the Nation; from the people than their chief men. Still, there was hope in what had been begun toward renewed agitation in Congress. The truce of silence had been broken.

There was another group of leading men that might have been of great service to the cause who were slow to endorse it. From his Harvard associates and the company of writers who were contributing to American literature Phillips soon found that he could expect little immediate assistance or sympathy, with two exceptions — Lowell and Whittier.

Lowell, from his college days, had strong humanitarian leanings. His note-book for the year of his graduation, 1838, is full of passages about slavery, and a letter com-miserating factory workers in England ends with the remark, "The abolitionists are the only ones with whom I sympa-thize of present parties." As with Phillips, this sympathy was strengthened by the encouragement of a young woman who eventually became his wife. Also a certain "Band" of kindred spirits seconded and supported this philanthropic influence. By 1840 Lowell was heartily committed to a cause which he had derided in his class poem two years·

before in common with several other 'isms. In November of this year he was a member of an anti-slavery convention in Boston, and from this time the slavery question appears frequently in his poems and letters. He even exhorts a Virginia classmate to join the abolition ranks. It is to be noted, however, that the poet never belonged to the extreme wing of the radicals, and in the years when he was corresponding editor of the *Anti-slavery Standard* he did not entirely satisfy some of the more rigid managers in the abuse they wished heaped upon slaveholders, whom he considered human. Yet his moderation reached some readers who had no liking for violent assaults upon their mistaken countrymen. Worn with the drudgery of fortnightly contributions, he wrote in 1850 that he had decided to turn for a time from politics to poetry, and two years later his official connection with the *Standard* had ceased.

With his growth as a professional man of letters and upon a larger acquaintance with the guild, following his appointment as a professor in Harvard, his early zeal became dissipated in the stress of his new occupation. Still, the primitive enthusiasm of the Biglow Papers period had not vanished so much as it had settled into an abiding principle of humane sympathy, which was to be enshrined in some of the noblest poems in our literature. As early as 1844 he had written the lines which Phillips never tired of repeating:

"Truth forever on the scaffold, wrong forever on the throne—
   Yet that scaffold sways the future, and behind the dim
      unknown
   Standeth God within the shadow, keeping watch above
      His own."

Through all the poems of war time, culminating in the Commemoration Ode of 1865, runs the same lofty patriotism, a broader stream from the fountain which bubbled noisily in the decade of ferment and unrest.

The support which Whittier gave to anti-slavery illustrates the differences of method that were employed by abolitionists. As a young journalist, inclined to politics, he was not at first greatly interested in this reform beyond others, all of which he regarded as tokens of a moral revolution that was setting in. Yet as a philanthropic movement its claim at length began to assert itself in the growth of public sentiment. Moreover, Garrison by a strong appeal aroused him to serious consideration of what he might accomplish for the cause. Still, he did not deem it needful to follow the leader in his uncompromising demands, nor to employ the severity of his language, nor even to join the "Boston clique." As a natural politician, who had already been of service at the State House, he had a practical sense of the value of time in all important changes, and of the gradual preparation of public opinion, and of its effective expression at the polls. By 1833, however, he was sufficiently committed to the cause to write a tract on Abolition as the Remedy of Slavery, urging its safety and justice, and that free labour would be more advantageous to the planter than slave labour. It was a moderate and reasonable argument, but it did not fail to stir up Southern resentment that any word should be spoken against the domestic institution of the section.

He had not been without political ambitions, but when he went as a delegate from Massachusetts to Philadelphia at the founding of the American Anti-slavery society he

necessarily broke with politics and with the journalism
which was its ally. Although he continued to write as a
contributor or editor for several papers, they were not
organs of the two great existing parties. Indeed, his health
during the period of the great contest did not allow him
to be in the thick of the fight. An occasional article or a
stirring poem, struck off when the day permitted, amounted
to much in twenty years, but to little month by month.
Yet these occasional efforts did good service by their sincerity and inoffensive presentation of a cause which was
oftener associated with narrow methods and violent words.
Later, the poet himself cared more for the reformatory
quality of his verse than for its artistic form, which
was not so severely judged in those stirring times as
afterward.

As a politician who had a keen sense of values he may be regarded as a connecting link between the theoretical abolitionism of the early period and the practical emancipation
through legislation of the final period. The first agitation was
needful in order to bring about the methods which are
essential to lasting reform in a republic. Whittier must have
the credit of pointing his radical companions to the legiti-
mate way in which their high purpose could finally be accomplished. On the other hand, he could not have had
reasonable hopes of the result by the customary political
management. The plow and the harrow were needed in the
springtime, and the sowing of the seed. The autumn
brought its own ways of gathering the harvest. Between,
something was to be done which looked backward and
forward; and Whittier, more than any other man of letters,
stood for that intermediate time and work.

From the literary coterie that gave Boston and its vicinity distinction leading abolitionists did not fail to observe that they received little encouragement at first. Longfellow was occupied with introducing Old World literatures to New England and the Nation; Emerson was absorbed in a philosophy with which he was startling his orthodox neighbourhood and parts adjacent; Hawthorne was musing on the severities of his ancestors in the Bay Province more than on those of the South; Holmes was busy with his medical lectures and Harvard anniversary poems, and confining his attention within the rim of the Boston Circle. Thoreau, indeed, added to the rest of his eccentricities, as they were reckoned, protests against human bondage, and upbraided a zeal for Kansas which he thought should have been turned against home indifference for the slave. After a time, when the war broke out, all of this company who were then living awoke to the importance of the issue which had precipitated strife, and fell in with its requirements with various degrees of assent and devotion; as did the chief men of the city, their associates. The same can be said of men of letters in New York and other Northern cities.

XIII

PROTEST AGAINST THE FUGITIVE SLAVE ACT

(1854–1855)

ACCORDING to the Missouri Compromise of 1820 slavery was to be forever excluded from the North-west Territories. In 1854 an attempt was made to cancel this agreement. Simultaneously, raiders from Missouri undertook to make Kansas a slave state. Free Soilers in Congress protested, and petitions flowed in from the entire North against the violation of a sacred pledge.

It is of great interest to note the effect upon abolitionists of this sudden awakening of Northern people. It was a surprise party, disturbing the family somewhat. Phillips did not pay much attention to the cause of it—Kansas troubles— being occupied with the arrest of Anthony Burns and his rendition to slavery under a guard of Massachusetts militia. For appealing to citizens to prevent this, he and Theodore Parker were indicted by the Grand Jury for "obstructing the process of the United States" in slave catching, but nothing came of it.

Evidently the great Northern awakening did not appeal to him. For one thing, it had been started at the political centre of the country and by men who were reckoned as politicians, if they were not statesmen. They had appealed to their constituents, instead of petitions coming from the people to their representatives in Congress, as had hitherto been the custom. Reform was not proceeding in the normal direction. A current had suddenly set in from the other pole. It started before its time, and threatened to make agitation useless. Besides, anything savouring of political methods or action in this abolition reform had been decried from the first by its pioneers. Therefore it is not strange that they looked askance at the crowd that all at once came flocking in their direction. An extremist wrote Phillips from " Cornville " deploring his mild toleration of political action.

Of course, there was the consolatory reflection that the way had been prepared for the new-comers by the labours of thirty years, and that the seed for this up-springing wheat had been sown long before, and had been lying in an apparent death, which was the condition of its life when the winter was over. But even this comforting assurance was not offered yet.

Instead, in a lecture in Tremont Temple in the last week of 1854 on the Character and Extent of Anti-slavery Feeling in New England, Phillips spoke in a strain of high faith in the future rather than in any immediate prospect for the present. " It is a question of free speech, all that the South has not beaten us in during its successive stages of political aggression — the Fugitive Slave Law of 1793, Louisiana and Texas, the compromise measures of 1850, and the abolition of the Missouri Compromise." But this last measure, which had aroused the North, he passed by in silence, keeping to his home theme of the North leagued with the South in perpetuating the profitable system of slavery.

The most Southern sheet in Boston said of this speech that,

"Never were the splendid abilities of this most accomplished and able fanatic more amply displayed than on this occasion. Sentiments most repugnant to the feelings of every patriot were absolutely applauded when clothed in the graceful and magnificent diction of this anti-slavery Cicero. The gross injustice of the matter and the exquisite felicity of the manner, topics such as the dissolution of the Union and destruction of the Constitution, were dwelt upon with such unparalleled force and beauty that disapprobation of the subject was lost and overwhelmed in admiration of the man. The vast hall rang again and again to rounds of enthusiastic applause. Great as has been the change since 1850, it is insufficient to explain the favour with which this abolition oration was received by an audience such as is seldom collected, even in this city."

In March of the next year, 1855, Phillips gave evidence of what he might have attained in the legal profession by an extended argument before the Committee on Federal Relations of the Massachusetts Legislature in support of petitions that had been presented for the removal of Judge Loring, who had issued the warrant to arrest Anthony Burns and was responsible, Phillips held, for his return to slavery.

A Commissioner of humane and just instincts would be careful to remember that he was both Judge and Jury. No jury would have sent Burns back to his master. The state declares that the fugitive is constitutionally entitled to a jury trial. Mr. Webster once prepared an amendment to the act of Congress securing jury trial. A judge who consents to act at all as Slave Commissioner should be removed from office. The hunting of slaves, then, is a sufficient cause for removal from a Massachusetts bench. For the sake of Justice, in the name of Humanity, we claim his removal.

This argument, occupying fifteen newspaper columns, closed with an appeal worthy of the orator's best perorations.[1] His narration of circumstances and citation of authorities were skilfully managed, but in closing he massed all their weight and force in an address to the legislators that would have moved a jury to let any bondman go free. " It is in your power to-day to redeem the judiciary of Massachusetts from the disgrace which this case has flung upon it. You will render it impossible that any but unprincipled and shameless men shall aid in the enforcement of a wicked clause in the Constitution." A few days later, at a third hearing, Phillips went over the ground again in reply to Mr. R. H. Dana, Jr.'s, review of the case, in a speech an hour in length. His recapitulation was spoken of as especially eloquent and powerful, and was listened to with profound attention. He said: " Judge Story and Professor Greenleaf used to point to the Bible and say to the students, ' Gentlemen, that book is the origin of all law, and its foundation. When you find a law which conflicts with *that*, it is *no* law!'" He then pointed out that the principles which the people held in their hearts had been defied by judges, until one had overstepped the limit, who, having had fair warning, should be removed for the execution of a law which was offensive to the majority of the Commonwealth.

Those who heard these arguments before the " Great and General Court" knew that they were not the extravagances of a wild fanatic. But some of them must have speculated on a possible career at bar and bench and in halls of legislation that had been surrendered for a cause unpopular and ridiculed.

[1]Afterward included in " Speeches, Lectures, and Addresses," First Series, p. 154.

By this reproof of a judge, who, as Slave Commissioner, had returned the last fugitive to be remanded to slavery from Massachusetts, the state had nullified the Fugitive Slave Law in all its progressive stages. And then it had the audacity to pass an " Act to protect the rights and liberties of the people of the Commonwealth " — without respect to their complexion. The Latimer case had secured a Personal Liberty Bill forbidding officers henceforward to take and detain fugitives; and now the law was made to match the Compromise of 1850. Habeas corpus was secured; burden of proof thrown upon the pursuer; issuing a warrant, assisting the claimant, or presiding at trial were fatal to official and professional careers. Counsel was to be furnished; police, sheriffs, jailors, and troops were to keep their hands off. Phillips led in presenting and supporting this bill, which was vetoed by the Governor, but passed by the Legislature over his veto on May 21st, the vote standing in the Senate thirty-two for, to three against; in the House two hundred and twenty-nine to seventy-six. Thus did the Bay state defy the South and the Constitution.

Phillips's third argument before legislative committees within a month was a long one on the abolition of capital punishment. Of the two common pleas in its favour he answered the first — to restrain the murderer from repeating the offence — by saying that a prison will do that; and the second — hanging a man for an example, as the forefathers did on the Common — loses its force because it is now done within prison walls in comparative privacy. The entire argument bristles with historical citation and legal learning. In closing, he enumerated barbarous practices that have given place to others more merciful — crucifixion, impaling, tearing by horses and hot pincers, the rack, the stake.

"Now we ask you to abolish the gallows. It is only one step further in the same direction. Take it because the civilized world is taking it, in many quarters! Take it because it is well to try experiments for humanity, and this is a favourable community to try them in."

As president of the New England Anti-slavery Convention (since June, 1847,) he becomes retrospective at its May meeting, saying:

For the twenty years these meetings have been held in the city of Boston no clergyman, no officer of the state, no man of any social standing or position of influence, has stood on this platform, Henry Wilson excepted — the first ray of light breaking over the mountains. Great men would have come in and swamped us by the magnificence of their aid long ago if slavery had left them any soul.

The next day he opened a long speech in the same strain with the words: "Mr. Chairman — Our distinctive policy is the necessity of a dissolution of the American Union, in order to abolish slavery. It is the one essential point of the anti-slavery movement out of which conduct and purpose and system must grow." For an hour he proceeded in his amplification of this proposition, showing why and how it should be done. "Dissolution was not an uncommon problem. The fathers dissolved two Unions. We can dissolve another by taking Massachusetts out. *South Carolina* threaten to leave the Union! Why, she cannot walk! She has not yet stood alone! Nobody will go out unless we go."

The value of these significant fragments is to show that the only remedy for the chronic malady appeared to him to be in amputation, six years before it was begun at the other end of the body politic in the South. But no man was prophet enough to see how Liberty *and* Union, in a fuller sense than was contemplated by Webster, was to be accomplished.

As examples of persuasive and convincing speech, and all the more because one-half his audiences did not accept their doctrines, these arguments stand in their unabridged fulness as models of popular exposition. They read well even now. That they were spoken well, contemporary testimony affirms by the notes of applause in the reports of them which mark the responses of throngs that were by no means sympathetic before or after his discourse. Built upon lines of strong logic, they were enlivened by frequent anecdote, illustrated by historical examples, and varied by question and answer, personal allusion, pointed reference and startling assertion. The effects of every rhetorical device are secured without the appearance of art. It is the sparkling conversation of a full mind, before a full house, on a subject of which the speaker's heart is full.

An interesting note occurs in remarks at a Fourth of July celebration at Framingham, which Hon. Henry Wilson had been invited to attend, but owing to other engagements he had sent a letter instead, deprecating mutual criticism and reproach in the working for a common cause. To this Phillips put in a demurrer, to the effect that criticism of action or principle is a great benefit, securing the cause against the possibility of being diverted out of its proper course.

Abolitionism is not like an old and organized political party, but made up of men who think each one for himself, who must welcome criticism even from their associates. Principles are to be maintained, whatever becomes of men. When the time comes that the advocates of any reform cease to criticize each other its efficiency is gone. Harmony and peace are not essential. Where confederates come in, criticism necessarily follows. If harmony is desired, it will be found in political parties where men's heads are cut off to make them all of the same regulation stature. Not so among independent reformers.

This announcement will explain some occurrences which threatened to shatter a loose organization a dozen times in the course of one generation. It was their cordial agreement to a guerilla warfare that kept various independents within sight of an occasional rallying place where they met, each one with his own musket, rifle, club, or fists, and in regimentals as unlike as Continental buff and blue, Quaker drab, and Indian toggery. In only one respect did they agree — that slavery must be abolished. Exactly how, was a question not so clear or so unanimously settled In the early 'fifties, disunion, by the withdrawal of the voter and politics, the separation of one state and another from the Union, and finally of the entire North from the South, appears to have been the programme, so far as it was formulated and endorsed. But immediate work and endeavour was by the individual citizen with his neighbour, from house to house, from village to village, county to county, city to city, state to state.

An example of this method is seen in one of Phillips's "abolitionizing trips," as his wife called them. Starting from home on November 20, 1854, he spoke in Lee that evening and on successive evenings as follows: Utica, Pen Yan, Rochester, Syracuse, Rome, Syracuse again, Hamilton, C. W., Detroit, Cleveland, Zanesville, Cincinnati, Elmira, Binghamton, Middletown, and three evenings in Philadelphia, ending December 10th. In this circuit of three weeks he made a dozen and a half speeches, which varied as the places and with the remarkable diversity which was a part of his oratorical skill; but the theme was always the same and as constant as his single purpose. Ten or twenty thousand persons meantime heard a voice they would not soon forget, and words to be remembered for years, and saw a presence that was photographed upon their vision, intent and fascinated as by a Periclean statue living and thinking and speaking before them, bearing them far away from their environment and out of their habitudes of life and thought.

It might be inferred that this one man alone sowed seeds that would spring up abundantly when the season should come. The temptation must have been great to attribute a new movement in political circles at this time to the agitation of thirty previous years. But as yet there was little boasting. On the contrary, it seemed to the leaders that no great advantage had been won beyond free speech and a doubtful difficulty thenceforward in returning fugitives to the South from Boston. Even men of good will toward abolition said, What care we about it? The Constitution, the Party, the Church are against us. Such half-hearted friends Phillips addressed at a celebration not far from Plymouth Rock in August of this year, 1855, telling them to stand "clear of party politics, of churches that were not disgracefully anti-slavery, and not to vote under a Constitution that protected the slave-catcher." Salmon P. Chase had just asked Dartmouth students to pledge themselves to "no slavery — outside the slave states!" "No slavery *in* those states was the only effective principle, and conscience the only living power against the institution," was Phillips's reply.

One thing upon which he congratulated himself and his co-workers was the admission of coloured children to the schools of Boston, a movement which was begun by himself and a few others petitioning the city government; and that had been kept up until it reached the state Legislature fourteen years later and was made law in 1854. Then the city followed the state's example. At the celebration of this event by a meeting on the 17th of December Phillips remarked that it was one of those rare days in the history of a hard struggle when there was something palpable to rejoice in. Men were always asking, What has the anti-slavery agitation done? He was glad they had this answer to make now, It has opened the schools! Without this agitation they would never have been opened. The best thing learned by these struggles is, how to prepare for another. They were in for the war. He should never think Massachusetts a fit state to live in until he saw one man, at least, as black as the ace of spades, a graduate of Harvard College. He did not go for annexing territory only, but all sorts of races and all sorts of customs.

Beyond this there is little congratulation. Closing the year with a speech at a dinner of the Pilgrim Society at Plymouth, he remarked that —

What the Puritans gave the world was not so much new truth as *action*. They planted, and the *oak* is the answer to all criticism. They are to be regarded in their possibilities. If Elder Brewster could appear to-day he would not be contented with the five points of Calvin. He would add to his creed the Maine Liquor Law, the Underground Railway, and the thousand Sharpe's Rifles, addressed "Kansas" and labelled "Books." To be as good as our fathers, we must be better. Plymouth Rock underlies all America. It cropped out at Bunker Hill, at the Declaration of Independence; Lovejoy rested his musket upon it when they would not let him print at Alton and said, "Death or free speech!" The Pilgrims said *death* rather than the compromise of Elizabeth. They voted that each man should build his own house. So, now; each one his own mental house, without having too much uniformity in the architecture and keeping clear of shams and delusion, smothering phrases and compromises.

This final sentence is most characteristic of Phillips. There was no conformity in his mental structure to that of other men of his time, nor did he make any apology for his idiosyncrasy. He was never blind to shams, nor open to suggestions of compromise, nor did he ever soften words that could expose and brand a popular delusion. In his desperate warfare he asked no quarter, and he certainly gave none. Yet he never descended to low abuse nor used language that was beneath Ciceronian invective. His spear was like Ithuriel's, his sword like the Saracen's, his shield unblurred, his armour radiant, and a knightly spirit pervaded all his strife.

XIV

THE MAIN ISSUE

(1856)

THE Kansas struggle between Eastern immigrants and Missouri raiders did not divert Phillips's attention from the greater contest for general emancipation. At first he was inclined to be supercilious about the minor issue of territorial occupation, saying that "Yankees had gone into a half-barbarous West to dispute their way inch by inch with the bowie knives and revolvers of vagabonds. What are the squabbles around the ballot-boxes of Kansas?" Reform was needed at the centres, where the root of the evil is more than on the outskirts, and by the agency of legislatures and the judiciary rather than by common politics and bayonets.

It is in this memorable year that the efficiency of Phillips's methods begins to get clearer, and to bridge over the dark chasm between his steadfast purpose and its accomplishment. First, he was for educating the individual and the community into the sense of an evil and the wish to remove it, in some way which would be discovered when the public conscience should be sufficiently awakened. Next, for disunion by withdrawal and separation of one state and another. This was to be hastened by checkmating the Government through an anti-slavery judiciary elected by the people. But this consummation must have appeared far off. However, it was something to have devised a possible way.

One disadvantage to extreme abolitionists in the score of years hitherto had been the destructive policy they felt obliged to advocate. *Delenda est Carthago* had been their battle cry; but how to destroy it, and what to build on its ruins, were equally indefinite visions. They held that it was first of all necessary to destroy; but this is always an unpopular process — in this instance exceedingly unpopular in the South, and in much of the North as well. If to the latter section it seemed a practicable or possible way to pull down and uproot an evil that from Colonial days had not ceased to be national in various degrees, it is doubtful if it would have been regarded with favour for a moment, except by the little band of abolitionists. Certainly, the destruction of slavery was not the purpose of the Northern rising in 1861. If in addition to a definite destructive method, the reformers could have shown a constructive plan, the question would have been more than half settled. But if they could have done this, their wisdom would have surpassed the teachings of experience during the forty years in which the Nation afterward wandered in the wilderness of reconstruction. It was enough for the early pioneers to determine to go forward. It might not be in the straightest line, but it was in the right direction. In any case, it was not sitting down in despair. Agitation was better than that. Doubt, however, was still brooding over one of the leaders, despite the open struggle for freedom in Kansas.

In what may be regarded as his annual report of progress — the customary address at the May anniversary of the

New England Society, Phillips was not jubilant. He doubted if there was public principle enough to save the experiment of civil government. Ignorance of true liberty prevailed and indifference to all but national interests, and even to the striking down of Senator Sumner, and to making a protest by the best of the city — the milk-and-water men that did not dare offend the South. "We, at least, can protest. When this generation is gone and a better one come, they will be glad to trace through us the line that connects them with an ever living protest against infamous tyranny. It is a great thing to keep alive a protest. The anti-slavery cause does not seem to move; like the shadow on the dial you cannot see it move, but it gets to twelve o'clock at last."

In his inmost heart Phillips did not think that the night had wholly passed. If there were dawn-streaks, there was a cloud-bank of materialism in the East; and the red and lowering sky in the West of yesterday was not a promise of fair weather. It was from a prairie fire on the plains of Kansas.

If Phillips could upbraid the half-hearted Northern denunciations of the assault upon Sumner by Brooks, he had just then no words strong enough for the Southern adulations of the outrage which were published in the majority of pro-slavery papers, nor for the chivalry of the South which sent the assassin gold-headed canes and silver plate with its endorsement of his cowardly and brutal attack upon an unarmed man, writing at his desk. A Faneuil Hall indignation meeting was addressed by "eminent speakers of all political parties." The most distinguished speaker of Boston, and of the Nation, being of no political party, was not invited. His sentiments, if not his language, must therefore be gathered from the anniversary speech three days later, the drift of which has been noted. Inwardly, he regarded the disgraceful attack upon the Senator as a surrender by slaveocracy of argument and a resort to club and knife, and therefore one step downward toward its final doom. Undoubtedly it hastened this event with the North at large.

By the Fourth of July he was ready to take a broad view of the situation in 1856, and out of the general gloom to extract a spark of light. On the Southern side every barrier to the extension of slavery in the Southwest had been thrown down: the Northwest, once consecrated to freedom, had been divided, and Kansas had been overrun by armed invaders backed by the Administration, who had driven Northern settlers from their farms and ballot-boxes. Nebraska would be the next ground to be occupied. In Congress, knockdown arguments had displaced the logic of Calhoun, while his prophecy of disunion was often repeated. This threat did not displease extremists at the North, although they did not take much stock in it.

Phillips had more hope in the formation and trend of the Republican party, because it was a strictly sectional party. Whigs, and especially Democrats, had belonged to the Southern states as well as the Northern. No Republican contingent could exist in slave states; and in the division of parties he saw the beginning of separation. He did not call the Republican an anti-slavery party; it had not risen to that, he said. But he hailed it as a sign — a little crack in the iceberg. In that light, recent political movements were a gain — a great gain — which had come unexpectedly early.

Aside from this, he regarded it as an absurdity. It was agitating for a political result when the times demanded *Revolution*.

In placing moral agencies before political, Phillips saw in the success of the latter nothing beyond the restriction of slavery to the states it already occupied, and with its bonds tightened by reason of this bargain for limitation. But he also saw, with everybody else, that it was not to be confined to its worn-out stamping ground, nor was the political equilibrium of power to be destroyed by giving the North an equal advantage with the South. This had never been and was never intended to be allowed. "Disunion first!" said the Slave Power.

The encroachments of politics upon the anti-slavery field in the form of the new Republican party was on Mr. Phillips's mind at the August anniversary of West India Emancipation, a day which had been observed off and on for twenty-two years. He valued politics for the discussion raised, more than for the men it put in office. The canvass was worth a hundredfold more than the election.

Two months later the opinion of the South with regard to Free Soilers was uttered by Preston S. Brooks on the occasion of receiving canes and goblets from his constituents in token of his bravery in striking down Sumner. "I hate them [Free Soilers] just as much as I hate abolitionists; nay, worse. I hate them worse than I hate the rattlesnake; for unlike it they give no warning of their approach, and seek to conceal their objects." And, further on, he overmatched the rankest Garrisonian: "The only mode of meeting the present issue is, just to tear the Constitution of the United States, trample it underfoot, and form a Southern confeder-

acy, every state of which will be a slave-holding state."
[Loud and prolonged cheers.] The infant party was having
hard usage from the tips of the right and left wings of the bird
of freedom. However, it was getting beaten into shape and
vigour for sundry efforts of its own in a similar direction.
And so the war of words went on until the election of James
Buchanan, which in South Carolina was regarded as
"emphatically a Southern victory — fought on Southern
grounds. . . . The Constitution reigns supreme . . .
and the South will rule the Union." "Through one more
administration," should have been added; "and then" —
but prophesying was unsafe, although there had been much
of it for many years and with ominous agreement North
and South.

Phillips closed the addresses of the year with a short speech
in New York at a woman's convention in which he uttered
some historical and social generalities, and advocated more
education and the franchise, if women were to be taxed.
He also lectured in Detroit for the third time, on the
"Philosophy of Reform." The press of the city agreed in
admiring his oratory, but questioned its useful tendency.
The reign of conservatism had been disturbed by his coming,
and "Republicanism, though far from being anti-slavery,
had opened many eyes to see the light." This evidently
had been the first advantage which it had brought to the
radicals, as the abolitionists were sometimes called; and
generally they were willing to accord this revealing power to
a growing political movement that was spreading along the
Northern border. But it was not after their own hearts by
any means. It did not go far enough.

As for Phillips himself, his idealism allowed him to take little comfort in the progress of any movement in his direction, since he always kept so great a distance between himself and the following host. To be just to him it should be said, that his remote and high standpoint was taken at the outset of his career, and for thirty years any approach toward his position by any party whose vote was worth counting was as slight as that of the earth toward the sun in the predicted swallowing up of the one by the other. At last there was an apparent absorption, so sudden that the radical had hardly time to realize it; but through all his fighting years he had little encouragement, on account of his discouraging distance from the army he was beckoning on. If some of the wild-eyed thought they had almost reached his standard, they presently discovered him at the end of its forecast shadow seemingly planting another. But it was always the same that he set up at the beginning of his crusade — the stars, without the stripes of the national ensign. These last, he used to say, represented its legalized bondage.

XV

DISINTEGRATION

(1857)

F ANEUIL HALL, on the second day of 1857, must have
presented a singular spectacle to conservative Bostonians. A chosen four hundred abolitionists assembled at a
dinner to celebrate the founding of the Massachusetts Anti-
slavery Society twenty-five years before. Mr. Garrison began
the after-dinner speaking by reviewing the growth of the
movement from colonial societies and later ones looking
toward emancipation in some indefinite period, and the
subsequent declaration for immediate emancipation promul-
gated in Baltimore in 1829, followed by the publication
of the *Liberator*, in Boston, January 1, 1831. He spoke of
the organization of two thousand societies in the next decade
before the unhappy divisions of 1840 upon the woman question, from which the cause had never recovered. Nevertheless, there was occasion for rejoicing in view of the
wonderful progress that had been made, as would be shown
by the speakers that were to follow. The only one whose
remarks can be noticed here was Wendell Phillips, and
the substance only of these.

He insisted that the abolition movement had been one of
education, revealing the state to itself. While politics had

advanced, it was still on the defensive; but abolitionism was aggressive, not apologizing, nor like congressmen, trying to explain its position. Massachusetts should be made too hot for slaveholders and doughfaces to tread her soil.

The chief note of the new year was not congratulation but disunion. The Slave Power, South and North, had won the country for its purposes in electing Buchanan; there was little or nothing to hope from the defeated Republican party; its chief speaker had been stricken down in the Senate Chamber; its fight for freedom in Kansas was uncertain, and if victorious would not touch slavery in its own states. The disunion threats which extremists in the South had made in case Frémont were elected were now echoed at the other end of the coast line when a Disunion Convention was held in Worcester on January 15, 1857, in reply to a call "to consider the practicability, probability, and expediency of a separation between the free and slave states." Letters from Amasa Walker, Henry Wilson, Theodore Parker, and Joshua R. Giddings were representative of as many personal views of the question. Senator Wilson wished to hold the Union together in order to protect the territories from the encroachments of slavery and to prepare the way for peaceful emancipation. Parker believed that the question would have to be settled by bloodshed. Giddings fell back upon the statement that "whenever any form of government becomes destructive of the ends for which it was formed it is the right of the people to alter or abolish it, and institute a new government," as the fathers of the Republic had done.

Phillips made his answer upon the platform as usual:

He was no worshipper of a Union which had merely preserved the peace between thirty-one states. " It had produced wealth but not men — greater than Daniel Webster,
Caleb Cushing, and Franklin Pierce; fair weather sailors
till the Kansas storm, and now men are skulking into harbour
for fear of being sunk! Free speech endangers the Government! Then the sooner it goes to pieces the better. The
Union has made slavery triumphant and has brought the
country to a lower point than the lowest in English history
— when Cromwell put his military boot on the speaker's
mace in the House of Commons — in the barbarism of the
assault on Sumner, mildly rebuked by the North and
applauded by the South. Take away Northern sympathy
and the South will set about getting a government, and
anarchy will not result." It must have seemed to the iron-
clad listener — if there could be such so long as Phillips
was speaking — that he failed to show how slavery would
necessarily disappear after the Union between the North
and South should be dissolved. Disunion was advocated
by Southern extremists for the very purpose of continuing
and extending slavery undisturbed and unrestricted. It
was the Union that still kept the bane within bounds, and
a Northern confederacy would not of necessity hold all
the territories free.

In 1857 the Union was not sure of a free Kansas. With
two independent confederacies, the war which was begun
there in 1856 might not have been delayed five years, as it
was, before it broke out between two sections of one country.
But abolition by force and arms was not a part of the abolitionists' purpose. The leaders were still holding steadfastly
to their hope of awakening the Nation's conscience, and so

changing its attitude toward an inherited evil that in some other way it would purge itself of the taint and corruption. Still, the way itself was not clear. Even the withdrawal of one state or several would give others more satisfaction than mortification. Therefore, Northern disunionists, while washing their hands of complicity in a national crime, were losing their hold upon the best hope and way of keeping it within present limits and possibly of exterminating it, if it became unbearable in its arrogance. Indeed, recent demands and encroachments were so fast hastening opposition to it that the South feared the result of the campaign of 1860, and foresaw plainly the end of their domination. Accordingly, they made the most of the four remaining years in getting ready for disunion in their own favour and for their own interest — as their leaders thought, but as many of the people did not think.

Against this meeting and its disunion sentiment there were opposing voices, calm and screaming. Sober-minded anti-slavery men preferred waiting for the progress of opinion and renovation of the Government; while conservative or pro-slavery newspapers ran the entire scale from the grumblings of caution to the screechings of ridicule. It was immediately evident that in Massachusetts a vote for withdrawal from the Union would be far from unanimous. The general sense of the Commonwealth would have dampened the zeal of any reformer who had not had cold water thrown upon him steadily for twenty years. Hydropathy, however, had been a favourite treatment with some radicals and a necessity with others — if they got nothing worse than a shower of water they were fortunate. More substantial and fouler descents sometimes fell. Therefore their sublime faith and undiminished effort in the face of another rebuff must be placed to their credit as indicating the elements of which notable reformers are made. Undaunted, Phillips said: "Cherish these meetings; repeat them; sound on in the discussion of this question; let the plummet down; try all the formulas of logic; it may be that, at last, as in the Arabian story, some fortunate tongue may pronounce, accidentally, the magic charm that will make the door of the Bastile to fly open."

President Buchanan's inaugural address voiced the determination of the slave interest, of which he was the figurehead, that every state and territory should have slavery within its borders, marking a long governmental stride from the constitutional restrictions of 1789, keeping the territories free from it forever. Nor was there any possible doubt to which alternative this Administration was committed. Kansas affairs were an open comment upon its pro-slavery bias and intent.

Two days later, March 6th, the immense weight of the judiciary was added to Executive pronouncements. Not of the full bench, but of a bare majority committed to the policy of the Administration, and who, through Chief Justice Taney, rendered the infamous decision in the notorious Dred Scott case, by which it was determined that a slave taken by his master into a free state and living there for years with his consent did not, as had hitherto been held, become free, but could be returned to bondage, and, inferentially, making every state a slavery-promoting or -protecting commonwealth. Incidentally, it produced a sentence, attributed to Justice Taney, which was the distilled essence of a long document, that "the black man

has no rights which white men are bound to respect." **It**
was regarded as fixing the high-water mark of a series of
slaveholding aggressions for seven years, beginning with
the compromises of 1850.

That Phillips's voice was heard beyond his own state,
and that he was a surprise to some, appears from notices
of lectures in Yonkers, New York, and Waukegan, Ill.
In these places they had supposed that he was "a ferocious
ranter, a blustering man of words, a bigoted, treasonable,
self-righteous fanatic, full of caustic bitterness" Instead,
they found him far from their preconceptions of an agitator;
"an embodiment of refined sensibilities, calm in temper,
polished in manner, full of common sense, logical in argument, concise and choice in language, a polished scholar and
a dignified gentleman." While deprecating the principles
and purposes of abolitionists, the local press generally
conceded that "all of them were not fools and fanatics,
but that there were men pure-hearted and noble-minded,
whom an over-acuteness of moral sensibility may have
impelled into the ranks." Such an estimate represents
the general view of a fair-minded journalism, free enough
from partisan animosity to appreciate qualities inherent
in the man and the orator, if not able to indorse his doctrine.

He was now being heard on other than anti-slavery
topics, as is seen in brief reports of a discourse one Sunday
in Music Hall, Boston, on a Living and a Dead Christianity,
relating to the treatment of criminal and perishing classes
in society, delivered to three thousand listeners. A week
later he spoke on Temperance. On both occasions the
halls were crowded. "Twenty years ago," he said, "you
had only to enter a hotel to see the character of an American

gentleman; now you had to go down stairs. Much had been gained in twenty years; a drinking life had come to be looked upon with disgust, public opinion was the controlling power in this country;— get the ideas right, and the customs will follow."

On the 26th of May Phillips took up the Dred Scott decision at the annual meeting of the New England Society.

When the Supreme Court lays down a Dred Scott decision on the anvil of the American heart, we want an energy and fixedness of purpose in that heart which shall shape it into a tool that will pierce the very heart of the Union. In 1789 the Government was launched with the *whole territory free*. At that same moment the devil hovered over Charleston and dropped a few cotton seeds into the soil. Presto! sixty years and the cotton seeds have annihilated the Constitution, the Revolution, and everything else, and we are nothing but a cotton-bag to-day. A generation rolled away to 1819 and another struggle, and our fathers yielded up *half* the territory for slavery, half for freedom. Another struggle in 1852 — the *whole* territory for slavery! That is the history of the Union. The South had not hardened into despotism twenty years ago — was not certain of victory. To-day the triumph of the Slave Power is written on the forehead of the Government! and that is why the necessity of the hour is revolution. There is the law made by the Supreme Court, and the North bows to this final interpreter of the Constitution. There is no course between submitting and rebelling but to say to the people, You must be ready for revolution. When they are ready, then you are ready for the first attempt to carry that decision into effect by refusing to submit to it. Convince Massachusetts men that it is not law to which they are bowing — that it is despotism, and they will not submit. Rebellion! — it is epidemic here. Hancock caught the disease and inoculated

us all. Remove the state from pro-slavery influences and
you will see her true character.

On the following Fourth of July he uttered once more
his independent sentiments in a grove meeting, to the effect
that abolitionism, like the grove meeting, had no roof,
with no institution or party to serve — a John the Baptist
in the desert to awaken conscience and stir thought, to
make the North love liberty, to make a highway for the
future to walk over to triumph.

With these utterances there is also an abundance of
criticism bestowed upon party leaders, from Banks in the
state to Wilson in Congress; but their usefulness is admitted,
and, despite their partial service, their education to higher
usefulness is hoped for. Furthermore, there is more than
a suspicion that the purpose which Phillips and his friends
had been labouring to accomplish might be effected, if at
all, by the imperfect, half-way measures of political action.
But not immediately. For in the call for a Northern disunion convention, issued four days later, July 8th, it was
printed: " From *mere* Politics there is little to be expected.
The Slave Power has always carried its measures and
always will. The attitude of Republican leaders is now
one of timidity and compromise, though the mass of voters
in many states is becoming more radically anti-slavery."
To create a united North was the chief hope and dependence.
Accordingly, three shades of opinion on the subject of
separation were appealed to: 1. Those who repudiate the
Constitution as essentially pro-slavery, and hence abjure
all union under it. 2. Those who, not accepting this view
of it, believe that there can be no permanent union between
free and slave states. 3. Those who believe in the ultimate

triumph of Freedom, without disunion, and still approve of agitation of the subject to strengthen and consolidate the North! [1]

The customary First of August Emancipation Address of Phillips was a skilful appeal for friends in a time of need and discouragement from those who were pledged for the long war — "between New England and the Carolinas." Massachusetts, he said, was not half so anti-slavery as it pretended to be, and therefore all the greater sacrifice and labour were demanded. He scored the inconsistency of asking the slaveholder whose social position, wealth, ease, and future consequence depended upon slavery to obey an abstract, rigid rule of right when its advocates were so reluctant in its service. Even the pulpit would be beggared if it preached radical anti-slavery, and politics was in fetters. Public opinion and Democracy were the worst of tyrants; commercial interest needed a resisting force of fanaticism to keep it from dulling the heart of the Nation. Therefore there was no rest ahead, and the day of agitation would never close in clouds of purple and gold.

It was in this long speech that he turned aside to answer the Unitarian clergymen who were "always pecking at him because he was Orthodox." He did this by comparing the free spirit displayed at a recent Yale Commencement with the restraint at Harvard, which he attributed to its affiliation with the commercial interests of Boston, and the silence they imposed on anti-slavery sentiments was illustrated by the striking out from an oration an inoffensive allusion to Kansas. Yale, too, had honoured Charles

---

[1] This call was signed by Thomas Wentworth Higginson, Wendell Phillips, Daniel Mann, William Lloyd Garrison, and F. W. Bird. The financial panic of 1857 prevented the holding of the meeting.

Sumner with a degree before Harvard had remembered her son and Senator. It was an ingenious and effective method of getting even with "the cloud of Unitarians who used to call him the one poor black sheep, the only one to represent all the swelling Orthodox sects." In it, also, as is to be observed in his recognition of the slaveholders' position, he could make allowance for a class of men while condemning the system which they inherited; and though he said that he "loved the pavement of his native city as Milton's Mammon loved the golden pavement," his broad mind admitted the virtues of the South and the West and particularly of the Northwest, " where they are all young, and, as Dr. Johnson said of Scotchmen, you might make something of them if caught when young."

At the Yale Commencement to which he alludes he had been invited to deliver the Phi Beta Kappa oration at so late a moment that he could not accept unless permitted to take for his theme, "The Scholar, in a Republic, Necessarily an Agitator." Some thought it of doubtful propriety to send for such a speaker where so many Southern men were likely to be present, but a good opportunity was afforded them to see the notorious abolitionist who had been often exploited in their newspapers in terms more graphic than classic. Nor was he sure to go beyond the license taken by sundry recent orators, one of whom had defended duelling. His own defence was of his chosen vocation — the Agitator's, " whose purpose is to throw the gravest questions upon the conscience and intellect of masses, because they are the ultimate governors in a republic, and therefore should be educated by agitation up to the idea of national and universal freedom. If the people do not rule it is because they are willing to have politicians rule instead. It is their indolence which has allowed the Government to drift toward despotism. This is the present danger in a country which is not homogeneous. One-half is seventeen hundred years behind the times, where the faggot and tortures rule. Argument only is found in an entirely Republican country, and its only safety is in agitation, and distrust of politics."

Whatever doubts had been expressed about the fitness of his topic, there were none with respect to the masterly way in which he handled it. Reporters wrote to New York and Boston journals: "His long practice has made him as nearly perfect in the art of eloquence as any other living man. We have never seen an audience charmed into a more absolute attention than the one which listened for an hour and a half. His eloquence has taken the town by storm. Much as people had heard about him, they did not anticipate so much pure oratory. He is undoubtedly the most brilliant man thrown up to celebrity by the abolition passion."[1]

[1] An aggrieved Tennesseean graduate protested in the *Richmond Enquirer* against Mr. Phillips's extreme views and President Wolsey's moderate remarks; as also did a correspondent of the Boston *Courier* the next week, when a similar oration was delivered by Phillips at Brown University, whose former president, Wayland, had inclined to the South side of the disturbing question. But the local press gave unstinted praise to the thought, diction, and delivery. An outcome of the Yale oration was a letter to President Buchanan on his Kansas policy by Professor Silliman and others, which was replied to by the President; to whom a rejoinder was sent, signed by most of the Faculty of Yale and the principal clergymen of New Haven.

XVI

RECALL TO FIRST PRINCIPLES

(1858–1859)

EARLY in the year 1858 Phillips attempted to stir up the flagging zeal and to rouse the failing courage of Massachusetts abolitionists by recounting the victories they had won. It had been recommended that they be indicted, and a certain Governor had urged sending them to prison. Instead, they came to the State House, where they had obtained one by one everything they had ever asked for in removing qualifications from universal freedom. Now, they wanted Massachusetts to stand up for her rights in Congress and to protect her representative on legal business in South Carolina and to redress the wrong inflicted on her Senator Sumner.

From sundry strictures made on the Republican party it was plain that Phillips had little expectation that it would follow his suggestions within the next twenty years, but the thought of political action was growing more familiar to him, and if it could be brought up to abolition standards something might be done to produce a catastrophe. If it could not uproot an institution, the North might be withdrawn from support of slavery and responsibility for it. But abolition by Congress, if it were possible, would be preceded by disunion. Therefore, the main result must have appeared to be hopelessly receding, and the slave system to be intrenching itself in its strongholds. This would have been still plainer if preparations which were being made in its favour had been known to the North as they were to the South. But just then Buchanan was diverting attention by his message recommending the admission of Kansas on the pro-slavery basis of the Lecompton constitution, which was "to put a final end to the slavery agitation in Congress." This finality had been attempted several times already, but never secured. It was not in 1820, nor again in 1850, and the last experiment in 1858 was far from quieting.

Before the month of January was over, the question of politics was once more introduced into the counsels of the old-time abolitionists. Some of the later accessions were looking with hope toward the growing Republican organization and its prospects for carrying the next presidential election. But Phillips placed no dependence upon the new party, nor did he wish his friends to be drawn into it, or to be deluded by uncertain, half-way policies and methods. He did not deny that a political movement might grow out of their own; but other men should inaugurate it. Their own mission was still to create public opinion, without which all politics is vain. Therefore they must stick to the old method — that alone could rightly attack the wrong-doing of the whole country. Agitation, as preliminary to politics, was their work. It was slow work,—perhaps for generations.

In all the darkness of their discouraging position three faint possibilities had dimly outlined themselves, which he stated more definitely in this speech than he had hitherto

done.   First, if in any corner of slave territory there should
be any considerable rising of slaves, it might inaugurate
some methods of emancipation. The institution that
sleeps on the edge of a volcano has doubtful permanence.
Second, if the South should stamp her iron heel on Kansas,
the Northwest might light the torch of war, as it was ready
to do twenty months before but for the timid counsels of
Republicans in the Frémont campaign.   Third, when
the Northern people are educated to abolish slavery at all
hazards, and to construe the Constitution to suit themselves
and to defy it, they may abolish slavery in the Southern
states by a law of the Union violating all compromises and
judicial decisions.

Thus did this man, who had given his hours and his days
for twenty-three years to thinking and speaking on a momentous question, come at last within a few points of the
way in which it was finally settled four years later "by a
law of the Union" which repealed all compromises and
reversed judicial decisions instead of violating them.   He
was also correct when, not knowing that civil war was imminent, he admitted that this last alternative of overriding
the Constitution by the will of a reformed public was in
the natural course of things far away.   It is furthermore
interesting to note that he and his friends either did not
anticipate or were unwilling to foresee, as contemporary
publicists did apprehend, that strife was brewing.   If
Phillips had admitted this, as Calhoun and Clay and Webster
did, he would not have excluded the dire vision from the
manifold aspects of the question which he was continually
presenting.   His non-resistant principles were not strong
enough to blind him, although his faith in moral suasion

was greater than his trust in politics or arms. As yet his disunion sentiment did not contemplate anything beyond peaceable separation. If it had included civil war, he would doubtless have turned to some other method of abolition. If, however, freedom to the slave could not have been secured without war, it is probable that he would have said, Let it come.

An instance of the occasional variety which came into a somewhat monotonous career, and of what he could endure upon such occasions, is found in a visit to the town of Cortland, New York, in February, where he lectured on "Street Life in Europe" on Saturday evening; on "Woman's Rights" Sunday forenoon; "Toussaint l'Ouverture" in the afternoon, and in the evening on "American Slavery." A correspondent wrote: "Such an intellectual treat is rare, at least, in the country." No doubt. It would have been a great city that would have got so much out of him; but trust a country town to exhaust a privilege, and a celebrity.

The anniversary of the Boston Massacre, considered as the dawn of the Revolution, and observed by the town for thirteen years as a precursor of the Fourth of July — which took its place in 1783 — was revived in 1858 by certain coloured persons in honour of the Negro, Crispus Attucks, one of the first men to fall by British bullets on the night of March 5, 1770. In front of the platform in Faneuil Hall were displayed a number of relics and tokens recalling the services and sufferings of several coloured men in the War for Independence. An excellent occasion was afforded for showing that the black race whose cause had been espoused deserved some consideration on account of what it had done for the freedom of white citizens.

Several spoke, among them Wendell Phillips. He reminded his hearers of the difference between reading history and making it; between imagining what one would have done and springing out of common life and doing it; that though Emerson had said the first gun heard round the world was that of Concord, the 5th of March, 1770, was when the Revolution begun with the populace, where revolution always begins; with Crispus Attucks and his four companions who fell in the affray that made the American Revolution something besides talk. It was right to remember him, because the coloured man has but one thing to remember in his life, that is, *slavery*.

There is no race that has not been enslaved at some period — Saxon was the mark of slavery for five hundred years. So of the Slav and the French race; and none of them won freedom by their own sword. The coloured race is the only one that has ever yet abolished slavery by the sword — in St. Domingo. The villeinage of France and England wore out; so may that of the South. As for his courage, the black man may cite Africa's independence for two thousand years; Egypt and the arts; St. Domingo with the sword. In that company he may hold up his head. Or nearer home; for the captain of a coloured company was the ancestor[1] of the richest family in Boston, and was rescued from imminent death by the devotion of his coloured troops, who made it possible for that family to exist to-day. They ought to be grateful. And John Hancock in giving a banner to coloured men recognized them as citizens and soldiers.

The entire speech was an illustration of the varied resources which the orator could bring into the service of his

---

[1] The father of Abbott Lawrence.

constant theme without tiresome repetition. No occasion was too insignificant, no occurrence too trifling, no historical incident too obscure to be made useful in setting forward the work of his life. All the gales might blow and all the zephyrs might breathe from every quarter in succession; he made them drive or drift him on his steadfast course.

The doctrine of States Rights has commonly been supposed to belong chiefly to the South. But Phillips found a use for it that matched the extremest view of Southern statesmen. This he set forth in a speech in New York on a Resolution asserting that, "Whereas, a central despotism exists at Washington whose purpose is to uphold and extend slavery; and Whereas, one of the readiest means to resist it is the machinery of State Government; therefore, *Resolved*, That we urge the Northern states to assume every attribute of unlimited sovereignty for effectual resistance to the Slave Power." It was turning the tables on the time-honoured dogma of Southern politicians. They had not supposed that it could be applied to the North. Its perpetual theme was the Union and the Nation. All at once this agitator had discovered that State Sovereignty existed north of Mason and Dixon's line, and that the Southern sword, which was always threatening to cleave asunder the Union, had a double edge. This the South had held over the united Nation from time to time; now he attempts to put it into the grasp of the new Northern party, which he admits is the prominent representative of *civil* resistance to slavery; but which "commits the capital mistake of letting the enemy choose when and how to fight, which is half the battle." He appealed to the Northern states to make their governments the refuge of liberty, and to use the loyalty of citizens to them, stronger than the love of Union, to checkmate the Administration in its support of slavery.

It is plain that a force was in the field which could not be overlooked, however far short it came of his own uncompromising position outside of all political methods. In all his speeches at this time the Republican party comes in for his criticism, with occasional and partial commendation. However, he admitted that it was improving. He was willing to acknowledge its moderate help in a sphere outside his own, into which he did not intrude.

In the beginning of the year 1859, casting about for some sign of progress in the movement for emancipation,[1] he notes the presence of insurrection in the air. It had been talked for the last five years in whispers of dread or hope in the South and the Southwest. The volcano and the earthquake were at work and they smelled the gas. Newspaper articles were drifting toward the subject and, like the flight of birds, it augured something that was coming. But, after all, it was only a sign of the general unrest and disquiet — one little flock prematurely dashing southward and ending in the discomfiture of Harper's Ferry. Ossawattomie Brown was not of the race of Toussaint l'Ouverture, nor were the blacks of the whole South so easily unified as in St. Domingo. The insurrection hope only showed to what desperate straits the pioneers were driven in trying to find a way out of the woods. A forest fire might make a clearing, but what would have been left if it could have swept from the Ohio River to the Gulf and from Mississippi

---

[1] Many Southerners, even, had cherished the idea of gradual emancipation; Benton, for instance. See Roosevelt's "Life of Benton."

to the sea! But he soon turned back to the better hope of the people's educated conscience and the adjustments of time. "There is not a Gibraltar rocky or fiery enough to stand against the united public opinion of the American people. They have acquiesced in bad measures enough for the slave interest; let them demand good ones for freedom and the state will enact them with an Amen, and the Supreme Court will cry 'Cuckoo!'"

On the 17th of February Phillips and others appeared before the Committee on Federal Relations in the hall of the House of Representatives of Massachusetts with a petition asking for a law to prevent the recapture of fugitive slaves. All made able arguments, each in his own distinctive manner. Phillips based his plea upon the traditions of the State of Massachusetts, the first either in Europe or America to abolish negro slavery immediately and unconditionally. Yet four hundred fugitives had fled from the state within a few years. With regard to the constitutionality of such a law, he cited Webster's early opinion and Adams's in 1819, the *Federalist* and other authorities to show on what unstable foundation the opposing provision in the Constitution rested, and that the acquiescence of the people is the surest sanction for a new enactment in a state that was a sovereignty one hundred and fifty-seven years before the Constitution was framed with its concessions and compromises. "And as for the Supreme Court, re-enact your law over its adverse decisions."

This movement received strong condemnation from at least two of the principal journals in Boston, which protested that it "is wrong to our sister states, which have a right to reclaim their property wherever found."

And by a few votes the proposal was lost in the Legislature.

Another speech on Education in Massachusetts is noteworthy as containing no allusion to slavery. It is also an instance of his versatility in discussion, itself marked by breadth of view and illumined by learning. He did not fail, however, to advocate another cause — the equal privileges of women in state provision for education. Altogether the address was good, but not comparable with the average of his speeches. He lacked the stimulus of opposition and of a great wrong to be righted.

Soon after, another example of his adaptation to the spirit of any occasion was afforded in a fitting tribute to the life and character of Charles F. Hovey, a Boston merchant who had been a generous and steadfast friend in the common cause. He possessed in a remarkable degree that quality of independence of which his eulogist admiringly said: "To be independent of the world, it has been well said, is little. To differ, when reason bids, from our immediate world, is the test of independence." This, it may be added, was a cardinal point and one of the first principles in the faith and practice of the band to which both belonged. In one thing only were they all agreed — the abolition of human slavery. How and where and by whom were questions about which there was great opportunity to differ, because these ways and means had in them so much of uncertainty and impracticability, improbability and impossibility. According to newspaper reports of the May anniversary in New York this year, difference of opinion, tending to general discouragement, and incidentally to criticism of fellow-workers, prevailed more than ever. The very broad-

ening of the movement disquieted them because it could not
be kept within pristine limits. Each man had his own
theory and laboured to establish its soundness. All together
they had stirred up some antagonism to the inhuman system
in forty years — and about as much toward themselves —
possibly more, when it is remembered that the South hated
abolition more than the North disliked slavery, and often
sympathized with slaveholders.

There is, however, little token of discouragement revealed
in Phillips's speeches at this time. He admitted that the
political and religious world were still antagonistic; that a
gulf divided the abolitionist from the sympathy of his
countrymen. But there had been an immense growth in
public sentiment. "Men are ashamed of the word slavery,
and call the thing by softer names, as 'economic subordination' and 'unenlightened labour.' There is hope for a cause
when a certain man, who never allows his name to be mixed
up with a hopeless cause, permits himself to be a candidate
of the Republican party. In so far he was to be taken as
a good sign. Nevertheless, no clergyman or politician of
repute puts his foot upon an anti-slavery platform; and
the great Christian societies do not commit themselves as
yet. There are political movements for territorial purposes
and state purposes; but only one to take a state out of a
slave-system Union." At the close of this speech he presented a petition for signatures, asking the state to put an
end to slave-hunting in Massachusetts.

If in his college days Phillips had thrown a wet blanket
on the temperance movement, he had made frequent amends
since, but never so conspicuously as by the open rebuke
in a letter to the Chief Justice of Massachusetts, the President

of Harvard, and the company who did homage to Paul
Morphy, the chess player, at the Revere House. The first
is reminded that intoxication is the cause of three-fourths
of the crime which he is called to pass sentence upon. The
second is told that the untimely end of many students is
due to the use of intoxicants. "Yet I find you both at a
midnight revel, doing your utmost to give character to a
haunt which boasts its open and constant defiance to the
moral sense of the state, solemnly expressed in its statutes."
In a crescendo of accusation the letter arraigns two of the
principal dignitaries of law and learning for lending their
sanction to a custom and an interest which the Commonwealth was trying to discourage. It could not be said
that the reformer confined his efforts to a single cause or
his rebukes to its adversaries far or near. Woman's position
and four sources of education — talk, literature, government, and religion,—was the subject of a lecture delivered
before a church fraternity in September. Under these
topics several men and measures get comments that are
spicy and adorned with illustrations from history, biography,
and literature in the profusion which marked Phillips's
lectures even more than his speeches. But underneath
such an effort as this, at home and among his friends, the
same cause of humanity comes to the surface as he moves
on through historic incident, English law, Greek art and
letters, closing with Æschines' words: "Beware, therefore,
Athenians, remembering that posterity will rejudge your
judgment, and that the character of a city is determined
by the character of the men it crowns." He had in mind
a statue of Daniel Webster recently erected — an honour
which the later policy of that statesman had greatly qualified,

not only in the speaker's estimation, but in that of recent
biographers, representing the changed views of the Commonwealth on a great issue.

Sundry journals intimated that Phillips was running low
for topics and resorting to criticism of persons instead of
institutions. The language used to denounce this criticism
appears to have been picked up in the gutter, and has long
since been discarded by respectable sheets. His sharp
invectives against specific features of slavery were turned
by his foes against himself, but lost their edge by their
added foulness. Therefore the man with the rapier was
not greatly harmed by the slingers of slime. Nor did they
have long to wait for a fresh topic to which he could turn
with the ready fulness of speech that characterized his
treatment of every important stage in the movement for
freedom.

The raid upon Harper's Ferry by John Brown and his
handful of comrades is now too well understood in its purpose,
and its immediate result too well known to need more than
passing mention. Its relation to greater events which followed
has given it an importance that has been repeatedly observed.
But, as in other critical junctures, it should be remembered
that the view-points to be taken must be the ones occupied
by the men of the time, and from the positions in which
they stood to the disturbing cause. They differed as
widely as the poles. Of them all it is only necessary here
to define Wendell Phillips's attitude. He made it clear in
a speech on the Lesson of the Hour, which he begged to
substitute for a lecture that he had been preparing on a
literary theme for the young men of Plymouth Church,
Brooklyn, a fortnight after the raid.

Its introductory thought was, confidence in the public conscience when the responsibility of deciding a great question is thrown upon it, after it has been educated up to a high moral plane; that education is the insurrection of ideas toward the absolute essence of truth and right which lives in the sight of God.

The natural result of this starting of ideas is like people who get half awaked, and use the first weapons that lie at hand. The element that John Brown has introduced into American politics makes them crystallize into right and wrong and marshal themselves on one side or the other. He has revealed a new element in the Northern mind. It is called madness. It will not be fifty years hence when it will possess, not a small band of abolitionists, but the civilization of the twentieth century. Free thought, in the long run, strangles tyrants. This is not an insurrection of slaves. Redemption will come from the interference of a wiser, higher, and more advanced civilization. Its first cropping out is in such a man as John Brown — his defeat the first step to something better. Your soldiers shot him, sixteen marines of the Union, "the sincerest, bravest, most resolute man I ever saw," says the Governor of Virginia, and the state has for him nothing but a scaffold! His deed was the opening of the sixth seal, the pouring out of the last vial but one on a corrupt and giant institution. His act was not spoken of as it would have been twenty years ago, but — "What a pity he did not succeed." Sympathy was wide-spread. The American people are beginning to be educated. Ideas strangle statutes. What is fanaticism to-day will be a creed to-morrow. There is hope everywhere. It is only the universal history.

> "Right forever on the scaffold. Wrong forever on the throne ;
> But that scaffold sways the future, and behind the dim unknown
> Standeth God within the shadow, keeping watch above his own."

This address and the favour with which it was received

caused much comment throughout the country. Southern papers began to talk of Northern conservatives as cowed by abolitionists and of disunion as inevitable. All at once the agitator was getting an unexpected tribute from the accusation of his enemies. He had not insisted upon so much credit for himself as the responsibility for the invasion of Viriginia, charged upon him by Southern journals. The hopeful tone of his last utterance was having an immediate fulfilment. Northern papers occasionally joined in the charge against him of exciting insurrection, and extreme Southern presses belched sheets of flame; but he turned this to account in the Boston meeting for the relief of the Brown family when he said, "Men say that he should have remembered that lead is wasted in bullets, and is much better made into types. Well, John Brown fired one gun, and has had the use of the press to repeat its echoes for a fortnight."

To those who said that the result would not be worth the sacrifice, he cited the example of the few farmers who flung themselves against the phalanx of the British Government: "It was the beginning of the end. Now and then some sublime mad man strikes the hour of the centuries — and posterity wonders at the blindness which could not see in it the very hand of God himself."

Phillips did not appear at the meeting in Boston on the day of the execution, Friday, December 2d, but the next day he was in New York waiting to take charge of the body on its way to North Elba, where its burial took place on the 8th. With the surviving members of the family before him and with friends and neighbours who had gathered in the mountain home Phillips, following Mr. McKim of Philadelphia, said:

How our admiring, loving wonder has grown, day by day, as he has unfolded trait after trait of earnest, brave, tender, Christian life. Your neighbour farmer went to tell the slaves that there were still hearts and right arms ready and nerved for their service. From this roof four, from a neighbouring one two, to make up that score of heroes. He has abolished slavery in Virginia. You may say this is too much. Men walked Boston streets when night fell on Bunker Hill and pitied Warren, saying: " Foolish man! Thrown away his life! Why did n't he measure his means better ? " That night George III. ceased to rule in New England. History will date Virginia Emancipation from Harper's Ferry. John Brown has loosened the roots of the slave system and has proved that a slave state is only Fear in the mask of Despotism, and men are trying to frame excuses for hanging an honest, heroic man. Others have fought for themselves and died for their own rights. This man died for a race in whose blood he had no share. This hour was the flowering of fifty years of single-hearted devotion. Could we have asked for a nobler representative of the Christian North putting her foot on the accursed system of slavery ? I do not believe it will go down in blood. Ours is the age of thought. His words are stronger than his rifles. They have changed the thoughts of millions and will yet crush slavery itself. Standing here, let us thank God for a fuller faith and firmer hope.

The next Sunday Mr. Phillips spoke in Music Hall on the Puritan Principle as illustrated by the life purpose of John Brown.

Like the Puritans of two hundred years ago, the muskets are on one side and the pikes on the other. He flings himself against the gigantic system which trembles under his single arm. What does Virginia fear ? *Conscience.* She stands on a volcano. Thought, the earthquake, is below her. She erects a gibbet and says it is necessary. One man goes up from it to God with two hundred thousand broken fetters in his hands and henceforth it is sacred forever.

The Puritans formed a state and achieved liberty for themselves and their posterity. John Brown goes a stride beyond them and dies for a race that was not his own. They taught him to trample wicked laws underfoot. He has taught us to practise the same principle. "If the crisis becomes sterner, meet it! If the battle is closer, be true to my memory! Men say that my act was a failure. Prove that it was not by showing a North ready to stand behind it. I am ready to plunge into the chasm that opens in the forum; only show yourselves ready to stand upon my grave."

Foolhardiness! was the exclamation with which many concealed their admiration for the motive of a rash attempt, often adding, "What a pity he did not succeed!" "Why did he not take his victory and march away with it?" But a few months revealed a significance in the wild venture which the mad prophet himself may have dimly foreseen, cast, like the spectre of the Brocken, as a portentous shadow of his heroic figure upon a gathering war-cloud, through which swelled the chorus of advancing regiments—

"John Brown's body lies mouldering in the grave,
But his soul goes marching on."

Among diverse judgments at the time and since, only Phillips's has been given here, which is, of course, that from his own perspective, and not that of the country at large.

No question can be raised about John Brown's bravery, sincerity, and general purpose to organize some sort of an exodus of slaves out of bondage as peaceably as possible, but effectively. He found at once that they were not inclined to second his quixotic attempt. Judged by standards of law and order it was most culpable. The best way to have shown him how futile it was might have been to let him go on into the mountains as he proposed, and to see how few would have joined him, and that his enterprise was unappreciated and ridiculous. Instead, a frightened state, recalling Turner's insurrection, conferred on him the crown of martyrdom and gave him the success which he would have lost in trying to carry out his plan. He was thus saved from ignominious defeat by his natural enemies. Later, men who would have scoffed at his wild scheme in its failure remembered only the daring and the heroic purpose which had survived his death, and were enshrined in a war song that inspired them with a more reasonable courage. So Virginia, building his scaffold, unwittingly raised for him an Arch of Triumph.

The following are from the Blagden MSS.:

Norfolk, 22d Nov., 1859.

WENDELL PHILLIPS, ESQ.

SIR: Enclosed please find a lock of Old John Brown's hair who is to be executed on 2d Proximo.

A SLAVE HOLDER.

Charlestown, Va., *2d December*, 1857.

I, John Brown, am now quite *certain* that the crimes of this *guilty land will* never be purged *away*, but with Blood. I had, *as I now think*, vainly flattered myself that without *very much bloodshed* it might be done.

On this envelope John Brown, the night before his death, wrote the names of hotel and towns as directions for his wife to return home. He gave it to her. McKim and I got it as our guide in going with her.

WENDELL PHILLIPS.

On an envelope inclosed in Mr. Phillips's letter was written:

MRS. JOHN BROWN,
                    Present.

American House, Troy. Get ticket to Morean Station, Glens Falls, or go by Railroad by White Hall to Vergennes, Vermont.

XVII

WAR IMMINENT

(1860–1861)

THE attitude of Phillips and some of his comrades when war clouds were gathering was of interest to those who believed these men to be precipitators of sectional strife. Agitators themselves had not failed to observe that anti-slavery sentiment was spreading, if it was not deepening under their peaceable efforts to inform the public mind and to create antagonism to slavery. At last this was getting to be strong enough to uphold methods not sanctioned by themselves, although they might prove more efficient than their own. The Republican party, by advocating non-extension instead of abolition, had discouraged some radicals and turned them from the polls to the rifle. This, Phillips declared, was not the way to put down slavery. "Give us the ballot-box and a church that is Christian and an honest press and the people will cleanse the nation."[1]

Here was an instance of Phillips's steadfast faith in the ideals of thirty years holding, and of patience and hope for years to come, with some tolerance for those who could not bide the delays of the time, and a qualified commendation

---

[1]"During the war the opposition to slavery, which originally had been abolitionist and political, gradually permeated the whole Church and made the conflict a crusade for the freedom of the slaves."—Hamilton's "Reconstruction Period," p. 461.

of the Republican party as "the twilight dawn of a better
day, whose sun was to be a radical abolitionist with lips
as unfettered as John Randolph's, an Arab in the United
States Senate with no President on his back." But there
was no open vision of strife, nor even in passages of rhetorical
fervor any presage of bloody conflict. It was in some
other Northern extremists' minds, and threats were made by
Southern fire-eaters; but either from respect to the peaceable
doctrines of non-resistants, or fidelity to his own methods
of intellectual and moral suasion, addressing the head
and heart, Phillips sounded no note of war. The failure
of force at Harper's Ferry warranted silence, whatever
prophecies might be inwardly deduced from the influence
of this foray upon the Northern and Southern relations,
already strained and tense. Probably a remark made in
his speech in New York before the American Society's
meeting in May, 1860, reveals his real sentiment as in a
flash-light gleam, with the obscurity of irrelevance prevailing
on either side of it, when with reference to a previous speaker's
words he said, " I should be disposed to say with Mr. Browning:

> " ' Shout for the good sword's ring!
> Shout for the thought still truer!'

I go for the sword; but I go for the thought which ploughs
deeper and lasts longer than the sword-blade in a reading
and thinking Nation like ours." But with the rest of the
inhabitants of the land he had little thought of how far
the sword might go when once it was drawn. Just then
the Republican party was uppermost in his mind and also
Seward, whose softening of the "irresistible conflict" idea

in his Rochester speech two years before encouraged Phillips to believe that the mission of abolitionists would not be ended until mere restriction of slavery to its present bounds should be supplemented by its total abolition; since fertilizers would prevent its hoped-for extinction on its old ground. He believed that the Republican party had the heart of the North behind it, and that it meant to strangle slavery as soon as it could; but that it must not think that the slaveholder or the abolitionist believed the lies it called speeches. " Jefferson Davis and Mr. Mason were not listening to Seward's real opinions when he said that John Brown was justly hung. The South paid him the compliment of believing that he lied. He must have other metal than that to draw sixteen million of hearts." Presumptively, Seward was to be the next President.

This partial overtaking of abolitionists by an anti-slavery movement in politics was heavy on Phillips's mind, as is evident in an address the next month, in Boston. His criticism of Republicanism is repeated, and his assertion of its shortcomings in not declaring its intention to attack American slavery. With it he contrasted the thirty years' war of abolitionists, despite which the Slave Power continued to have such a hold on the Nation that no politician or party dared to declare a purpose to overwhelm it. This speech was made two weeks after the Chicago convention, in which Abraham Lincoln passed William H. Seward on the third ballot and was unanimously nominated as the Republican candidate for the next presidency. Phillips's attention was at once turned to him and the platform of the party. Of this he said, that with a few changes on the territorial question Douglas might as well have stood upon it; and of

Lincoln, proclaimed to be the only man capable of uniting the anti-slavery sentiment of the North, he had arrived only at the point that he would favour the gradual abolition of slavery in the District of Columbia when the slaveholders asked for it! This represented the high-water mark of Northern anti-slavery sentiment. Sumner and Wilson, the best specimens, had never attacked the institution in its strongholds. Therefore no reliance could be placed on anything outside radical abolitionism. It would be better to elect Douglas and let Lincoln and Seward agitate, free from the restraints of office, and create a public sentiment able to deal with the great question. As it happened, the people said to Seward after he called John Brown a felon and said that the worst of our states was better than the best of Europe: You are not available; we want a cleaner man. "And they took Lincoln, an infinitely more hopeful sign. His past is a blank. Seward's is not. He said what he did not believe. Men are politically dead when they whisper in Washington what they would not have heard at home, and *vice versa*."

If Phillips had looked up Lincoln's record he would not have found it much more promising. Before his election he was not in favour of the unconditional repeal of the Fugitive Slave Law; was not pledged against the admission of any more slave states into the Union; nor of a new state with slavery, if the people choose; nor against the prohibition of the slave trade between different states. "Impliedly," he said, "Lincoln was pledged to a belief in the right and duty of Congress to prohibit slavery in all the territories. This was a very mild, safe, and available political creed in 1860. Northern Democrats might have swallowed it."

But it was a red rag in Southern pastures, as was the Chicago platform; and the candidate who stood upon it was a black Republican, or a red one, according to the lights reflected from different sections of an inflamed South. And there were dire threats of what would happen if he were elected in November.

On the seventh of that month Phillips spoke at length upon the election of Abraham Lincoln the day before. His opening sentence was characteristic:

If the telegraph speaks the truth, for the first time in our history the *slave* has chosen a President of the United States. We have passed the Rubicon, for Mr. Lincoln rules to-day as much as he will after the 4th of March. It is the moral effect of this victory, not anything which his administration can or will do, that gives value to this success. Not an abolitionist, hardly an anti-slavery man, Mr. Lincoln consents to represent an anti-slavery idea. He is before the curtain: John Brown behind it. A freedom-loving Whig, to bring back the Government to where it stood in 1789, who does not believe that the Negro is his political or social equal, nor that he should sit on juries, nor vote, nor be considered a citizen. But this standard bearer is enough gain for once. First the blade, then the ear, then the full corn! His election is a milestone marking prog- ress. There are hopes in growth. The Republican party will be forced on to abolition, and to believe with Napoleon that there is no power without justice. But for us, the pioneers of a Christian future, it is for us to found a Capitol whose corner-stone is Justice, and whose cap-stone is Liberty, where One shall dwell who is no respecter of persons, but hath made of one blood all Nations of the earth to serve him.

The significance of this entire speech may be gathered

from these lines. It is hopeful and ungrudging. The new party got all the praise it then deserved, and though its proposals were below the orator's own advanced standard, he believed that the people had reached the foot-hills and were beginning to set their faces toward the mountain tops. But not all of them, as he could see in his own neighbourhood. For although the mass was turning, there was the inevitable clashing and the desperate resistance by those who could not all at once be moved from the holdings of a lifetime. Proof of this was near at hand.

On the anniversary of John Brown's execution "a number of young men unconnected with any organization" undertook to hold a meeting in Tremont Temple, and had invited leaders and representatives of anti-slavery societies to be present and speak on the question, "How Can American Slavery Be Abolished?" The account of a long and stormy meeting may be given in a few words. It was broken up by a mob, hissing and howling, jeering and interrupting, no one able to utter five sentences, the police indisposed or not caring to keep order, and finally commanded by the Mayor to clear the hall after three and a half hours of pandemonium. The orderly element adjourned to Joy Street Church, where Mr. Phillips appeared as one of the speakers, although his name does not appear in the account of what he termed "the morning's convulsive spasm of mercenary scoundrelism." He took up the mayoralty of Boston, remarking that abolitionists were accustomed to live without government. With two exceptions there was not a city north of Baltimore in which abolition meetings had not been broken up. In regard to the main question, he was in favour of all methods of abolishing slavery, but principally of free discussion. "Free speech is what we want and what we will give."

His adhesion to this peaceable method of working out a great reform cannot be observed too often. In all the phases of political progress, or of sectional violence, he held fast to the efficacy of ideas and ideals, presented without fear or apprehension. His words were as strong and his vision of sin as clear at first as now, and at last as in the beginning, twenty-five years before. And, judging by the way his speech was received in December, 1860, the broadcloth mob, for such it was, had not advanced much beyond the malignancy of their fathers in 1835; it was more violent than on the occasion of the Alton riot meeting. It cursed negroes, cheered at mention of the Slave Power and slave states. The best explanation of a seemingly retrograde movement, in a generally forward one throughout the country just after the election of Lincoln, must be found in the final wrath of commercialism over its impending loss of Southern trade. Like the demon in the gospel story, when it saw the end coming it threw the possessed down, tore him, and he wallowed, foaming. It pursued Phillips returning from the Joy Street meeting by a side street, but finding him guarded by a cordon of forty men, vented its wrath in yells of execration.

A fortnight later Phillips addressed the late Theodore Parker's congregation — as had been his frequent custom since the death of their minister in Florence on the 10th of June — and upon whom he pronounced a fitting eulogy, quoting Mr. Parker's words: "When I am fifty, I will leave the pulpit and finish the great works I have planned."

God ordained it so. He has gone to finish the great
works that he had planned — gone full of labours if not
years; "old in hours, for he lost no time." Of his theology
it is not for me to speak. Mine is the old faith of New
England. The lesson of his preaching was love: his
pulpit a live reality and no sham. His criticism not
so much censure as the creation of a nobler pattern, broad
as humanity, frank as truth, stern as justice, and loving as
Christ.

Other qualities were enumerated in terms that the eulogist so well knew how to employ in portraying the character
of one who had served and sacrificed in the unpopular
cause. Despite differences of belief, the people had asked
Phillips to supply the pulpit when he could do so. On
the morning of Sunday, December 16th, he found policemen
stationed in the ante-rooms and a detachment in the hall,
in consequence of a rumour that the speaker was to be
mobbed and assaulted. Requesting the audience of thirty-
three hundred to abstain from expression of sympathy with
his sentiments by applause — hisses never troubled him —
he proceeded to speak on "Mobs and Education." He
characterized the recent mob as "made up of young rogues,
society snobs, rotten before they were ripe. Like the two
tailors who undertook to tear down the throne of George
the Third, calling themselves 'We the people of England,'
these are the House of Nobles whose leave we are to ask
before we speak. And the city government — small men
with not grasp enough for business and therefore with leisure
for politics, could not quell the mob which attempted to
silence men who were forcing this question of freedom
upon statesmen. To avoid such disorders in the future,

plant in the heart of masses the conviction that the right of free speech is sacred."

During the discourse the speaker was frequently interrupted by hisses and clamour from the rear of the hall and upper balcony; but these sounds died away before the masterly eloquence to which the great assembly was compelled to listen. But as Phillips left the building accompanied by friends a crowd cried out, "There he is! Down with the abolitionist! Bite his head off," etc., surging toward him. His friends, aided by the police, finally forced the crowd to give way and proceeded up Washington Street, followed by a yelling and hissing mob until they reached the house in Essex Street, where by the request of the deputy chief of police the pursuers reluctantly dispersed. One of the two hundred policemen who assisted in guarding Phillips said that they were all needed to get him home alive through a crowd of merchants' clerks whose interest and very living compelled them to trample him down in the street. The cotton trade was behind them in a city where, as one of its clergymen said in the same month, "it had been a source of pride that all might speak. Its halls are open to Senator Toombs, Yancey, or Jefferson Davis. If men did not wish to hear what they said, they remained at home; but if slavery is discussed, the mob cries, Stop! When it strikes down the right of free speech, it strikes down all of us and we are at his mercy. But this one was composed of Boston gentlemen, men of wealth, church members, a gray-haired deacon among them, and a candidate for whom twenty thousand people voted to put him in the Governor's chair." And prominent journals endorsed the two mobs of December, 1860. It was the last argument of a weak cause, the desperate upholding by force of a system which was tottering to its fall, anticipating a final rally for its defence by armed states.

A month later Phillips again addressed a great congregation in the same hall on the Lesson of the Hour. Reckoning years as minutes, he said that the clock of the century was striking twelve, and signs of dissolution were patent to observers at home and abroad — in January, 1861, the year of secession and rebellion. There were more lessons than any one man could read or expound ; but the man who had watched the Union for thirty years told what he saw plainest, although he was the last to see or to predict the worst, as he exclaimed:

The Lord reigneth, let the earth rejoice.   The chain which has held the slave system since 1787 is parted.   Who dreamed that success would come so soon ?   South Carolina flings her gauntlet at the feet of twenty-five millions of people in defence of an idea.   I would New England could count one state as fearless among her six.   The mistake is in fancying there is more chance of saving slavery outside than inside.   Three states have followed her example.   If the rest of the slave states follow, the whole merciless conspiracy of 1787 is ended.   Before the Union was formed nine out of ten were proud to be called abolitionists, and Washington and Jefferson uttered anti-slavery opinions for which they would be mobbed to-day in every great city of the North.   The best way to get rid of this evil is not by the slow progress of Government patronage, which the South has controlled for sixty years, but to let all connection with it be severed immediately and it will die for lack of Northern support.   The North pays for the plantation patrol, and other expenses.   Launch South Carolina out and let her see if she can make the year's ends meet.   Slavery will drop to pieces by the competition of the century.   That is what we mean by disunion! That is *my* coercion: Southern pulpits commanding the Southern conscience; Northern competition emptying its pockets; educated slaves awaking its fears; Civilization and Christianity beckoning the South into their sisterhood.

Such was Phillips's view of settling the question which was dividing the Nation and states, disturbing sections and neighbourhoods, creating feuds in families and alienating friends. It was a method as good as any where none could avail anything. Compromise had been the sedative hitherto, and the leaders of the Republican party were now desperately trying every form of it, knowing that it was not a cure, but hoping to induce quiet until they could be as high-handed as the Slave Power had been for half a century. This oligarchy saw the inevitable turn in control, and that its only assured dominion was by itself and over its neighbours in its own domain. The day of compromises was gone forever, because the South would no longer accept them. In its coming kingdom of self-sufficiency it had no use for a Northern partner whose sense of justice and human rights was struggling with its commercialism, and whose willingness to permit the existence of slavery did not include its extension.

Therefore the lower states were seceding and trying to draw the upper ones with them. Abolitionists began to rejoice over the prospect of a Northern confederacy, freed from longer responsibility for the protection and continuance of a system of bondage — a republic made consistent through the simple and peaceable process of sloughing off a diseased section by its own choice. It seemed all at once to be an unlooked-for solution of a question which had vexed anti-slavery people for years. There was no longer need to withdraw Massachusetts and Ohio and the rest, since they and all the Northern states were to be left in the lurch. Slavery, to be sure, might be prolonged when the growing Northern opposition to it could not attack the slaveholding power in Congress; but it would die of starvation and competition. So they reasoned and so they talked and wrote for five months.

The next time Phillips spoke in public, on the first of February, 1861, the disturbance in the galleries was so great that for over an hour he could get only an occasional sentence heard until the appearance of policemen secured comparative quiet — that is, for an anti-slavery meeting. The most noteworthy remark made by him was, that "time would bring South Carolina back into the Union a free state. Economic reasons would bring her back when the poison of slavery that causes a temporary convulsion is gone." Its casting out he also expected would be by similar reasons of profit or loss, not at present by any high moral view of a long-standing system of injustice. "How could South Carolina be expected to take higher views than Massachusetts, which was then considering a repeal of her Personal Liberty Bill as interfering with the working of the Fugitive Slave Law?" This concession to the Slave Power Phillips opposed in a long argument before a legislative committee as late as the 29th of January. It was one of a number of propitiatory offerings after secession had begun, to keep the integrity of the Union on any terms. The Personal Liberty Bill had greatly offended the South and had hastened disruption. It provided that the Supreme Court might command that whoever holds a person in custody should come before the court and tell why he holds him. If the arrest was illegal, he should be discharged; if facts were disputed, a jury would be summoned. This was well enough for a white man, but it might interfere with catching a fugitive slave. Accordingly, Massachusetts on the eve of secession was holding out a repeal of *habeas corpus* in black letter to bait back disgruntled pursuers of runaway slaves, who, however, were now scorning the proffered concession.

The argument which Phillips made before the legislative committee, crowded as it is with legal and historical lore, is another instance showing to what eminence he might have attained, and what he surrendered for the cause he had chosen to champion. If not more than an agitator, he could be something besides an abolition orator.

His optimism, which had prevailed in varying degrees through twenty-five years of slow advance, was strong and encouraging a fortnight before Lincoln's inauguration, when in an address to four thousand people crowding Music Hall to overflowing, he asked:

Why is the present hour sunshine? Because, for the first time in our history, we have a North, asserting and claiming, no longer cheating and buying. Out of the popular heart is *growing* a Constitution which will supersede the one *made* in 1787. The North elects the President, the South secedes. Despite the danger of compromise and the belief that disunion is ruin, twenty millions of people are loyal to the idea of justice to a dependent, helpless, hated race. Notwithstanding mobs in every Northern city, no man wishes to be charged with a willingness to extend slavery. Now the North is willing to compromise to gain time; but that delays emancipation. A thousand slaves are born each day. Hurry emancipation three years and

you raise a million into freedom. Delay risks insurrection
— the worst door at which freedom can enter. The ballot
should supersede the bullet. Let there be a peaceful solution of this question. But war is no more sickening than a
hundred and fifty years of slavery. With the Union ended
we part friends, and the South no longer hates the North.
Laws of trade will bind them together as they do other
lands, and disunion could not make them any more at war
than they are now. The South cannot make war on any
one; they will have enough to attend to at home, and slave
states will soon be fewer. Disunion is honour and profit.
Why then offer the South a whole bundle of compromises
and beg her to condescend to indicate her preference?

But the South was beyond offers of compromise. She
either saw the incidental delay for Northern purposes or
was too busy with the scheme of secession, upon which
some states were engaged in enlisting others, to pay attention
to Northern proposals for reconciliation. Nor had Phillips's
optimistic vision of peace a sound basis. The hope of
years was father to a prophecy which men less studious of
the times than he were not making. Mr. Lincoln's inauguration was at hand, and threats of his assassination were
heard, with plots that made necessary a change of route to
Washington and military surveillance of the city on March
4th. And yet in the first paragraph of his inaugural address
the Republican President declared that he had "no purpose,
directly or indirectly, to interfere with the institution of
slavery in the states where it exists"; that he had no lawful
right or inclination to do so; and that he was elected with
this understanding. In the second paragraph he defended
the returning of fugitive slaves as a Constitutional obligation,
recommending care that free men be not surrendered as

slaves. He spoke of disruption of the Union as formidably attempted, but not to be lawfully accomplished without the consent of all parties concerned. He asserted that resolves and ordinances to secede are legally void and acts of violence revolutionary or insurrectionary; that he should consider the Union unbroken, and that it would defend and maintain itself without bloodshed or violence unless it were forced upon the National authority. Secession might be repeated in a seceded section. Its central idea is the essence of anarchy, the rule of the minority. Slavery is the only substantial dispute, and would be worse after separation than before. Aliens cannot make treaties easier than friends can make laws. If two sections go to war, after much loss on both sides and no gain on either, the identical questions are again upon you. "In your hands, my dissatisfied fellow-countrymen, and not in mine, is the monstrous issue of civil war. You can have no conflict without yourselves being the aggressors."

Lincoln did not refuse to see what was imminent; but his vision did not penetrate far beyond Phillips's in these first days of disturbance. He evidently thought of an evenly matched strife and the old question unsettled in the end. It was not easy to prophesy in the spring of 1861. Boasting was easier when men were putting on the harness for a three months' war. When they put it off after four years, they had learned that it is as unsafe to boast as to predict. The new President surveyed the entire country with sadness and misgiving, but also with calm determination to stand for the plainest rights of the Government, the letter of the Constitution, and the integrity of the Union. Doubtful questions might be settled later — slavery among them.

XVIII

THE CULMINATION OF CONTROVERSY

(1861–1862)

IN FORTY days from the inauguration war had begun by the attack upon Fort Sumter, April 12th. Three days before, rumours of impending strife reached New England. Phillips, lecturing in New Bedford on the evening of the ninth, commented on the tidings in these words, which are at least consistent with his position for a quarter of a century:

I am sorry that a gun should be fired at Fort Sumter or from it. A series of states think that their peculiar institutions require a separate government. They have a right to decide that question. Standing with the principles of '76 behind us, who can deny them the right, and what good to deny it? Years hence we shall have gone through a war, spent millions, required the death of a hundred thousand men, and be exactly where we are now. There is no longer a Union. My proposition is: Go out, gentlemen: you are welcome to your empire; take it. Let them try the experiment. But there is another element in the problem: we can then no longer extend to the black race in the South our best sympathy and our best aid.

Furthermore he thought that the North would not endorse such a war; that sympathy for the South would follow; that it could injure the North more than the North could harm it; that provoking war was to bring about another compromise, and that the end would be another Union under a worse Constitution.   Altogether there was not much to choose between his outlook and the President's; and other prophets saw no clearer through the war-cloud that was rising.

Twelve days later, and nine after the first shot was fired, Phillips addressed four thousand people in Music Hall, where he was still occupying the place left vacant by the death of Theodore Parker.   In these few days his position on the question of armed conflict to which he had always closed his eyes was materially changed.   For the first time he was with the majority and the majority was with him. Together they had been swept into a solid phalanx by the cannon blast from Charleston.   Throughout the North the uprising was as general as it was unlooked for; volunteers were assembling by thousands, and three hundred millions of dollars had been offered to the Government.

It was a question of curiosity or concern to his fellow-citizens how Wendell Phillips would meet the flood of popular excitement.   Would it move him from the rock on which he had stood for a quarter of a century?   Would he be surprised and a little disturbed by the sudden throwing down of the barriers that had kept back accumulating waters? Could he keep ahead of the wild rush and direct its course? These and other questions, thousands flocked to hear answered on that Sunday morning of April 21st, and other thousands more who could not be admitted to the hall.

Many times this winter, here and elsewhere, I have counselled peace — urged the expediency of acknowledging a Southern confederacy, and the peaceful separation of these thirty-four states. It has been announced that I come here to retract those opinions. No, not one of them! I need them all, every word I have spoken this winter — every act of twenty-five years of my life, to make the welcome I give this war hearty and hot. The only mistake I have made was in supposing Massachusetts wholly choked with cotton dust and cankered with gold. The South thought our patience and willingness for peace were cowardice; to-day shows the mistake. Any man who loves either liberty or manhood must rejoice at such an hour. The anti-slavery enterprise started with peace written on its banner, believing that the age of ideas had come; that if statesmen would devote themselves to a great issue it might be accomplished. Our mistake was in counting too much on their wisdom and on the intelligence of the masses. It is the nineteenth century in the North; the fourteenth in the South, baron and serf, noble and slave. The struggle is between barbarism and civilization, to be settled only by arms. The war is not aggressive, but defensive. For thirty years the North has exhausted conciliation and compromise, has left the helm of government to the Southern states. It offered in vain to meet in convention the sister states and manage the terms of peaceful separation. The South knew that the Government could not acknowledge secession. It is revolutionary. The Nation offered in convention to meet the question. It was declined; an evidence of intention to provoke war. Let it be short and thorough. We are to rebuild the Union down to the Gulf. War means one of two things — Emancipation or Disunion. Establish *Justice* and secure *Liberty*. It is Freedom against Slavery.

In this address there was no indication of veering from his course toward emancipation, steadily pursued for twenty-five years. The only change was in accepting the arbitrament of war for the persuasive methods which he had vainly hoped would prevail in some far future when the educated conscience of the majority should vote slavery out of the Union, with or without compensation to slaveholders. Plans could not be clear with the day of deliverance so remote. These he trusted to the coming time. The present duty had been to create the right sentiment, and much had been done; but all at once, before the people were half convinced or converted, they had started up with one accord and were marching an armed host to defend the integrity of the Nation; but in a direction and possibly with a half-formed purpose that together made the perpetuity of African bondage in the South extremely uncertain. Therefore the agitator said, "If it is to be swept away by war instead of peaceful methods, let the shortness of the process and the early coming of the kingdom of righteousness compensate for the violence of the means." Speedy amputation might be surer than slow and unwholesome absorption. Nor was there any note of regret that the credit of victory was likely to pass to those who had arrived at the eleventh hour to carry by force what milder methods had not more than begun to accomplish. Instead, he fell in with the new movement and did what he could to shape its direction and add to its efficiency. This work, tributary to his constant purpose, gives a new phase to his future utterances, which are as independent in their criticism of policies and politics as in the days when he stood alone or with a forlorn hope against the sentiment of the entire country. And it was sometimes as unpopular and dangerous to disagree with the new fervour as with the old prejudice. But in this address of April 21st, the multitude was with him, and the mob outside that threatened his life three months before now wanted to draw him home in triumph. Nevertheless, Boston papers, having a full report of the address, did not

publish it. An extra edition of the *Liberator* containing it
was struck off and nearly sixteen thousand copies sold. The
press was waiting to be led by the people, who were for once
nearer in accord with the orator than ever before or even
afterward, at least for a long time. All had been uplifted as
by a tidal wave of patriotism, which soon swept printing
presses also to a higher level.

There was no attempt at reticence in the Southern press.
Virginia papers spoke of besotted fanatics, including now the
entire North, bloody and brutal abolitionists desecrating her
sacred soil, who were to be welcomed with bullets and
bayonets as a horde of thieves, robbers, and assassins. In
Tennessee journals, Northerners were a rabble of vagabonds
and cut-throats, mercenaries and murderers. In Louisiana,
a greater sanity was shown in admitting disappointment of
the expectation that a conservative element in the North and
West would overwhelm the Administration and extend aid
and succour to the South, or at least decline to take up arms
for the Government. Jefferson Davis fell into a similar
strain when he told the citizens of Richmond, June 1st: "To
the enemy we leave the base acts of the assassin and incendiary; to them we leave it to insult helpless women; to us
belongs vengeance upon men." Wise and Wigfall discoursed with equal truth and valour, assuring the crowd that
a Yankee would never face cold steel, and that genuine courage was a Southern monopoly. And Beauregard's fling, in
his proclamation on June 5th, was the charge that "Beauty
and Booty was the war-cry of the abolition hosts"; all of
which was the bluster, bravado, and falsehood of apprehen-
sive Southerners.

With his inflexible and advanced ideas, Phillips found

much to criticize in the conduct of affairs, and on the Fourth
of July, 1861, he took up the role of public censor once more.
Events, not men, were the objects of interest. These events
were brought about by the masses rather than by statesmen.
Seward, in his opinion, was not honest enough, Lincoln not
bold enough, and there was no statesmenship anywhere in
the sense of understanding the times. He had advocated
disunion as a peaceable method of freeing the North from the
guilt of slavery and of planting in the South the seeds of
emancipation, but no man should flatter himself that he can
mould the world exactly in his method.

Discussion is over; war has begun. The South has preferred bullets to debate, which I should have chosen. I bow
to the masses and welcome emancipation by war. The South,
in its ruling elements at least, is in earnest. The North is
only awake, not yet in earnest, groping its way, like the
Administration, saying, What shall I do? but proposes
nothing. It should scan the cause of the disease, and indicate the remedy. Assure that half of the South who would
be rid of slavery that the Nation will shield them from ruin,
free the slaves, and success is sure. War is a stain on the
country if it means only the Union as it was. The Government is not strong enough to announce emancipation now;
but let it declare its purpose not to propitiate the Slave Power
and to secure liberty. Shut the Administration up to its
duty of emancipation. Give it sympathy and all the confidence you can. It means Union at present and is willing
to mean anything now. Change the Republic from hypocrisy
to honour. Point your muskets at the Slave Power. Shame
England. Help Lincoln. In five years the slaves will be free.

Phillips continued his criticism after the first battle. The
Bull Run blunder and disaster, murder and butchery was in
all minds. He scored the Administration.

The Government deserved to be defeated. Its half-way measures, its traitor subordinates in every department of the Capitol furnishing information and aid to the enemy, delaying emancipation — the only way out of the war and the only refuge for the future, demanded by the North because Slavery is the kernel of this dispute — all this is to be ordered anew. The blacks not to be returned to bondage, but received within army lines and armed.[1] Public offices to be cleared of men who have refused to take the oath of allegiance, hoping for the defeat of Union soldiers, making duplicates of plans for rebels to inspect — what is such a campaign but sending regiments to be butchered. Let the Government dare to give free rein to the ardour of the people and strike at the cause of rebellion by protecting fugitives and freeing the slaves.

Within five months from the opening of the strife the leading journals of the North were voicing a general conviction that there ought to be a definite purpose rather than a divided policy. Compromise, concession, and strict observance of property-rights in the Negro had failed to have a modifying influence on Southern war policy. Instances of rebel barbarity worthy of aboriginal savages were reported in letters and reprinted in newspapers, convincing pro-slavery or indifferent people in the North that the Slave Power was more earnest than chivalrous — an opinion which at length began to possess the composite brain of a mixed Administration, but not entirely or immediately. Southern leaders fired soldiers' hearts with the duty of striking for the sanctity of their homes, as if there were any need of it, and the safety of wives and children, not much mentioning their slave interest; while the Northern leaders held up a Union of all

---

[1] Twelve or fifteen thousand Negroes were already employed by the Confederates in throwing up intrenchments and digging trenches.

sorts of states and a National Government to be kept intact. Both sides said little about four million blacks who had been the irresponsible occasion of a growing alienation, culminating in fratricidal war.[1] Gradually this disturbing cause was coming to be recognized, and the opinion to prevail that it must be removed. Abolitionists had always insisted upon it; and now in the first year of the war influential journals in the chief cities were telling the Government what the better portion of the North had concluded ought to be done: Strike down slavery and the Union will take care of itself when the disintegrating canker is removed. But the President, bent as he was on the suppression of the rebellion, had not begun to entertain this measure as tributary to his purpose. Petitions were circulating in Middle and Western states as early as August that he would proclaim abolition under war power. Frémont in Missouri had declared slaves of the enemy free, for which, however, he was rebuked by Lincoln, but justified by his later action; and Marshal McDowell of Kansas was instructed to execute the provisions of the Fugitive Slave Law. If Lincoln was moving in the same direction as the Nation, it was slowly and in the rear of press and people. He was still careful of slaveholding interests in September, 1861, as was Congress.

As early as May, General Butler at Hampton had interrogated three Negroes who had entered his camp, and deciding that they were what their rebel master claimed — his property — confiscated them as "contraband of war." By the 30th of July he had nine hundred more of them on his

---

[1]"The Negro was the cause of the war and the subject of three amendments to the Constitution."—Thorpe's "History of North America," p. 405. "The cause of the great War of the Rebellion against the United States will have to be attributed to slavery."—"Personal Memoirs of U. S. Grant," p. 659. See also Chadwick's Causes of the Civil War, "American Nation," xix.

hands, when he applied to the War Department for further instructions.

Twenty days before the able-bodied had been set to work upon military works of the army at $10 per month with rations and clothes, and had become heirs to American citizenship and all its chartered rights without all of its privileges. Emancipation had begun in the army as a war measure before it was proclaimed at the Capitol.[1] There, property in slaves was still regarded as more sacred than in cattle and provisions. The domestic institution was kept out of sight while war was discussed. Putting down a rebellion was considered more than the conditions of a perpetual peace. It was the first thing to be done.

Meantime there was one more outcry against abolitionists as enemies of the Government, dissatisfied grumblers, and obstructionists, or as prodders of the Administration. In turn, they regarded spurring as their special duty.

There was little bitterness in Phillips's address on The War before the Mercantile Library Association of Boston on the 27th of November. As a mere abolitionist his interest in the war had ceased, for slavery had received its death wound, and the rest of its life would be a process of dying. Whether conquest or compromise ensued, the slave would go free and there would be a peace born of justice. Abolish slavery and save the Union. He had been a disunionist in order to take nineteen states and consecrate them to justice. He would rather take thirty-four.

Phillips closed his speaking for the fateful year of 1861 with a lecture at the Cooper Institute, New York, on the

[1] See an article in the *Atlantic Monthly*, November, 1861, by the first superintendent of this auxiliary labour, Edward L. Pierce.

19th of December with The War for his subject. He came upon the platform no longer as a despised abolitionist, but as a national man above political creed and party, the champion of human rights and the advocate of whatever measures would soonest secure their respect by the country at large. At the opening of his address he recognized that the old work of creating public opinion was over, and the time come for making evident and intense the matured purpose of the Nation that slavery as the cause of the war should be exterminated; a result that would follow either one of two possible issues of the strife. He did not accept war as the best solution, nor even as a good thing, except as compared with the standing evil of the craven past. A debt of three billions of dollars and a disbanded army were evils to be dreaded, with tendencies toward unlimited domination at Washington.

The alternative is that the country remain as in the last thirty years under Southern control. It means that some three hundred thousand slaveholders befooling seven million poor whites into being their tools shall dictate terms to millions more in the North, with our commerce and foreign relations at the mercy of Southern demagogues. If the South should emancipate, England would make haste to recognize and help her. If we could have one hundred thousand blacks we could cut the rebellion in halves. Congress has all powers to carry on a war, despotic, if need be; power to root up an evil which has culminated in rebellion. Let it abolish slavery throughout the Union, with compensation to loyal slaveholders. A Union founded upon justice, existing for the liberty of all, is the only permanent Union. Democracy accepts the struggle, confident that she has power to execute her will, she sends her proclamation down to the Gulf — Freedom to every man beneath the stars and death to every institution that threatens the future of the Republic.

Eight months' reflection on the kaleidoscopic shiftings of events had not greatly changed Phillips's position. He was an abolitionist still, but one who saw his teachings of thirty years suddenly springing up like seed that has waited a generation for deep plowing to bring it to the surface soil. He was talking disunion no longer because he was in good hopes that the Union would come out of the war purged of slavery. The country was moving toward his standard, and while it loved to say that Mahomet was at last approaching the mountain, the reverse was true; and the multitude was drifting like clouds before the " slow, unwilling winds " to conclusions which were once regarded as the height of wild fanaticism. The logic of events corresponded with his word of prophecy. But the Administration was lagging behind the people and holding them back.[1]

This was Phillips's charge when he reviewed the nine months of strife in the first week of 1862.

The Cabinet could explain why Sumter fell, and why Norfolk Navy Yard and Harper's Ferry were lost, and why the defeat at Manassas happened — through the timidity, incapacity, and ill-timed ambition that has brought the eager country into humilation and jeopardy. If the Nation survives, it is because the people are vital and sufficient for the hour. The Government's purpose, so far as can be learned, is to put back the Nation to 1789 and 1860, and save slavery. The South so far has shown the better right to succeed and more statesmanship, subsidizing every press and court in Europe. She fights for her idea — slavery. Liberty is our idea, and the Government is trying to tread on eggs without breaking them. We must avoid war with England and

[1]Phillips's advanced position is recognized in a letter from George William Curtis, written December 25: "If I differ from you, it is never at the bottom, but only on the top; and if sometimes it seems to me that you want a law before you have the public opinion which makes law valid and practicable, why — I am sometimes singularly mistaken."—Blagden MSS,

servile insurrection. Say to Europe, We can manage this quarrel. We can ask Congress to override this Cabinet, to give it courage to blot out the disgrace of '61 and conquer with better cannon than McClellan's.

In March Phillips started on a six weeks' lecturing tour through Washington and westward. At the Capitol he was graciously received by Mr. Lincoln and welcomed on the floor of the Senate by the presiding officers of both Houses; speaking at the Smithsonian on Seizing the Opportunity. At Philadelphia he was hissed, but at Cincinnati a paid crowd of whiskey-filled ruffians made such a disturbance that the papers of every party made haste to efface the stain of the city's record for vulgar and dangerous demonstration. A bottle of vitriol was left behind unthrown, but a paving-stone from the third tier of boxes crashed among the footlights near the speaker and rotten eggs decorated the platform. The police had been told by the Mayor to keep away from the expected scene. The speaker was not in the least disturbed, and of his discourse, constantly interrupted, a leading paper said: "It is due to him to say that his speech was inoffensive in terms, dispassionate, argumentative, and patriotic. The infuriate mob was stirred by the presentation of the fact that the poor whites have been degraded and oppressed to sustain the despotism by which they are debased." It was himself more than his sentiments that the mob attacked. In Chicago no attempt at disturbance was made, ample police force being provided by the city on the two evenings in which he lectured to the delight of decorous and appreciative audiences, as also they were in Madison and Milwaukee. It was the general impression throughout his circuit that the orator had abandoned disunion sentiments

and was now for the Union because it would cast out slavery
and also keep its own integrity. But sundry pro-slavery
sheets, West and East, kept up the old howl, as dogs do
after the object of their hate has passed by, turning to their
kennel with a growl at the remembrance of their foe.

By the 17th of April Mr. Phillips was speaking again in
Boston on Washington and the West. The day before,
the first step toward emancipation had been taken by the
abolition of slavery in the District of Columbia after twenty-
eight years of agitation. He had not expected to live to
see so much, and it gave him good hope that those in middle
life might see the whole continent free. "The bold word
that the President's message had spoken telling the South
that now was the time to sell slaves to him: he would buy
— was the first anti-slavery act of the Government. Enough
to accomplish in a year. He is appealing to the people.
How far may I go? Answer him. The Gulf states want
slavery without the Union. The Border states want slavery
and the Union. The North wants Union without slavery.
You cannot save slavery and the Union. Support the
President; endorse Sumner and say, Death to every institution that makes war upon the Republic and liberty to
every man under its flag."

The speaker's recent tour of Western states had enlarged
his vision and given him national views, which made prejudices and policies of his home city appear narrow and
timid, and its support of the war, while loyal, was without
enthusiasm and tempered by cautious conservatism. He
feared they were not moving now so fast as the slow President. He tried to move them to speed the Administration,
while they in turn were "looking back toward burning

Sodom to see if there were a possible chance of saving dry goods and bad debts."

He spoke in New York next, declaring that the abolition of slavery was a foregone conclusion through the military action of the Government, which had already suspended the Fugitive Slave Law and offered to buy slaves. The heart of the people was set on emancipation and would accomplish its purpose. The help of the blacks was needed as a breakwater against the barbarism of the South. They only ask justice; "use us to save your liberty." Everybody in Washington looks forward to ten years of military despotism. Shorten the time. Hasten the Government in order to save it, uphold and strengthen it in declaring the liberty of a race."

The next day Phillips made another long speech in New York in which he remarked that the Nation after a year had discovered that this was a war and not a family quarrel merely; that the anti-slavery movement had always held that we were a civilized people and could lift the slave into liberty without a drop of blood, but forgot that the North was linked to a barbarous South. But the Nation is one, though part of it is under military governors, in two camps, one of which will go to the wall.

Two days after this speech was made Gen. David Hunter, at Hilton Head, S. C., proclaimed, May 9th, that, "Slavery and martial law being incompatible, the slaves in Georgia, Florida, and South Carolina are therefore declared forever free." Ten days later the President annulled this order and held up to the rebellious states the offer of gradual "abolishment" with compensation, urging them to accept it as the change which would not wreck or ruin anything.

Once more he told the army men to wait his time, and once more begged the South to consider a last offer, thirteen months after the firing upon Sumter, May 19, 1862. But in this appeal there was an intimation that it might be indispensable to the maintenance of the Government to follow the example set by commanders in the field, although as Commander-in-chief he could not allow them to ante-date him. He pulled ardent generals back and behind him while he called to the Davis Cabinet, like an auctioneer, "Going, going," but before he said "gone!" he called for three hundred thousand men in response to the suggestion of nearly all the governors of the loyal states. But this voice of the people President Lincoln waited for, as Phillips said in his 11th of July address in closing Music Hall for the summer. Remarking upon the time as the first real trial of Democracy and the delay in decisive action, he believed in the President's honesty and good intention; but being what most presidents before him had been and had to be — followers rather than leaders — he was waiting for the demand of the masses to go forward. These, in turn, had not quite made up their mind for emancipation, but if he would proclaim it they would say, Amen. And so between President and people the only measure that could crush the rebellion and save the Union was halting.

Meanwhile the same waiting policy kept a fine army decimating itself by its own picks and spades until its training in swamps and trenches should enable it to sustain a morti-fying reverse instead of taking Richmond, all the while refusing the help of the only men that could stand the climate. The demand upon the Government to employ them soon began to be positive, and to admit this race among the three hundred thousand recruits now called for.[1]

On the 26th of July the President issued his proclamation, in accordance with an act of Congress approved nine days before, entitled, "An act to suppress insurrection and to punish treason or rebellion," — by seizing and confiscating the property of rebels and freeing the slaves of such persons. Fines, however, were to be levied upon other property than slaves. By this proclamation, President Lincoln had provided for the emancipation of those bondmen only who were held by rebels, and incidentally recognized slaves as no longer property. But between the act of Congress and the welfare of the country, the lives of loyal soldiers and the sentiment of families all over the free states demanded such a proclamation. The nation was pushing him forward.

Phillips voiced the impatience of the majority in his speech of August 1st, when he said of the Administration's partial emancipation act:

I do not think that the Government has any purpose to get rid of slavery; only to end the war and save it. It is a political war and its policy is to extend that clemency to the South which they call cowardice. We all need courage to use the weapon ready at our hands — a million negroes. There are bright signs — when people begin to believe that McClellan is made of mud and answers no question; and that Lincoln has no backbone and cannot say, No. Banks does not know how to handle an army, but he would have pressed it against something, and that is all it needed. With five chances to enter Richmond he would not have sat down and dug. When the war makes us all over into men we shall conquer.

[1] On the difference of attitude toward slavery among army officers see Henry Wilson's "Rise and Fall of Slave Power," iii., 384.

On the 22d of August Lincoln, in reply to Greeley's open letter, stated his position at that time: "If I could save it [the Union] by freeing all the slaves I would do it; and if I could save it by freeing some and leaving others alone, I would also do that." But whether his preference was in the order indicated cannot be said. Possibly the second and third hypotheses should change places to make an orderly climax — no freedom, partial freedom, complete freedom for slaves. There was a significant sentence that followed: "I shall adopt new views so fast as they shall appear true views." To find the truth and advisability of all the propositions urged took time and caused the delay which made many impatient.

By the 22d of September he showed that his mind was moving on toward the crowning act of the war and his own career, when he proclaimed freedom of the slaves in states which should be in rebellion on the first day of January, 1863. Slow as his progress toward this war measure had been, the country was surprised in different ways when it was at last announced. Some rejoiced, many were doubtful, and a strong minority cried out against it. The Confederates went wild, and talked of retaliation under the black flag. Its effects were seen later to justify the wisdom of the act.

It was as late as the 19th of November when Phillips spoke on public affairs — at the opening of the Mercantile Library Association Lecture Course. He did not dwell upon the President's Proclamation, for a wonder, but instead insisted upon the necessity of carrying Northern civilization into the South. He believed in the President but not in his Cabinet, who were not supporting him. He believed most of all in planting the vacant slave states with schools, churches,

primers, and sewing machines.   "After long inaction what
is needed is a Cabinet, a General, and Confiscation."

It is plain that, as always, Phillips was looking forward
beyond the present to the future; beyond the war to reconstruction.   Like the halcyon day in February, he suggested
the coming hopes of April long before the stormy days of
winter had passed.   Possibly, too, he was waiting for the
President's message, and to see what it would do with the
threat of emancipation before the recent proclamation should
go into effect.   It held out one more offer of delaying emancipation for thirty-seven years, or till 1900, with compensation
to slaveholders.   From them there was no answer but that
of contemptuous rejection of all proposals.

Therefore by the terms of the Proclamation slavery went
out with the year 1862.   The long protracted, "going,"
became "gone."   But the institution lingered on till the end
of the war.

XIX

REFLECTIONS ON GOVERNMENT POLICY

(1863–1865)

THE Emancipation Proclamation seemed to many of Phillips's friends to announce the successful issue of his labours for twenty-six years. He did not himself regard it as a victory so completely won as to need no further attention. On the first week of 1863 he spoke in Music Hall to a crowded house, from which hundreds were turned away who wished to hear how he would take the triumph of his life. After reading the Proclamation he discoursed for an hour on How to Make it Efficient. He called it the retort of Freedom upon the onset of the slave system against our nationality. The people had driven the Government to abandon its policy of conciliation and submission and to abolish an institution inconsistent with the perpetuity of the Republic. With no slavery there can be no disunion. But there must be vigilance and work to secure the freedman his new liberty, lest it be set aside by the next Administration. "To three millions of slaves this Proclamation is sunlight, scattering the despair of centuries, and the blessings of the poor bear it up to the throne of God."

An even more enthusiastic audience of four or five thousand intellectual people assembled in Cooper Institute on the

evening of January 22d in a howling storm, crowding the hall
to its aisles and platform to hear Mr. Phillips say Amen to
the Proclamation. "It does not annihilate the system.
In the gospel the devils come back to the swept and
garnished chambers. Unless free institutions are put
in the South, the old order will return in some form.
Confiscate the lands and colonize them with Northern men
and schools, ploughshares and seeds. Send a new Government there. Organize the South anew if you can have the
right leaders."

A week later, in Boston, he called attention to that minority
in the North which was industriously using every means to
restore the supremacy of the Southern states over the Nation.
He cited outbreaks in Harrisburg and Albany, the press in
some places opposing the Government, a threatened change
in the House and Senate to block the action of the Executive,
and beyond all, the Supreme Court and its possible adverse
decisions about war measures. In view of such possibilities
his hope was in a proclamation which, while it covered only
half the ground, planted the whole idea — that slavery is
incompatible with the safety of the Union. This idea would
grow and bear its own fruit. The future would reveal the
danger from treasonable pilots through which the country is
passing, which should be defeated by the Government assuming control of the territory and using the blacks for its purposes. It had made mistakes and they were all in the interest
of the South. The rebels had been treated as if they were
half right. Twenty thousand Negroes had been returned to
slavery since the war began. Two hundred thousand were
now to be armed by a Government at last in earnest, and
beginning to assert that there is but one power in the Nation

— the North. Public opinion was to insist upon this, congressmen to back the President.

General doubt prevailed with regard to the ability of the blacks to be of much service to the Government, unless in throwing up defences. Spades and shovels rather than muskets were considered their only weapons. To disabuse the popular mind of this prejudice Phillips began to repeat the address on Toussaint l'Ouverture — a sketch made some years before, which its author called "at once a biography and an argument," a comparison and weighing of races, in which he placed the black close by the side of the Saxon; an unmixed black, his father stolen from Africa, who by the testimony of enemies relating his achievements, accomplished under adverse conditions results which had been honourable to Cromwell and Napoleon, with a spirit of noble generosity which contrasts most favorably with the malignant jealousy of Bonaparte.

This address, delivered in New York on the 11th of March, was repeated in many Northern cities at a time when public confidence in the Negro needed to be strengthened. The question was arising, What can be done with four million inhabitants who have inherited the traditions and received the crushing treatment of their race for eight generations? Was it safe and expedient to give them freedom and put arms in their hands, to say nothing of the rights of citizenship? It was not so easy to answer this confidently in 1863 as to-day, nor has the entire problem been solved after forty-six years. But if the possibilities of a race are to be estimated by the attainments of its best examples, the African made a fair showing in the hands of his advocate and champion. The eulogy was received with delight and acclaim by thousands, and their confidence in the future of the Negro during war time and after was amazingly strengthened. As a piece of rhetorical art, the closing paragraphs of this address have never been surpassed by anything which the writer has had the fortune to hear, nor has the aspect of the orator on that occasion been greatly dimmed by the subsequent years. It was a vision of lofty inspiration under masterly control. And the assembled throng was powerless except to thunder its applause.[1]

Another instance of the readiness with which Phillips could turn his attention to local needs was seen in his address on the 5th of May, when he spoke in Music Hall on the need of a Metropolitan Police for Boston. The laws, he said, had failed of execution when great and grave interests were involved, and the city had failed to do its duty. Its officials were a committee appointed by its grog shops. Restraining laws on the sale of liquors had been enacted; the city did not execute them, and three thousand shops were open, producing poverty and crime. Every known vice was fostered by drunkenness, and twenty-five thousand men were reduced to poverty or relieved by the public every year. Shut up the grog shops and throw a third of a million dollars into the sea and the city would be better off. Free speech was not protected. For five years he had been able to make a speech in New York, with the unsolicited protection of the police, which he could not make in Boston without being surrounded by armed friends.

"Liquor shops are responsible for this. City officials are their servile tools. Liquor dealers are on our juries and laws are made of no effect. The Mayor cannot put down riots —

---

[1]Printed in the first volume of Speeches, p. 468,

when they do not wish to.   Latimer, Sims, and Burns were arrested illegally.   The entire state has interests in this city and ought to regulate its conduct.   London and New York have been saved by the states of which they are the chief cities.   Agitate! and we shall see the laws of Massachusetts rule over Boston."

It looked as if Phillips was at last getting entangled in politics when he spoke before the Sixteenth Ward Republican Association in New York on the 11th of May, 1863.   But it was in Cooper Institute, to a crowded audience, and on The State of the Country — "a very respectable ward meeting," as he remarked.   The topic of the hour was broad and full of interest.   In this depressing time he asserted that he had no doubt and no despair in this strife, which was a part of the great struggle between free and caste institutions the world over.   But the South rebelled against a divided North, which surprised it by rallying for the Union and then for emancipation.   He believed in the Northern conscience, in events, in the tendency toward liberty and union.   "Our leaders have lacked earnestness — did not want to fight, and the generals did not know how.   There has been but one general, and he a Democrat, who has dared to hang a rebel.   The President is hampered by half-hearted politicians.   A Massachusetts general mutinied, and Massachusetts senators made him a brigadier-general.[1]   Lincoln may do anything to save the Union.   Let them put the blacks in the field before the Rebels do it as their last chance to secure the assistance of England.   Never otherwise shall the North deserve victory."

The war had been dragging wearily on for two years.

[1] T. G. Stevenson.

The return of Independence Day was not celebrated with boisterous confidence as of old. The Republican experiment was plainly on trial and many were beginning to doubt its issue. Phillips at the usual Framingham gathering felt the need of cheering the despondent in his address.

It is a day of hope. There is hope in the newly appointed generals, sober, brave, and able, three qualities never before united in the field. Thirty thousand black troops are now under the flag, giving colour to an idea. Time has brought round its revenges. Justice must conquer. Even the Cabinet cannot resist events. Iron in the current of Niagara is tossed like a chip. Our second enemy is at Washington arranging for the next election by saying that the Negro may fight for us and work for us and afterward be kicked out, and the whites enjoy what he has won. The New Zealand chief said, " I have a clear title to this land, for I ate the former proprietor." That is the compromise bid for the next nomination to peace Democrats and half-awake Republicans who would be glad of any way out of the strife. Negrophobia is the worst enemy the Union has, and a speech recently made at Concord, N. H., aimed to keep it alive in order to make a base and ungrateful use of it. General Butler said, " Before I ask a Negro to fight for me he shall have his rights." Remember that the people rule; let them have the facts and checkmate the Cabinet. The next year will decide whether this is a revolution or a political war. Hold Lincoln to his pledge and discard this political bid for office.

Phillips was watching with tireless vigilance every scheme that was alien or secondary to the main issue of a war for liberty to all the inhabitants of the land. No speech was made, no editorial of consequence printed, that he did not measure by this standard. Nor were there any forms of criticism or invective unused by this master of public speech.

Men high in the Administration were scored as if they were ward politicians. A watchman on the citadel, he descried the approach of danger afield and caught with quick ear the whisperings of conspiracy beneath and within the walls. The close of the year was marked by his address at Cooper Institute on the danger of nullifying the President's Proclamation by decisions of the Supreme Court, and on its limited reach in declaring slaves free instead of abolishing slavery as an institution. As beyond the possibility of its return he would have an amendment to the Constitution demanded by the people, providing that "no state shall make any distinction among its citizens on account of race or colour"; and, further, to provide the Negro with land and education as the first steps toward good citizenship, and, incidentally, the cotton crop would be trebled. He was already looking forward to the problems of reconstruction when the war was, in his opinion, but half over; and with a prophet's vision he discerned the drift of events and saw the channels through which the tide of affairs must flow. Few men had their predictions more faithfully fulfilled. Not all of them, to be sure, but enough to justify him as a wise observer of the times.

On the first day of 1864 a Boston paper said: "If ever there was season of dire distress, it is now. Victory flutters on our standard, but sorrow and gloom sit on the heart of the people. As long as Negroes are the principal class for whose interests the Government contends, so long will public discontent continue. Abolitionism has ridden into power and promises to enthrall all those true friends of the Union who dare desert from its revolutionary doctrines." A Milwaukee paper asked, "Will the American people never give over their systematic worship of humbug and look upon preachers and lecturers who seek to overthrow the Union as moral monstrosities?" A New York journal charged them with "preserving the Union only to help the Negroes," and an Albany sheet declared that "Radical Abolitionism and Radical Democracy were of one accord in denouncing the conduct of the war, but for different reasons." Certainly the entire North was not in accord with the agitator.

Phillips's view of affairs is clearly set forth in his speech of January 25th, supporting resolutions to the effect that, "In our opinion, the Government, in its haste, is ready to sacrifice the interest and honour of the North to secure a sham peace; risking the introduction into Congress of a strong Confederate minority to embarrass legislation, and leaving the freedmen and the Southern states under the control of the late slaveholders, embittered by their defeat in war, entailing feuds for another dozen years; and we listen in vain to the Republican party or press for any protest sufficient to avert the sacrifice. The Southern quarrel is for aristocracy — it is a war of ideas. Let it be ended by cannon, not politics. Overbearing pride expects to govern if it comes back, not to coöperate. What will become of the black men who have been tempted to the unpardonable sin of helping the North? Their technical liberty is of little worth. Unless slavery and the aristocratic element that gave it birth be rooted out the cause goes backward. Let the rebel have anything the Nation can give him in safety to itself."

Among the newspaper comments on the times, a Hartford journal declared that a discussion between Phillips and Garrison on the merits of the Administration was considered of sufficient consequence to be telegraphed all over the country, and added that the policy of the war was shaped to suit the abolitionists. Doubtless this assertion of their influence at Washington had more of truth than other newspapers were willing to admit. Certain it is that in the war years Phillips had interviews with the President and conveyed to him his ideas of public questions without reserve. The difference between the two leaders of abolition was small, Phillips contending that the Administration was not moving so fast as popular opinion and Garrison believing that it was. The temperament of the two men was somewhat pessimistic and optimistic, respectively; but there was no such radical disagreement as sundry public sheets proclaimed.

A reception given to the old-time friend from England on his third visit to this country, George Thompson — who was the indirect cause of the " mob in broadcloth " of twenty-nine years before — gave Phillips an opportunity to speak of the English attitude toward this country, and particularly of its opinion-making press. But Bright in Great Britain and Grant here, he observed, were fast settling that opinion right. Even the English abolitionists had sympathized with the rebellion, having been taught by their American co-workers that disunion meant the overthrow of slavery; and they had not unlearned the lesson so fast as American agitators had discovered another way out of the difficulty. Thompson could understand and explain this better after his visit in 1864.

About this time a great miscegenation outcry had been raised out of sundry "amalgamation-of-the-races" remarks by Phillips on the 4th of July in the year before. The whole matter was best disposed of by the *Boston Journal's* remark, that it knew of no abolitionists who advocated it, but it was widely practised in that portion of the Union where an abolitionist, if caught, would be hung to the nearest tree.

In his review of the year at the annual meeting of the American Society in Cooper Institute, Phillips remarked upon the recent gain which once would have required a quarter of a century to secure. The work had almost been taken out of anti-slavery hands, and the laurel was worn by a man whom the world believed was an abolitionist. The President was moving but had not reached the goal; the army was subjugating but not converting; Russia was the only foreign power on our side; all Unionism was gone in an exasperated but not conquered South; half every man's income from capital was going to pay war expenses; and the issue doubtful. Therefore he demanded of his fellows to push on the Administration by the minority which always rules in a Nation — as slavery had for seventy years. He was not speaking for the rights of the Negro, who was linked with the future and will share the country's fortunes. Altogether he took a cheerful and hopeful view, believing that the goal of universal freedom and equality would be reached.

A few days later he asserted that he had not an element of despondency, but was as full of faith in God and Democracy as ever, and believed that the North would eventually give law down to the Gulf and make the South over in its own image and establish not a seeming Union but a perfect Republic. And then followed an example of that extravagance of speech into which his personal preferences sometimes led him. "It would have been done already, if the man who is asking to be reëlected in November had not lagged behind public opinion. If Frémont or Butler had been at the head of affairs the rebellion would not have lasted twelve months. The people panted to be allowed to act while they submitted to the dull burden of McClellan — and now the war is waged with a view to the next presidential election. What does Mr. Lincoln mean to do in the future? Let him build the State; give the black man a vote, education, and land; look up to justice, to the rights of every man under the law."

Meantime Lincoln was receiving commendation from abroad and at home for his steady advance, though slow, toward an abiding peace through complete victory, although condemned by Copperhead leaders who nominated Mc-Clellan; and maligned by rebels as a despot whose policy had separated the Union into two nations essentially foreign.

After four months of silence, on the eve of the election, October 20th, Phillips spoke in Tremont Temple on the issues of the presidential campaign. Of the war he said, that it was the death grapple of irreconcilable ideas brought face to face in 1789, which had contended with arguments and votes for weapons for seventy years, with at last an appeal to arms by slavery; a struggle that would go on until it or freedom should gain a complete victory, how soon none could tell. The present question was to see that the Nation reaped the greatest possible advantage from the war and secured freedom forever for every one. Lincoln's plan of reconstruction put all power into the hands of the unchanged white race, making black freedom a sham, continuing the war at Washington after it was over in the field. Lack of purpose had brought about a united South and a divided North; an aristocracy *versus* a Democracy.

Leave a square inch of the slave system and we shall be ruled as before. The South in '61 expected Northern submission as usual; but the abolitionists by thirty years of agitation have lifted the people to a higher level, who clutched at the opportunity to reconstruct the Union on an anti-slavery basis for permanence; and now the fight is for Union and the liberty of the Negro. But Mr. Lincoln's halting policy for the last four years is not to be desired in the next four. Positive and vigorous in everything else, he has been wavering on the slave question and may be still tender toward the slaveholder and unjust to the Negro. His emancipation act he knows might be easily set aside by a Supreme Court. He will obey the strongest if elected. Support any man who is resolved to end this war so as to establish justice for all men of every race.

It is plain that there was no candidate adapted to Phillips's standard except Frémont, whose resignation from the army to accept nomination the great agitator could not approve, in view of the temper that his hero had at last displayed, although with some justification. Moreover, his criticism of Lincoln was regarded by Garrison as ill-timed and unjust in representing the President in the worst light; damaging his chance of reëlection, and tending to further the schemes of the Copperheads.

Notwithstanding Phillips's strictures the President was reëlected, and in his message gave great encouragement to the abolitionists by his avowal that he would not permit the return of slavery in his administration. On the 31st of January, 1865, the House concurred with the Senate in

passing the amendment to the Constitution which abolished
and prohibited slavery in every part of the Republic.

Although Phillips saw difficulties in the way of immediate
realization of a hope long deferred, he turned at once to the
coming question of reconstruction in his address before the
annual meeting of the Massachusetts Society, in which he
criticized the unfairness to the Negro in what he called
"Banks's Freedom" in the Louisiana plan of reconstruction,
with no liberty for the freedman to make a contract for his
own labour and the time and place of it. "This was not
liberty according to Northern interpretation. Freedmen
are not apprentices."

In view of the approaching fulfilment of their hopes and
labours for a generation there was some talk of dissolving the
Massachusetts Anti-slavery Society at its meeting on the 28th
of January, 1865. Garrison had prepared a resolution calling a special meeting to commemorate the passage of the
abolition amendment to the Constitution after it should be
ratified, and then to terminate the Society's existence. Bronson Alcott, in a short speech intended to be complimentary
but also discriminating, pointed out Phillips as the leader in
new methods, and that Garrison was falling behind the times.
This criticism called out protests from both men. But in
Garrison's the note of dissolution was given plainly in these
words: "What do we want of an *anti-slavery* society when
there is no slavery in the country ? The thing is an absurdity.
There will be other work to be done, but we shall unite with
great mass of the people in carrying forward the struggle for
equal political privileges." Phillips disclaimed any pleasure
in allusions to himself and Garrison as antagonists, and accorded all praise to the pioneer who had been the inspiration

of the movement and was still its leader. He then called attention to his view of the main question before the meeting: The ballot for the Negro to be demanded of any rebel state as the condition of its return to the Union. He wanted not only emancipation but the ballot; and the anti-slavery body to stand behind the weak Republican party. "We who have given thirty years to the study of one question understand it better than the converts of yesterday. Shall we now sit down and trust everything to novices? They may help or hinder the great question of righting a race. Justice and absolute equality before the law is the high-water level of American politics and no Nation can be safe till its labouring class is contented."

In the midst of continued advocacy of freedmen's rights he could take up other issues, as when on the 8th of February he appeared before a legislative committee to urge the enforcement of the law against the sale of intoxicating drink, showing how old such enactments were, and that the special temptation of country towns was strengthened by nearly two thousand open places for the sale of liquors. "Hide their sale and men are saved." In a different strain and an example of his versatility was an address of welcome to Rev. David A. Wasson on his becoming successor to Theodore Parker.

April was to be filled with historic events for abolitionists and the rest of the country. The fall of Richmond on the 3d; Garrison's sailing on the 8th as a guest of the Government to be present at the re-raising of the flag at Fort Sumter on the 14th, four years from the day when Major Anderson was compelled to lower it; the surrender of General Lee on the 9th; the last speech of the President discussing the questions of Reconstruction on the 11th, in which he expressed hopes of a righteous and speedy peace, and announced the preparation of a call for a National Thanksgiving— which was suddenly turned into a day of mourning by his assassination on the evening of the 14th — these were more memorable occurrences than had been crowded into any fortnight or single year of American history. The chief event, however, was the last of personal demonstrations in behalf of the "domestic institution." The opening act of private hostility was the cowardly assault upon a Senator; the final, the greater cowardice of murdering a President. And all the acts between were not entirely chivalrous. It was fitting that Garrison should pronounce its doom, when, standing by the tomb of Calhoun he said, "Slavery has gone down into a deeper grave than this, and there is no resurrection for it."[1]

Phillips was not among the notables who went to Charleston. At the mass meeting in Tremont Temple, April 23d, "to consider the great question of our country and its perils," he began by remarking that these were sober days when the judgments of God have found us out. The sin of the Nation had been passed by, but God had set it before the world in

---

[1] What it cost to bury it may be noted here. In reply to an inquiry of the War Department it is stated that "the whole number of deaths among officers and enlisted men as shown by official records was 359,528. The actual number must be somewhat larger because many of the records, especially those of Southern prisons, are far from complete. The wounded on the Union side is estimated from surgical reports at 280,040, also below actual number. No statement can be made concerning Confederate losses that would be at all reliable." Dated, Washington, D. C., March 9, 1907.

From the careful and trustworthy computations of Colonel Thomas L. Livermore in his "Numbers and Losses in the Civil War," Boston, 1901, p. 63, the following summary is taken, in abridged form: Number of enlistments in the Union army, 2,808,304; in the Confederate army, 1,239,000. Killed and wounded in the Union army, 385,245; in the Confederate army, 329,000. A total of 714,245.

In reply to an inquiry of the Treasury Department as to the financial cost of the Civil War the following was received: "In the year 1879 it was estimated, and reported to Congress, that the expenditures then amounted approximately to $6,190,000,000. This sum has been increased since that date by payments for pensions, interest on the Civil War debt, and for miscellaneous charges and claims growing out of the war to approximately $10,000,000,000. Dated January 4, 1908.

dazzling light. Barbarism had culminated in assassination of the President.

The martyr sleeps in the blessings of the poor whose fetters God commissioned him to break, and he has sealed the triumph of the cause he loved with his own blood. Who among the living may not envy him? leaving a name immortal in the sturdy pride of one race and the undying gratitude of another, withdrawn at the moment when his star touched the zenith, and the Nation needed a sterner hand for the work God gives it to do. . . . With prejudices hanging about him, he groped his way very slowly and sometimes reluctantly forward; let us remember how patient he was of contradiction, how little obstinate in opinion, often forgetting justice in mercy. Coming time will put him in that galaxy of Americans which makes our history the day-star of the nations, with a more loving claim on our gratitude than those who were not called upon to die for their cause.

The entire tribute[1] is characteristic of its author. He could praise virtues for which he himself was not distinguished, and while he did not recant his criticism of official tardiness — as he understood it — he showed the fullest appreciation of Mr. Lincoln's personal qualities of patience and kindheartedness, all the time bating no fraction of his own inflexible consistency. Men and brethren alike, living or departed, were measured or remembered by their conformity to his own inexorable standard of righteousness and humaneness.

In his unflinching gaze at the course of events he was not blinded by the fearful tragedy. He saw an impending amnesty, approaching compromise — the old weakness of the Nation — put aside, and a sterner régime promised, if

[1]Printed in the second volume of his Speeches.

not secured. As a Copperhead journal in New York said, "We are now twenty-five millions of abolitionists." The trumpet had sounded a final note, gathering in the entire North and some of the South, repudiating the plot of a few barbarians. Its recoil finished the rebellion and its chances of resuscitation. All this has been more evident to the Nation since April, 1865, than it was then; but the man who had pressed straight on for thirty years toward a goal which even then was not quite attained saw just how far the race was run and that complete success was still an arm's length away.

For this reason he protested against two measures advocated by his abolition comrades — the dissolution of anti-slavery societies and the discontinuance of their organs. In a card addressed to the members of the American Society he asked, "What right, under its pledges, has the Society to disband while the *system* of slavery remains legal under the Constitution, or while slavery remains, both substantially and technically, and before any decisive action has been had on the Constitutional Amendment? When every slave is freed and the system itself legally ended, it will be time to *consider* what is then our duty." To this the editor of the *Standard* replied in substance, that the Nation had taken up the work which the Society had prosecuted for thirty years, and that there was little left for it to do alone except by making distinctions without a difference from the work of the country at large.

The question at issue between Phillips and his followers on the one side and the editors of both the principal anti-slavery journals and their followers on the other was as to the sufficient completeness of their work, and if nothing more could be done by the Society as such. Time showed that there was need for the efforts of every agency. This question was thoroughly thrashed out at the annual meeting of the Society. There it was proclaimed by the advocates of dissolution that Negro suffrage was not one of the primary purposes of the Society, but emancipation only. This being practically accomplished, it was absurd to continue. Abolitionists were not the special and only advocates of ballot for the Negro.

On the other side, Phillips held that the Government of the United States did not at that date acknowledge the existence of the Constitutional Amendment, and slavery was a logical element of the Constitution. Moreover, the system of slavery lived still in the statute book. In the eye of the law it was untouched; and as a matter of fact there were hundreds of thousands still labouring under the lash and in the same bonds as in 1860.

Neither the sword nor proclamations have reached them. We shall reach them, but we have not yet. It is no time to disband while there is a slave to free on any plantation this side the Gulf of Mexico, and land and the ballot to be given him. Continue the persistence and devotion of thirty years. There is no substitute for it in the new organizations. While there is a single slave and one act to be done to ratify the Amendment, this Society has no right to dissolve.

After further discussion, which came near being heated, it was voted to continue the Society, and Garrison was elected president. He declined the compliment as inconsistent with the position he had taken, and Phillips was elected, as the chief advocate of continuing the organization.

His next appearance was at the annual meeting of the Emancipation League in Boston on the 29th of May, when he discussed "the great question of the hour"—How large a step forward will give absolute security? — and advocated demanding of the Administration "reconstruction on a basis of equality for both races."

On the 19th of December the announcement was made upon official authority that the abolition of slavery and its prohibition forever were engrafted upon the United States Constitution and had thus become a part of the law of the land. The Senate had adopted this measure in April, 1864, by a vote of 37 yeas to 6 nays; the House of Representatives passed it on the 31st of January, 1865, by a vote of 119 to 56. The year closed with ratification by twenty-nine states, more than the required three-fourths; California, Oregon, Iowa, and New Jersey being added later. Of it the *Liberator* said: "It is the final crowning and completion of the labours of the American abolitionist as such. It is that great end for which they have toiled so earnestly, so perseveringly, so uncompromisingly in dark days, in evil days, amidst obloquy, persecution, ridicule, violence, and amongst an unbelieving and unwilling people. It is a triumph which they saw in the distant future, but never expected to see in the mortal body. . . . We cannot express the feelings of gratitude and joy with which we think upon this grand result of all anti-slavery effort. . . . We repeat, the *anti-slavery work is done*. The Nation, by a vast majority, has confessed the principles of the movement to be just, and has overthrown slavery." It added, that though so much had been accomplished there was no warrant to relax diligence, and that the emancipated must be shielded from the suffering which must accompany the transition from bondage to manhood and to the rights and opportunities so long withheld, and in making freedmen freemen and citizens.

This change in the Constitution would mark the close of the *Liberator's* thirty-five years of labour. Accordingly, in the issue of the 29th of December, 1865, Mr. Garrison wrote his valedictory, reviewing its history from humble beginnings as a "disturber of the peace," maligned by the South, and repudiated by the North, while opening its columns to opposition and denunciation and vilification, and also to free discussion of all sides of every question. Meantime, he had the satisfaction of frequent testimony to its elevating and quickening influence upon many lives and its aid in abolishing a gigantic evil in the Nation. This extermination of chattel slavery having been consummated, it was best to let the paper's existence end, and leave the rest of the work to other instrumentalities under new auspices, with millions instead of hundreds for allies.

Better to be in a minority of one with God — branded as madman, incendiary, fanatic . . . mobbed by the populace, in defence of the *Right*, than like Herod, hearing the shouts of a multitude crying, "It is the voice of a god and not of man!"

And then, with a paragraph of affectionate and grateful farewell to friends and patrons, he dropped his pen.

XX

CONTINUING THE CONTEST

(1866–1867)

A S HAS been observed, Phillips did not think the time
had come to discontinue organized effort for the
welfare of the Negro, nor to suspend publication of a recognized organ of the movement. To be sure, there was not
so much to be done in the way of freeing blacks from bondage as before the passage of the Thirteenth Amendment,
although in several remote districts they were still practically
in thraldom; but there was much to be accomplished before
their condition could be compared to that of the poor whites
even. So, likewise, there was no public journal that quite
filled the place of the *Liberator* and the *Anti-slavery Standard*.
Accordingly, as Phillips had consented to be president of
the surviving Society, he also became the sponsor for its
surviving organ, the *Standard*, of which Aaron M. Powell
took editorial charge.

The question of dissolving the Massachusetts Society
also came up at the annual meeting in Boston, at
which Phillips again prevailed over all opponents, thus
saving it for special service during the stormy period
of reconstruction. It was a cloudy time for abolitionists
on account of their divided host and differing counsels,
when the old approach to unanimity would have been

better for their common object, whatever their methods. But Phillips kept cheerful and charitable till the end was attained; and then everyone could afford to follow his example.

Meantime, a noteworthy change occurred in the attitude of the city of Boston toward him. His fellow-citizens, represented by the School Committee of his native city, had in 1865 recognized him in a public way for the first time by asking him to address twelve hundred children of the schools at their annual festival. It was a good introduction to a new generation, which would be in greater harmony with his purpose than the one to which he had been a wild prophet of an impossible kingdom of the future, as they believed. Both generations together listened with delight to an address which the older hearers were afraid might contain something incendiary. But it did not. It was reminiscent of his own school days; of the welcome to Lafayette, of the Latin School, of the good name Boston had borne from the Revolution down, enforcing the obligation of upholding its fame by being better citizens than the fathers and making the city stand for good learning and character, love of liberty and a refuge for the oppressed of all lands. The children were delighted and parents were relieved that nothing more radical had been uttered than the generality of the closing sentence about "the oppressed of all lands."[1]

The policy of Lincoln's successor justified Phillips's feeling that organized effort for freedmen's rights could

---

[1]In this address occurs one of the remarkable prophecies which he made in science as well as in politics: "We have invented a telegraph, but what of that? I expect if I live forty years to see a telegraph that will send a message without wire, both ways at the same time." If he had lived thirty years he would have seen the old problem of Winckler, 1746, and his successors, solved by Marconi, in 1895.

not safely be abandoned. The sudden change that came over Andrew Johnson's republicanism, such as it had been, was as disappointing to his party as it was encouraging to the Confederacy. Whether he feared his predecessor's fate by the assassin, or was planning to succeed himself, or had both contingencies in mind, he certainly entertained only as a second or third purpose any advantage to the race which had been formally declared free. "Johnson governments," set up with unseemly haste in several Southern states, not only excluded coloured people from deputations to frame constitutions, but regarded loyal men in the South as enemies, and white men from the North, who were exercising their right to settle anywhere in re-united country, as intruders. With malign ingenuity codes were framed to keep Negroes under the control of planters, and secluded from the reach of any who could tell them of their new privileges as citizens of free commonwealths. Once more all blacks in the Gulf states were practically bondmen and subject to stripes and the pillory; all their friends were vagrants liable to fines and imprisonments. The shadow had gone backward on the dial of freedom, and reconstruction needed reconstructing from the start. Congress undertook the difficult task with no little hesitation, on account of the superhuman wisdom needed, but also with no long delay, because the headstrong and partisan precipitancy of the Chief Magistrate had made immediate and corrective measures imperative. Even then, his obstinate partiality to rebel states vetoed wholesome legislative acts as often as they were passed, which, in turn, were re-passed over his vetoes.

While the majority in Congress was trying to neutralize

the waywardness of the President, himself backed by a minority in the Cabinet, Senate, House, and by a South from which he hoped support in the next election, and while the whole country was in dissension and distraction about the future, Phillips, with his unwavering and lifelong principle of justice for all men, laid his course unchanged; helm and prow were in the line of the long, straight wake behind him, and the haven for which he was making was the same as in 1835. In that year he put forth with a little company derided by everybody else; now, a Nation was looking on as he neared port and all were asking, What will he say and do? From Congress a Massachusetts Senator called to him, "Hold the Societies together; the crisis is grave. You and they are doing indispensable work; in this I express the conviction of every Senator and Representative on our side of pending questions."[1] Thus by the highest authority his determination to prolong the Societies' efforts and life was justified. The situation they were to meet was pointed out in one of his resolutions offered in May, 1866:

The Rebellion has not ceased; it has only changed its weapons. Once it fought, now it intrigues; once it followed Lee in arms, now it follows President Johnson in guile and chicanery; once its headquarters were in Richmond, now it encamps in the White House. The President has betrayed the loyal North, is bent on giving it over into the hands of its unconquered foe; he should long ago have been impeached for the use of his powers to aid rebellion, etc.

[1] In a letter to Mr. Phillips dated "Senate Chamber, 1st May, 1866," Mr. Sumner wrote: "I trust that the Society, which has done so much for Human Rights, will persevere until these rights are established throughout the country on the impregnable foundation of the Declaration of Independence. This is not the time for any relaxation of the old energies. Slavery is abolished only in name. The slave oligarchy still lives and insists upon ruling its former victims." — Blagden MSS.

In his speech on these resolutions he noted the hindrances to the complete reaping of just results of the war by reason of disagreements between Congress and the President who, if he had fulfilled the hopes of his party, would have settled the questions of rights for the freedmen in addition to the privileges which had been won for them.

At this time Phillips's signed editorials were frequently appearing in the *Standard*. That of August 4th on the Adjournment of Congress preferred against it the charge that, having full power in its hands, it left the Negro without protection in the rebel states and that the Freedmen's Bureau was checkmated by the traitor President.

The exhortations that came to him from congressmen to keep straight on with his life work were echoed by the North at large in calls to tell towns and cities what he thought should be done in that time of perplexity and disquiet. Turning his back on solicitations to accept a nomination for Congress from his district in 1866, preferring the wider range of the lecture platform and the independence which no political alliance should hamper, he went forth once more, early in 1867, on a circuit of twelve thousand miles, in which he delivered over sixty discourses on the crisis, interspersing them with temperance lectures on Sundays. To have accomplished this tour and what it involved entitles him more than any other man of his time, if not of all time, to the distinction of public instructor at large, especially when the size and variety of his audiences are considered; not to mention the exceptional charm of his eloquence, which won him engagements months in advance, and hundreds more of invitations to speak than there were days in the year.

There were diverse views of Phillips's decision in September, 1866, not to accept the nomination for Congress by the Workingmen's Convention. He preferred the independence of irresponsibility to a constituency, and the freedom to criticize those who were responsible. His friends thought that the position of congressman would add to the weight of his utterances, and his foes expected that, plunged in practical work with legislators, his extreme views might be modified; especially since he had shown wisdom and caution equal to the best politicians whenever occasion had required deliberation. Others hoped that the severity of his words might be lessened, to accord with the genuine benevolence of his disposition and character, if he were associated with other Representatives. He himself feared such restraints upon his freedom as the leader of public opinion which he chose to be, rather than an interpreter by legislation. The press of his section urged his acceptance; that of remoter regions, for different reasons, commended his declination.

The words he spoke on a hundred platforms now found thousands of readers in many journals, but the *Anti-slavery Standard* had become the recognized and authorized reporter of his speeches. A bequest of $10,000 by Francis Jackson might have gone to this paper in its battle for the enfranchisement of the blacks; but a minority of the executors diverted its funds to the Freedmen's Union prematurely, and added to Phillips's burdens a financial responsibility which would have been relieved by another interpretation of Mr. Jackson's will. Fortunately, his private resources, which had helped him in all the years of his warfare, were sufficient to keep the *Standard* from extinction; while his contributions to its columns on important questions in that disturbed time became increasingly frequent, as well as upon the minor but ever-present topics of intemperance and labour troubles, the one often causing the other. He could, however, turn aside upon occasion to academic address; as when he charmed the literary societies at Vassar College with a talk on Street Life in Europe. But the doings of Congress were his chief concern, and his criticism of them sharp and bold. It is probable that the speeches and opinions of no one of the national legislators were so read and heeded as those of this free-lance, faring forth alone to attack whatever wrong provoked his righteous ire, and to defend whatever cause or person needed protection and friendly help.

It was not an extraordinary feat to attack Andrew Johnson, whom his own party was ready to impeach for obstructing legislation which was working to complete the destruction of slavery and to reëstablish the peace and integrity of the Union. Naturally, the busy vetoer did not escape Phillips's tongue and pen.

If Andrew Johnson had done his duty, if he had stood where the country supposed he would stand when they placed him in power, this question would have been settled at once. But he has endeavoured to provide for himself a special place in the future of the Nation, and the battle is between himself and Congress. He does not look upon the South as conquered territory. The public has stood, until within sixty days, affecting to believe that Johnson was a leader to be followed, whereas he was an enemy to be hated, a snake to be crushed, an obstacle to be removed.

Meantime one and another are defying the power of the Administration, a spectacle in Congress such as has never before been seen by the American people, a party standing up against its own President, with an unbroken front.

At the Cooper Institute, October 25, 1866, he said that the South had resumed her old purpose, and failing in the fight against the flag, meant to rule beneath it, to be the Government, with Johnson her willing and avowed tool, betraying the Republic to rebels. "Hand and glove with Jeff Davis, a prisoner in Fortress Monroe, the President has been the agent of leading rebels to continue the war on the phase of politics. . . . The real friends of the South are the radicals, who for a quarter of a century have stood upon her borders and told her that she was running a race that would end in bankruptcy and blood. They now stand ready to help her to prosperity, but not to make bank presidents of state prisoners." Then followed the suggestion to "impeach the rebel at the White House, the inspirer of mobs, and depose him, that the loyal part of the Nation may manage its own Government without waiting for two years for a mobocrat to build up Southern aristocracy and put it back in the Senate and House to manipulate us into submission." He was only a little in advance of the foremost Republicans, proclaiming in public what they were whispering among themselves. A petition for Johnson's impeachment was already circulating in the West.

One thing Johnson accomplished to the satisfaction of the party which had elected him Vice-president, whose policy of reconstruction he had steadily opposed, namely, his own political death. Who should succeed him, became a question of immense consequence in view of the unsettled

state of the South.   Battles were over, but the spirit
which inaugurated them was only scotched and still stirring
and vengeful.   Its chief demonstrations were made by a
secret, mysterious order called the Ku-Klux Klan that for
two years had committed outrages upon loyal citizens
and Negroes with impunity.   In Tennessee alone its membership was estimated at forty thousand, and included prominent rebels in that and other states.   A reign of terror was
established whose extent and malignity is partly indicated
by the incomplete summary of five hundred and twenty-six
murders and two thousand and nine whippings in different
states, besides other methods of intimidation and torment.
A committee of Congress stated that in Louisiana alone in
the year 1868 there were more than a thousand murders,
most of them chargeable to this atrocious confederacy of
ghouls.[1]

In view of these and other evidences of a rebellious
temper the loyal part of the Nation demanded a strong
hand to hold what had been saved at great cost, and the
man who had settled the first difficulty was considered as
best able to regulate the second.   The storm was over,
but Andrew Johnson had shown that it was not time to put
the helm into a civilian's hands.   The waves were still high
and the troubled sea was casting up mire and dirt.   Besides, a
natural sentiment of gratitude won much support for General
Grant.   Phillips was not sure that he was all that could

[1]For detailed account of the organized "ghosts of the old Confederate army" see Hamilton's
" Reconstruction Period," pp. 434-442.
    In his new paper, *The Issue*, of Jackson, Miss., ex-Governor Vardaman urges the erection
of a monument in honour of the Ku-Klux Klan, and would have its history taught to Southern
boys and girls.   It was, he says, "the most orderly, law-respecting, law-loving body that was
ever organized and maintained in violation of the law, and drove from power a band of human
vampires who, under the guise of law, robbed and plundered and oppressed an outraged
people."   That is a strange view of law.—*Independent*, April 30, 1908.

be desired, but trusting his long-tried theory of educating the people the agitator believed that they would force the nominee to follow the advanced position, up to which he himself strove to lead them. At first, however, he was opposed to Grant's candidacy because the soldier had been trained in military rather than in civil affairs. Moreover, the General's taciturnity had not permitted him to declare his position on vital questions. He was not in the habit of making promises. His policy was revealed most often by its issues.

Coupled with his opposition to Grant was the more popular advocacy of Negro suffrage, which was soon to be secured by the Fifteenth Amendment, an improvement upon the Fourteenth, which had left each state to determine the privilege of ballot. Without this, the condition of the coloured citizen was unlike that of any other, and to be regulated by everybody but himself. It was the final question of great importance, still unsettled after forty years. But all that could then be done by national legislation was accomplished. The execution of constitutional provisions and obedience to them are responsibilities belonging to the present generation of rulers and citizens. To the initiative legislation Phillips's voice and pen contributed more than any other single influence of the day, as they had to the effecting of the two preceding changes in the Constitution, which recognized the manhood of the blacks as distinguished from their old status, either as creatures or property.

The year 1866 had been full of work for Phillips. The dangers of reconstruction on a bad basis, with little gain, for the coloured population, and its abuse by former slaveholders, Johnson's schemes, and congressional legislation kept him alert and active.   On the platform he was as ubiquitous as ever, helping more than any other man to create public opinion; in the *Standard* his editorials appeared with increasing frequency and were copied, quoted, and commented on by leading journals of wider circulation. In the most of them, whatever the point of view, there was the admission of leadership and of an advanced position which would presently be occupied by the Republican party.   He was no longer standing alone on the mountain top, calling afar to indifferent or hostile throngs below. These had always admired his silver speech and wondered at its far-reaching power, and for the time some had believed in his sincerity; but they now saw that his predictions had been fulfilled and his demands justified by events; accordingly they followed him faster than before.

Early in 1867 the press of the country was publishing Ashley's resolutions for the impeachment of President Johnson, "for combining with the South to resist the lawful legislation of Congress and other high crimes and misdemeanors."   He now had the Supreme Court as his coadjutor; Congress only, through its Republican majority, backed by the best of the North, standing for the just results of the war through loyal reconstruction.   Meantime slavery was being reëstablished upon the foundation of a clause in the Fifteenth Amendment whereby persons convicted of crime were excepted; and it was easy to trump up a charge against any likely Negro without money to pay his fine, and to sell him for the amount of it, until gangs of slaves were at work under the lash on many plantations, with no court to favour them.

In the spring Phillips sent editorial contributions from
Grand Rapids, Michigan, Muscatine, Iowa, Alton, of Lovejoy fame, and from Fort Wayne, Indiana, in which he commented on the Southern situation, the restraining of the
President, and the question of his successor. "If he should
be a Democrat, two-thirds of the fruit of the war would be
lost; if a compromiser, one-half; if a radical, two-thirds
might be saved. Would Grant's military record encourage
trust for a similar civil performance?" The reason of the
tour is found in reports of lectures which he was delivering,
published in the papers of many cities. One of them
remarked: "An opinion of his speeches should not be
passed until twelve hours after their delivery. His words
grow more effective and convincing hours and hours after
you have gone out from his presence. You are pleased
and interested while he speaks; it is not till afterward that
he becomes wonderful to you. His great strength is his
transcendent apperception of principles, and his clearness in
stating them; the most entirely plain, common-sense, and
practical man we ever heard."

XXI

RECONSTRUCTION AND OTHER ISSUES

(1867–1870)

PHILLIPS, as President of the American Anti-slavery Society in the thirty-fourth year of its existence, called it the advance guard behind which was the great body of earnest people determined to support its principles. He reverted to the beginning of his career when he pronounced the shibboleth of the Society with buoyant enthusiasm, perfectly ignorant of what slavery was and how strong its system. In those days he regarded Webster as a great statesman and almost an orator; and from afar worshipped Clay as a great orator and almost a statesman. Mobs and the murder of Lovejoy made him conscious of a Slave Power whose motto was Victory or Death, living as a tree whose trunk was in Southern soil, not yet realizing that its wide-spreading roots ran as far as New England. By and by he saw the death grapple into which abolitionists had been drawn. "Thirty years of fighting revealed the depth of the disease and prepared the North to understand the struggle to which it had been summoned. Now that it is over, we are told to take off our armour and be content. But with an interest as broad as humanity all great questions still concern an American. Momentous issues are before this and the next generation. The race question, temperance, woman's position, capital, and labour furnish toil for years."

The release of Jefferson Davis furnished Phillips's pen, as it did many other writers whose memories were over two years long, with a stirring theme.

Davis at large and Wirtz in his grave proved the Administration a cowardly murderer, wreaking its spite on the miserable tool instead of his master. Treason is no crime if he goes unpunished. He can be overlooked; but what sort of a future this course will make for the Nation cannot be doubted. In the event of another civil war there will be no risks to rebellious leaders; and no amount of barbarity will harm any man who orders it. He knew of attempts to burn Northern cities, poison communities, of plots to assassinate. Belle Isle and Libby prison were within his sight and Andersonville existed by his order, a chief of a savage horde, rivalled only by fiendish aborigines in his warranted atrocities. Now Horace Greeley goes to Richmond to contribute to a $100,000 bail and congratulate him on the Administration's cowardice. Crime ceases to be something to be checked and punished.

The motive of this clemency is indicated in one of the resolutions at a meeting in May: "*Resolved*, That in the release of Jefferson Davis, we see proof that the South is still triumphant in the Executive council; and lamentable evidence of a disposition to postpone the safety of the Nation to the supposed interests of a party." In a speech upon these resolutions Phillips asserted that the Republican party did not dare exclude the Southern states from the next election, hoping that they would support its candidate, who would be suited to their level — a non-committal man would do. Instead, it was the business of agitators to keep the people up to the demand that there shall be no recognition of race by the United States or state law, accomplishing the work begun in 1831 by securing the ballot for all citizens, with law, land, and the spelling book.

His fears for the immediate future are prophetic of a more distant future than ever he imagined. "Demagogues will be just as bad in the thirty years to come. After forty years the crop of Andrew Johnsons is not exhausted. We must expect such men to grow out of the South in the future. How shall we make them do justice to the Negro as the Northern politician does to labouring men from Europe? Through fear of the German or Irish vote. Give the Negro franchise and he will be well treated."

By July, the Raymond-Weed Club of New York had inaugurated the question of the next President by naming General Grant. As Secretary of War, taking Stanton's place by Johnson's act, the General became a target for Phillips's criticism as a candidate for the Presidency. If Grant was a Republican, by what rule of party fidelity, he asked, did he accept the office out of which Stanton had been turned simply for being a Republican? By this acceptance he declared himself not a Republican and accordingly should not be a candidate of that party. Meantime every political move was for campaign purposes. The burning question of persecution of Southern Unionists and freedmen was growing worse through the delays which Johnson's double-dealing encouraged. Anarchy and assassination were rife. Whippings and hanging were common. "Regulators" and desperadoes prolonged a reign of terror.[1] Congress was timid and the Southern states hoped to get back

[1] On the guerrilla evil see Speed's "Union Cause in Kentucky." On the Ku-Klux Klan and Knights of the White Camelia, Hamilton's "Reconstruction Period," p. 434

and so shape the laws that the coloured race would be thrown back into substantial serfdom, as had been repeatedly declared on the floor of the Senate. The "Dawdling Congress" Phillips arraigned in a lecture with this title in Music Hall, Boston, on the 31st of October, in which he said that Congress allowed the President to defy its power and encourage rebellion — the man who stands in the most prominent position as the next candidate says nothing and nobody knows what he thinks. "Impeach Andrew Johnson, clean out the nest of unclean birds, the Cabinet. Grout down into the Constitution the principle that the Negro has every right that any white man has on the continent. Do it now! Do it at once! Be just to the dead. Register by the faith of their memories the entire success of the Nation for which they died. Exact to the uttermost all that the South lost and the North gained in that fearful struggle." And in an editorial he urged a resumption of forfeited lands returned by Johnson's pardons to men who were driving freedmen from their neighbourhood and the ballot-box.

The President's message urged repeal of reconstruction acts, withdrawal of military from the South, repudiation of Negro suffrage, and intimated forcible resistance if an attempt were made to depose him. This failed by a small vote despite a majority report in its favour from the committee on impeachment. Phillips, in an editorial on "Congress Surrenders," came nearer billingsgate than in any of his printed utterances hitherto.

Convinced that he is guilty and deserves impeachment, the Fortieth Congress refuses to impeach on the ground that Johnson is too strong for the Republican party. . . . If the lackey who bloomed out into a Democrat only after a long and fruitless effort to make slave-owners admit him into their society; if the drunkard of March 4th, the swinger round the circle, the mobocrat of New Orleans, the demagogue, the pardon broker, coxcomb, second-hand rebel — if this is the Conqueror, how shall we describe the threescore Republican Shallows and Aguecheeks who disgrace the consistency of their Democratic brothers in the rebel 109 of the state vote?

The Republican press seemingly deplored the surrender of the Capitol to the White House.

In an address in Philadelphia, November 8th, on The Perils of the Hour, he defined his method of criticizing parties and men as having no motive beyond benefitting the Republic and to secure the end which every good citizen had in view. He believed that the South had not been made over by the war; death only could remove mistakes, to be followed by new ideas in time — perhaps a long time.

Just now it is hoping for compensation for its slaves, if elections go to suit them. Grant, the reticent, is the coming man; but one who either has nothing to say, or dares not tell what he thinks; neither is good timber to make a President of. Why was he not in New Orleans quelling the riot with Sheridan? I would impeach the President, pass a law that his pardons are void, and that the land south of Mason and Dixon's line belongs to the Nation. A radical measure? Yes, a measure to teach one section that never again should the land be filled with widows and orphans, nor Libby and Andersonville make idiots of sons that came out half alive.

Phillips enlarged upon this theme in a lecture at the Brooklyn Academy of Music on December 19th, in which he said that the Republican party had made its record, but not a Union man holds his life safe in the South, because the

White House is held by a second-hand Jeff Davis. And
this with Grant as Secretary of War and the press engaged
for two years in explaining his reticence! Butler, Sumner,
Wade, and Stevens do not need explaining. He knew he
was treading on hot ashes when he touched the great soldier,
but the harvest of his lavish sacrifice of men ought not to
be risked by hapless confidence in *any* man. And in his
next editorial in the *Standard* he upbraided a reassembled
Congress for not restoring Stanton, whose removal a subservient press was justifying because Grant was lessening
expenses. But Johnson had his own reasons for keeping Grant
in the War Office, a willing or unwilling cat's-paw, and the
Senate its own for reinstating Stanton at the next session.

Phillips was often criticized for his strictures on General
Grant. To this he replied that he dealt with men as they
were true or false to the principles he advocated, freedom
for freedmen first and temperance next. The freedom
of the blacks was still the subject of controversy, and the
struggle for it had passed from the battlefield to the sphere
of politics, where it was losing ground under Johnson's
administration. Therefore the agitator saw no reason for
slackening his efforts and his vigilance so long as misrule
and murder were rife in some Southern states and reconstruction was lagging in Congress. By his editorials in the
Standard, and, as in the early spring of this year, 1868, on
the platform in several cities of the West, as far as St. Paul,
he was stirring up the country to reap the full earnings of
the war for national freedom.

These were fast being wasted by the policy of the
President toward those lately in rebellion, when he was at
last impeached for resisting the acts of Congress, and other

crimes and misdemeanors, escaping conviction by one vote. His second removal of Secretary Stanton precipitated this action, though far from the chief cause of it, on the part of a thoroughly incensed Congress, which, however, materially weakened on the vote to convict.

At this time, according to Republican metropolitan journals, anarchy and unrest prevailed in the South, where there was no safety nor assurance of personal liberty. Capital did not dare to meet the enmity awaiting it; rebels looked to the President for help, and loyal men leaned upon Congress; the strife of the bullet was followed by the strife of the ballot. The Democratic press opposed impeachment, a Western paper urging renewed rebellion in terms that were too bloody to be of any account, the frothy rage of extravagant partisanship.

Technical failure to impeach by one vote was disappointing to the hopes of Phillips, but the encouragement he extracted from a bare defeat was characteristic.

Our whole success for thirty years past has been fed by just such defeats as this. The annexation of Texas, the Compromise of 1850, Kansas trampled in blood, Bull Run, the second election of Lincoln, his murder; all these seeming defeats were victories in disguise. The traitors who plotted them were the only men who died by them. Polk, Seward, Pierce, Webster, Clay, and their fellow-conspirators all died by their own hands. In the light of such history we should read this hour.

His explanation of this failure of the Republican senators from Maine and Illinois, and others, to seal the conviction of Johnson was their eye to the next election, political preferment, and safety of the party, with the suggestion of feminine spite and ambition in the background, as had happened before in political history at home and abroad. Of the President he said: "The question is not whether Johnson is a sinner. He is an obstacle. There is no pathway down South except through the White House; he bars the door and I want it open to the farmer, the merchant, the mechanic, the schoolhouse, and New England ideas, to men who create and invent, surrounding human nature with comfort and lifting it up into the sunlight."

The nomination of Grant was regarded by Phillips as the expression of the mixed motives represented at the Chicago convention. Therefore the duty of radicals was the same as in the last twenty years — to rouse and educate the people, and with fearless criticism of parties and their leaders to put blocks under the wheels to keep the carriage from going back and to drag it up higher if possible. He accepted Grant and the probable success of the Republican party as the salvation of the Union and the best hope for the Negro, with the loyal North in the saddle, to ripen the problem of reconstruction day by day, with justice and equal rights for all. Meantime seven Southern states had been admitted with the voting privilege restored, to be used by white voters chiefly, since control of the polls was in their hands and of legislative assemblies, as in Georgia, where twenty-four coloured members were expelled on the third of September, not without good reason.[1]

Phillips was not so completely occupied with wrongs of the black man that he could see no other. It was in the midst of all the perplexities and perils, after failure to oust

---

[1]That there was another and a white side to reconstruction rights and wrongs cannot be denied by any who know the history of the period. In brief, it is a story of violent reactions: first, by freedmen from two hundred and fifty years of bondage; second, by whites against the unwise abuse of unaccustomed privilege by ignorant Negroes and their unprincipled instigators to partisan legislation. The Northern carpet-bagger was a poor successor to the Northern soldier, and came near undoing his work for the Union.

Johnson, that another plot against certain Indian tribes called out a vigorous protest and arraignment of the white man's policy toward so-called savages. By felicitous examples he showed how much more chivalrous had been their treatment of white captives than our soldiers' instant murder of red men; and also cited sundry treacherous dealings with friendly Indians who were watching the roads at the request of United States troops. A brief summary of our general treatment of a vanishing race is concluded with comparisons which closed with the remark, "What a scene for Christianity! God bless such barbarians and make us like them!" In the removal of troops to the plains he also saw rebels freed from military rule and loyalists left to the mercies of the Ku-Klux Klan — another Johnson move.

An instance of the breadth of Phillips's sympathies and of the reach of his thinking occurred when he delivered an address in Tremont Temple on The Relation of Religion to Philanthropy and to Social Science. Organized Christianity he regarded as the ice formed above the flowing river, a fixed principle embodying this dogma and that, good to stand on and walk over, but the force is in the moving current below it, and when that falls the ice breaks, or if it rises it breaks up the binding crust and carries it away. Religion is principle applied to every social need of the average man to make his life worth living, dividing his day into thirds for labour, rest, and sleep, giving mind and soul a fair chance; helping him to be temperate and to use the opportunities that are offered, and to share the profits and leisure that result from the combined industry of labour and capital. The Church had come to recognize this because the sentiment of the people had lifted it up to this level, as the anti-slavery sentiment had raised it to a plane to which it never came of its own accord, but instead, protesting against such radicalism for thirty years. Therefore in the Republican party, faulty and defective as he regarded it, was the only chance of safety, since the loyal masses of the Nation were within its ranks. Behind Grant, its candidate, was a broadening purpose and resolve, and his election meant progress. If not elected, the spirit of slavery would reverse the results of the war. Negroes were now voting the Democratic ticket and saying, "Do not blame us — we had to do so, else be shot or starve."

When, in spite of seven rebel states and their compulsory votes, Grant was elected by about 6 per cent. majority of the whole vote, Republican success did not diminish the agitator's vigilance and his efforts in educating the masses to demand every right thing of the victorious party. He did not expect that the effects of slavery could be razed out in one generation. It would require a century of civilization of Christianity to remodel the complex social or political system arranged around it. Many Southerners were blindly honest, living in darkness; they needed light, not honesty. We should be patient fifty years, if forces are allowed to ripen their minds. His appeal in this movement was to the people rather than their religious and political rulers, just as Christ addressed the common people who heard him gladly, while Pharisees and the Sanhedrin lagged behind and opposed every advance.

This need of principles underlying our Government Phillips emphasized after the election of Grant — a clear, square, unequivocal statement of the relation between men and laws, capital and labour, and a full repudiation of any legal recognition of race distinctions. The moment our laws take note of Negro, Indian, Chinese, Irishmen, and forget the *man* hid behind each, the seeds of discord and weakness are planted. "Forget the race, remember only the *man*. Contrast Canadian treatment of the Indian by the laws and ours by arms — statesmanship with folly. So, too, hasten the day when coöperation shall make every capitalist a labourer and every labourer a capitalist. Anchor these principles in the Constitution."

It was now six years from the act of emancipation, and Phillips said that he had no particular reason to rejoice over January 1, 1863, and while there rested such a cloud upon the present and future condition of the coloured race his anxiety was greater than his joy. The Negro had suffrage as a man has the rights of going to law— if he care to pay for it. He had voted at the risk of starvation and death. It was impossible for him to outweigh all the forces ranged against him. He stood alone against the Government. And there was no protection for person or property in the South to induce men or capital to go to the help of the blacks. Still, he did not despair. He had fair faith that justice would triumph, but was not absolutely certain that it would in the next forty years. "It all depended upon public opinion, upholding the radical element in the Republican party in amending the Constitution to guarantee suffrage beyond any possible state legislation. Chattel slavery is gone, but political slavery still remains."

At last an amendment which Phillips had been urging upon Congress was passed by the Senate on the 9th of February, 1869: "No discrimination shall be made in the United States among citizens of the United States in the exercise of the elective franchise, or in the right to hold office, in any state, on account of race, colour, nativity, property, education, or creed."

Phillips had frequently complained of General Grant's reticence, but when the brief inaugural was published he found little to criticize. Endorsement of the Fifteenth Amendment, the promise of a vigorous execution of law, the policy of citizenship for the Indian, the payment of the national debt, were measures to be thankful for, and he added, "Now, Soldier of the Wilderness, *hammer* the rebellion to pieces so that the name of a 'Union man' may be as ample protection even on the Del Norte as that of a 'Roman citizen' was to St. Paul at Jerusalem." Then he turned to urging the ratification of the Amendment by state legislatures. "The peace of the whole section and nation demands it. Congress, three to one, recommends it. The President begs for its ratification. Besiege your legislatures. One effort now is worth months of common work."

In the winter between General Grant's election and inauguration, 1868–'69, Phillips was pleading on the platform for Negro suffrage. So, too, as he had turned aside to advocate the cause of Crete against Turkish despotism in the preceding summer, now in April, the Fifteenth Amendment having been passed, he could listen to the appeal of sundry women, whom he had put off until greater questions were settled, and appeared for them before the Massachusetts Legislature to set forth their claims for female suffrage. This was not altogether intended as a gallant reparation for postponing their request. As far back as the defence in London of delegated women he had declared his championship of feminine assertion of civic rights, thus proving himself in one more respect in advance of his age and Nation; farther indeed than in the matter of slavery, as the lapse of time has proved, since in no large part of the land has woman suffrage been established, or even greatly desired by the majority of the sex, who seem to be uncertain or unconcerned about their rights and wrongs, despite occasional instructors. With respect to his position on the subject he had said in May, 1866, before the Eleventh National Woman's Rights Convention in New York, that he did not feel by any means that keen agony of interest in this question that he did in the slavery question or the temperance cause. He placed the difficulty of woman's advancement not in lack of legislation, but in the sentiment that made it unfashionable for women to make their own living, and the starvation wages with no chance of rising in the future. Fashionable women could take off the ban from their poorer sisters and could dictate the legislative policy of their husbands and fathers if they would. " Woman's influence does not need to be increased, but educated and made responsible, counted, and criticized. She ties her own limbs, corrupts her own sisters, demoralizes civilization, and then folds her arms, and calls it religion, or steps back and christens it taste. She could make her own opportunity if the women of a state so determined."

This courtesy performed, he took up another cause which he had previously espoused, and addressed the Massachusetts Legislature on the labour question, to get a commission appointed to inquire into the condition of labour in the state — rates of wages, rent, prices of living, hours of employment. He urged that a labouring class divided from the rest is inconsistent with the safety of the Republic. It has to combat corporations to which legislatures are subservient. The Legislature of New York sits in the counting-rooms of its railroads. Corporations cannot be spared, but they should be made consistent with the welfare of the state. Workmen had to defend themselves by co-operating, which they could not do without more education than ten hours of work would give them. Eight hours would give them a chance at the night schools. Trades-union, though a great power, has provisions which are indefensible — makes slaves of its members and interferes with business and has a bad spirit behind it. The proper resort is a commission to learn, discuss, and decide this question. Coöperation will end all quarrels between the capitalist and the labourer. But the only consideration that could be expected to have weight with the committee was this: You must show that a man can do as much work in eight as he can in ten hours. He might have added, and that he *will* do as much.

A month later in New York Phillips spoke in a reminiscent strain, contrasting with the present the days when indifference toward the abolition cause was so great that the press did not condescend to notice its meetings; when men said, The work is too vast; all your waiting a dream.

And now they are saying, "What is there left to do? What can be your pretence for coming together?" It is a great change. Literature, the Government, the Church, so tardy in coming to our help, all are on our side. To be sure, as the Tory sentiment lingered in England and the Bourbon in France, so in sly corners, in the musty study of a Doctor of Divinity, in the empty attic which fashionable woman calls her mind, there will remain for a very long while an unexpressed prejudice against the black race. For fifty years you will find the ghost haunting his old home. But national forces are all moving in one direction — the equality of all races. Therefore the wisest work to-day is to go forward to teach the American people the absurdity of trying to found an empire on a single race. The great forces of society — not the brainless boys and aimless girls, the self-conceited set who imagine they are the fashionable world — but the men that work, mould, achieve, and manage the brains of the Nation, will comprehend this. Somewhere there is a power that has put this Nation forward infinitely faster than its leaders either purposed or dared to go. We will have a politics as broad as humanity. Nothing that interferes with the rights of a great class deserves the name of government. No state deserves it until it acknowledges the Fifteenth Amendment.

Phillips began an editorial in the *Standard* of July 3, 1869, with this sentence: " Grant has now been President four months; still there is no safety for loyal men in the South." He closed it as follows: "The blood of murdered loyalists is on the skirts of this Administration. Why is not martial law proclaimed? Is the promise forgotten? Is it a King Log with a paper sceptre that sits in the White House while loyal men flee for safety and rebels fire salutes under the Confederate flag?" In a single county in Texas there were ten murders in three weeks of July, 1869. With inactivity at Washington, while diplomatically "accepting the situation," the South was passing under rebel control again; the new voters surpassing their fathers in rebellious feeling. Almost discouraged, Phillips called for vigilance and preparation for the next election, in the betrayal of the freedman's cause by Grant — "a second Buchanan, temporizing while the enemy gets into battle array."

On the 23d of March, 1870, Revels, a coloured Senator from Mississippi, in the first paragraph of his first speech said: "Sir, I stand to-day on this floor to appeal for protection from the strong arm of the Government for her loyal children, irrespective of colour or race, who are citizens of the Southern states, and particularly of the great State of Georgia." After citing the Negroes' fidelity to their masters and their families during the war instead of fomenting insurrection, and their services in the army after their emancipation, thus proving their loyalty to the entire Nation and their help, he reviewed their subsequent treatment in being disqualified to hold office, and depicted the persecutions to which as a people they had been subjected. At the close, Morton, of Indiana, joining in congratulations of many senators, remarked that in the exchange that had been made in the place once occupied by Jefferson Davis, the Senate had lost nothing in intelligence, while it had gained much in patriotism and loyalty.

On the 30th of March, 1870, the President proclaimed that the Fifteenth Amendment had been ratified by the requisite three-fourths of the states and in a special message called upon Congress to take all means within their power to promote and encourage education, and upon the people to see to it that all who possess and exercise political rights shall have the opportunity to acquire the knowledge which will make their share in the Government a blessing and not a danger.

Then Phillips wrote: "For the President we have hardly any words but those of gratitude. He has done

more than his friends pledged him for. We wish he could see his way to a more prompt and decisive method of dealing with Southern murderers; and think he has full powers. He has done his full share to give coloured men the ballot. May he soon draw the sword to protect them in its use."
In the next and last number of the *Anti-slavery Standard* are the remarks he made at the disbanding of the American Society in New York, April 9, 1870.

I congratulate you that we are met at last in the full noon of that day whose very dawn hardly any of us believed we should live to see; that at last the nation in its organic law adopts the original pledge of this Society to secure to the coloured race of the United States all the rights and privileges which belong to them as men and as Americans. Our work as an organization is accomplished, our pledge redeemed, our promise fulfilled, and we have nothing to do but to thank God and to throw our exertions henceforth into channels more fitting the hour which dawns upon us.

Later in the day he made a concluding address of similar import, adding:

When I was absorbed into this great movement I remember well that it found me a very proud man; proud of the religious, proud of the civil institutions of the country. Thirty years have not brought back the young pride nor renewed the young trust. I go out with no faith whatever in institutions. I see a Government lashed by the iron hail of necessity to a great step. I see a Church shamed by the rising public opinion about it, at last, into a decent observance. My only joy to-day is that I can look into the face of the world and read the first line of the Declaration of Independence without a blush and say in the presence of Nations: At last there is no enormous, portentous crime which you can point at to mar that declaration.

XXII

NEW CAUSES AND OLD

(1871–1876)

IT WAS natural that Phillips should not be entirely carried away by the enthusiasm of his audience at the last meeting of the American Anti-slavery Society. He afterward recalled the ovation he then received as the crowning joy of his career and a compensation for all its labours. But, as his speech declared, and as subsequent events have proved, the equality of rights which the Declaration of Independence asserted, after the manner of French Revolutionists, and which the Constitution repeated in an amendment almost a century later, was far from reality — a promise and a hope only, which have not even yet been fully realized. All that legislation could then accomplish had been secured; the rest must be left to forces and influences of another kind and to time, the gradual moulder of peoples. As long as he lived the champion of one race's rights would concern himself about them; but henceforth he would also turn his attention more fully to other issues which were assuming a new importance.

After thirty-three years of unwearied activity, without much encouragement in the first two-thirds of that time, he might consider the eventide triumph of his main purpose

a signal to retire from active service at the age of sixty.
But the habit of a lifetime was as strong as his mind and
body. He was in the prime of maturity when the accumulated wisdom of years was for him at the disposal of an
intellect undimmed and of a vigorous physique. He
could not stop so long as there were evils to be discovered
and wrongs to be righted or thoughts to be spoken. The
inertia of the cannon ball keeps it rolling after it has slain
the foe, sometimes to the harm of other foes in its way.
Phillips could always find them. To a friend he said,
"Now that the field is won, do you sit by the camp-fire,
but I will put out into the underbrush."

First, he found intemperance, and without going far.
It was not a new evil nor the first time he had met and
attacked it. Prohibition he regarded as the best remedy for
general drinking, and he pleaded frequently for the enactment
and enforcement of laws to stop the sale of liquor at every
tenth door in Boston and in the taverns of every village.
Yet he was broad enough to state the other side; that the
saloon was the workingman's club-room, and that his twelve
hours of labour left him but twelve more for eating, sleeping,
and such diversion as he might get, which was not likely
to be intellectual. Beer with the boozy at nightfall was
the height of his anticipation. Excessive labour was one
of the causes of common drinking, and this, in turn, of the
poverty which made continuous toil imperative. Prevention
was connected with shorter hours, giving a margin for better
things than dram-shops — opportunity to make a home
attractive, to read, to see interesting and improving sights,
to think about something higher than grog, and for the
younger to obtain the elements of education in the evening

schools. To obtain all this he urged the value of organization, notwithstanding the ability of capital to wait longer than labour. It could control the nation if it were in earnest and kept united. This was forty years ago and a newer doctrine than it is to-day; but progress beyond his panacea has been slow, and the best achievements have been in the direction of his recommendations.

That he could view social and reformatory movements from the highest point was seen in a lecture on the topic of In Christianity No Substitutes and No Mustering Out, given in June, 1870, at the closing of a Sunday afternoon discourse.

There are many grave issues which the community must grapple with in the coming years needing all the reserve forces of social science and religion. Once man was regarded as a wild beast to be restrained; later, to be developed by implanting a motive principle and giving him opportunities, lifting him from subjection to temptation; opening to woman fields of labour that shall remove the necessity of vice, and bringing into society the reserve power of womanhood. Social science is wise selfishness. It does n't teach religion. I want to add to it a higher lesson. In the presence of the New Testament every human being is sacred and infinitely precious. Ten men are not to be ground up in order that nine hundred and ninety may be happy. Children are to be put right at home, not in houses. Young men, not in one Christian Association Building, but in as many and as costly as the devil's palaces on every corner. Newspapers to be as good as one which Wall Street consults, without its immoral tone. Give your millions and your presence in the lobby, in the suffering street, and supplement law with your sympathy and religion, and wherever the devil is go to fight him, without asking him to come up on level ground. Under-

neath you is surging the immense power of human vice;
how rotten civilization is! Then fight the devil with his
own weapons; fight him with greater inducements, grapple
with the same element of human nature. In order to do
this I want all Boston, in the court, in the prison, in the
grog-shop, every man and woman, not substitutes bought
by money. Give me that, and I will show you a city redeemed from vice.

These lines are only as the occasional words that might
be heard through a door ajar, needing all the rest to show
their full import; but they indicate the thoroughness of his
reformatory spirit and the absolute surrender which he
demanded for effectual saving of society. It was no 10 per
cent. method. Moreover, he practised what he preached,
whether in benefactions or in rescue from evil ways.

An immediate result of his agitation of social questions
was his nomination for Governor by the Prohibition Convention on September 4, 1870, and four days later by the
Labour party. It was an appreciation of his services in
behalf of the two causes he had championed; but the hope
of success was so forlorn that he cannot be said to have
at last indulged in politics after a lifetime of abstinence. It
only gave him an opportunity to publish his sentiments
in a political creed whose first sentences were: "We affirm,
as a fundamental principle, that labour, the creator of
wealth, is entitled to all it creates. Affirming this, we avow
ourselves willing to accept the final results of a principle
so radical, such as the overthrow of the whole profit-making
system, the extinction of monopolies, the abolition of privileged classes, universal education or fraternity, and the
final obliteration of the poverty of the masses. *Resolved*,
therefore, That we declare war with the wage system and

the present system of finance, with lavish grants of public land to speculating companies. . . . We demand a ten-hour day for factory-work, and eight hours hereafter; that women receive the same wages as men when employed at the public expense to do the same kind of work."

In a speech supporting these demands and in his letter of acceptance he placed the value of the movement chiefly in its attempt to protect human rights, to insure peace, and as a guarantee against the destruction of capital; since labour and capital are partners, not enemies, and their interests are identical, in order to bring about a fair decision of the common profits. The best minds should give themselves to the work of changing the vast inequalities in the social system. And to the Prohibitionists he wrote: "The law cannot make men temperate, but it can shut up dram-shops which feed intemperance, double our taxes, treble the peril to property and life. The *use* of liquors rests with each man's discretion. But the *trade* in them comes within the control of law. Whatever lifts the masses to better education and more self-control and secures them their full rights, helps the temperance cause. Thoroughly as I dislike to have my name used in a political canvass I have not the right to refuse it if it will strengthen your party."

As the candidate of two parties Phillips received over twenty thousand votes, enough to show that temperance and labour reform were issues that had begun to be of some interest in the Commonwealth, which was his reward for consenting to a predestined and expected defeat. Doubtless among these voters there were many who wished to compliment him for services to another cause. Others

did not let the opportunity pass to malign one who had
exposed himself to attack by entering the political arena.
Worse than the onsets of those who denied his fitness to be
a political leader was the provocation given him to strike
back. The violence with which he did this confirmed the
wisdom of his hitherto unbroken resolutions to keep out
of politics. He did not' need their rough methods to call
out his own sharper words, which were sometimes pointed
with bitterness and feathered with unwarranted fancies.
The lists which he had entered were unworthy of his steel,
and ward-meeting tactics did not become the hero of a
thirty years' war.

Nor in the opinion of his friends did Phillips gain anything
by urging the claims of General Butler in 1871 as a guber-
natorial candidate who had allied himself with temperance
and labour reform, and who at least represented an idea,
but also was a disturbing element in the Republican party.
This, however, was his recommendation to the agitator of
labour interests and the "great question of money against
legislation." It is noticeable that Phillips already foresaw
dangers that would threaten the social fabric in the next
generation, as he predicted in words like these:

Republican institutions will go down before moneyed
corporations. Rich men die; but banks are immortal,
and railroad corporations never have any diseases. In the
long run with Legislatures they are sure to win. This is
the battle which General Butler represents, the battle of
Labour. He has been charged with about every sin that can
be imagined, except of not doing what he said he would do.

On this account Phillips gave his support to the candidate who was pledged to work for his favourite reforms,

although he was again deserted for a time by friends and comrades. But this was an old story, and he kept on his way unswervingly without them until they chose to come back.

He appeared to better advantage in a newspaper controversy over Mayor Lyman's attitude toward the Garrison mob of 1835, having been an eye-witness of the occurrence. The dispute served as a landmark to show how far the city had advanced in one generation, recalling the year when it was neither respectable nor safe in Boston to speak against Southern slavery. Thirty-five years later a coloured Senator, occupying Jefferson Davis's seat, was the guest of the Governor of Massachusetts and of the Speaker of the House of Representatives, and was received with distinguished consideration by the Senate and the Judges of the United States Court. Phillips being called for, after an address by Senator Revels, reminded the large audience of an attorney-general who, thirty-three years before, spoke of emancipation as a letting loose of hyenas, and added, "Gentlemen of Boston, I introduce you to a hyena." The applause that followed was another token that the city had moved on from the day when this attorney-general's remarks in Faneuil Hall gallery incited Phillips to make the Lovejoy speech which made him famous in a day.

Not discouraged by Butler's rejection by two-thirds of the Republican Convention, Phillips gathered up the substance of his campaign speeches into an elaborate address on the Labour Question which he delivered in Boston and New York before the close of the year 1871, and published it later under the above title. He saw the same drift of wealth into the hands of a few here as in

England; and that the survival of republican institutions depends upon a successful resistance of this tendency by the masses roused to grapple with this danger through political action. His remedy was graded taxation, doubled riches to be taxed fourfold, and corporations made co-operative for associated labour and capital. "One-third of Christendom never had food enough to make them what they should be; they spend the day merely in getting bread enough to live, with a stunted mind and no aspirations beyond supper, grog, and sleep. The system that makes five thousand dependent upon one is faulty in its foundations. Coal is double its value because of corporations. Labour is too poor to own a journal, but its votes can command the press. Organization and education of the masses will win in the future."

Phillips lent his voice and pen to the Republican party in the campaign of 1872. Neither its politics nor its candidate suited him in all particulars, but Grant had done better in his first term than the abolitionists feared, and the great issues were now embodied in party measures. Perhaps the President's critic of 1868 was ready to atone for his strictures of that year; at any rate, his opinion of Horace Greeley, the opposition candidate, was as unfavourable as it was freely pronounced. Sumner had urged coloured men to vote for Greeley; and while Phillips sympathized with Sumner's injured feelings, he would not restore "the scandal and wrangle of Andy Johnson's years, with secession encamped in Washington." His acquaintance with Greeley in the old anti-slavery contest had not prepossessed him with the Democratic candidate's courage and political honesty; and he believed that principles were now being traded for the Presidency, and that the Negro was being decoyed into danger to be left doubly defenceless. This and more, in a long letter, was his answer to the coloured people who had asked his counsel in a year when their two best friends differed in a way they could not understand. He made his own position unmistakably clear, and also the risk they ran in voting for the great editor of the *Tribune*, who was snowed under in November, 1872.

James Anthony Froude volunteered, in 1873, to cross the Atlantic and explain to Americans in a series of lectures the ill success of England in dealing with Ireland. The reason which he mainly urged was the dogged incapacity of the Irish; that God left them unfinished, and that no wit of man can make citizens out of them; that the Celtic race lacks the elements that go to make up self-government, statesmanship, and a law-abiding community willing to associate with the great movements of the British people, who have furnished a government for the poverty-stricken, demoralized millions of Ireland for the last three hundred years.

If the eminent historian and pamphleteer had not heard that an able and eloquent defender of Ireland lived in the city where his explanation began, his unfortunate ignorance was presently revealed to him. Possibly he had assumed that all knowledge of the Irish question that was to be credited belonged to a certain Parliamentary party, and that American opinion was the outgrowth of immigration and needing correction by himself. Phillips dispelled that illusion without delay. Taking the platform as the defender of Ireland once more, he drew some Inferences from Froude, as he entitled his address, which were extremely disastrous to the purpose of that expounder and his statements. Thanking him for lifting the Irish question into public notice, he was not surprised that any Englishman should clutch an opportunity of wiping away the eclipse on the good fame of his country, and of explaining its lack of justice and statesmanship toward the sister island.

If Mr. Froude could convince the world that England had accepted the obligation which had been forced upon her, it would have gone half-way to wipe out the blots on his country's fame. No wonder that he did not make the attempt. Ireland has made itself the pivot on which the destiny of England turns. The would-be intermeddler in the affairs of all Europe did not dare draw her sword in the Franco-Prussian war for fear of Ireland behind her back. She knows that she would be checkmated if a foreign power should land men and arms on the opposite coast. The wickedness of the Tudors and Stuarts is punished by the weakness of Victoria. In the essential statement of the case Ireland has conquered England. And Mr. Froude comes here to explain the situation on the ground of Irish incapacity — a bad choice of a jury, for since July 4, 1776, our political faith has been that all men are capable of self-government.

The distinguished apologist for English government in Ireland had not counted on an antagonist of Puritan descent, and, surprised and discomfited, soon abandoned his enterprise of enlightening America.

Phillips appeared with some of his fellow-reformers at a meeting of the New England Woman's Suffrage Association in Faneuil Hall in December, and closed his year's work in a speech appropriate to the occasion.

Temperance and the labour question were frequent themes with him in the lectures which he delivered in the

early part of 1874, showing that the grave issues now before
the nation were clearly foreseen by this far-sighted observer
of events and tendencies. A temperance lecture of his
brought together the largest audience in Tremont Temple
that he had seen there since the outbreak of the war. He
hoped it foretold the rebellion of New England against the
tyranny of the grog-shop. More likely it was the tribute
of Boston to his eloquence on any subject in which he was
deeply interested. A letter to George J. Holyoake indicates the start which *incorporated* wealth had fully a generation ago:

Two or three united railways (*one* president) will subject
a state to their will. It is cheaper and surer to buy legislatures than voters. This is the peril of universal suffrage;
rum rules our great cities. One hardly sees whence the
cure is to come. I *believe*, I don't *see*. I never expected
to see any success of our anti-slavery struggle. The
gods made men mad and hastened them on their way
to destruction. I shall not live long enough to see any
marked result of our labour movement. I trust there will
never be a class-party here, labour against capital;
for three-fourths of our population are to some extent
capitalists. Limitation of hours is almost the only special
measure.

Southern ferment recalled Phillips's attention to the
Negroes whose position was full of doubt and danger along
the Gulf. The Governor of Louisiana had been elected
by them and stood by them before an opposition Legislature, but finally had to call upon the President to
help him keep the peace in New Orleans. Sheridan was
sent down and order was restored. Whereupon Southern
sympathizers in Massachusetts, for the tribe was not

extinct in 1875, called a meeting on January 15th, in Faneuil Hall, to denounce Grant and Sheridan. Phillips in the gallery listened to one speech after another, interspersed with calls for himself, which at the close grew so vociferous that he rose in his place, to be summoned to the platform, where he vindicated the administration and the commander in a speech that was applauded by Republicans and hissed by Democrats, after the former fashion. But the orator turned the tables on the promoters of the meeting, and an amendment to the denunciatory resolutions was passed, commending the course of Grant and Sheridan. He was certainly doing effective service for the cause at sixty-four, the military age of retirement. Also for the Government when he took up the currency question, which at this time was becoming a serious one when a gold dollar would buy two or three greenbacks, and when financial disturbance prevailed.

Without pretending to be a political economist, he urged the plan for relief which seemed to him most promising before the American Social Science Association meeting in Boston March 3, 1875. It was, in short, to make the nation's currency good as gold, and its bonds a good investment for capital, with interest at low rate for borrowers, who would thus develop the resources of the country. These principles of finance he set forth in a lecture with this title here and there for some time, not without the controversy which attends all economic theories, not all of which, however, are enforced with the vigour and plausible logic of his sincere argument. Even sincerity itself, he admits, may be at fault when tried by the wisdom of experience; as in the instance of his early belief in free trade contrasted with his later belief: " Any boy can see an abstract principle. Only threescore years and ten can discern when to make an exception to it. This explains the influx of college boys into politics with marvellous and delightful ignorance of affairs."

The world-wide celebration of the hundredth anniversary of Daniel O'Connell's birthday on August 6, 1875, afforded one agitator an opportunity to eulogize another, and one orator to characterize another. It was not the first time that Phillips had extolled his compeer when speaking upon kindred themes, but this occasion and audience permitted undivided attention to a favourite character. As an eloquent appreciation it is unsurpassed, and stands as one of the highest achievements of his oratory. His sympathies were with the Irish reformer and his work; his admiration sincere for his methods, and for the power of his masterly eloquence. The man and his cause, his purpose and abilities, appealed to one of similar aims and powers, who of all men found it easy to render such a tribute as one man seldom gives another. Faithful, generous, and without reserve, it stands, all in all, as one of the best examples in the language of true and honourable eulogy. For the eulogist himself it may be regarded as the acme of a climax, reached just as he had passed his grand climacteric year.[1]

Yet he found at this summit no signal to slacken his hand. If the causes he championed lacked the stimulus of anti-slavery discussion, their number and variety compensated in part and must have afforded a certain relief. Temperance, Labour, and Woman were themes on demand

[1] Printed in the second series of his speeches, p. 384.

for his lyceum audiences, and sometimes united as a composite subject of a single discourse, which was delivered when called for. The Indian problem also interested him as that of another race wronged by American greed, with a sadder destiny awaiting it than that of the Negro.

Under military restraint, provoked to useless revenge, robbed of one reservation after another, decimated by whiskey and bullets, the remnants of aboriginal tribes were vanishing into the mists of sunset. In Canada a white man could ride unharmed from Quebec to Vancouver. Gall and Rain-in-the-Face trying to reach the Canada line were attacked in their wigwams, and when the worms turned, a Christian nation grew indignant over General Custer's death. He might have been better employed in restoring law and order farther south. But he was obeying orders of a Government whose barbarous policy had cost hundreds of millions, many lives, and more dishonour — all to be repaid in land seized, largely for immigrants and speculators.

After the winter's lecturing tours Phillips hastened to the rescue of the Old South Church, a landmark of Colonial and Revolutionary times, whose destruction was threatened by the commercial value of its situation. The appeal he made on June 14, 1876, for its preservation was addressed to the historic spirit and civic pride of Boston, and as revised by himself remains among his published speeches as a choice example of what he could frame for an occasional address with an immediate purpose in view. It was a persuasive beginning in raising the requisite $400,000 that saved the venerable building. As a contribution to the same purpose he opened a lecture course in May, 1877, with an address on Sir Harry Vane, repeating it with great success before many audiences. In full sympathy with his hero, he placed him in the constellation of worthies whom Massachusetts delights to honour, and his personal admiration produced a memorial discourse of whose charm only newspaper reports remain.

In the opinion of many contemporaries — some of them his personal friends — Phillips would have left a more desirable record of his declining years if he had hung up his armour and had withdrawn from the field at the military age of retirement. The cause which he had championed had triumphed so far as legislation could give freedom to an enslaved race and the privileges of citizenship; but laws, like wealth, cannot endow men with capacities, abilities, and qualities essential to eminent social and civic attainment. In his later warfare he was opposed by hindrances as obstinate as natural laws which no amount of benevolent intention can overcome. Of these he could not have been entirely unconscious, although it was a part of his heroism to banish the thought of them. It might have been better to admit the limitations of a good purpose and to contend only for what is possible. At the same time it must be said that the most of his contention was for rights which are conceded to every grade of immigrant as soon as he can be naturalized, even if he is not denatured. As a rule, the African whose ancestors were here three hundred or one hundred years ago will make as good a citizen as the exile, voluntary or otherwise, from the slums of Europe, Asia, or the Orient.

There were other causes and reforms, however, in which Phillips was not so proficient a fighter and to whose success he did not so largely contribute. He always was ready to enter the lists in behalf of any worthy movement, but his ideas of it were sometimes too impracticable to be of the greatest value. Often they belonged to a future too far removed, to the present day more than his own; views and measures which time has vindicated, but not the best for his own day. And yet something ought to be accorded the prophet who discerns and advocates ideals that lift men's eyes to the hills while they are plodding along the lowland road which leads to the delectable heights. This idealist was sometimes impatient that the laggards did not mount up with wings as eagles.

Worse than this, the ideal which he proposed was not always absolute, and lacked the sanction of successful experiment. The element of friction is frequently left uncounted in mechanism that looks perfect on paper, and many airships have fallen by the weight of their driving engines.

The reforms advocated by Phillips were all good, but the methods he proposed were not in every instance as commendable as the causes; still, they usually had features that saved them from utter repudiation and uselessness. In conference with other men he might have furnished valuable suggestions; but as a lone dictator of policies from an irresponsible platform his opinion on debatable matters of currency and finance, labour and capital, for example, was ideal rather than practical. What is to be most admired, if it cannot be commended, is the continuance of the brave spirit which sent him abroad in quest of adventure. That which had kept him in the field engaged in single-handed conflict for forty years did not die when Giant Despair was slain. Other men turned to the pursuits of peace;

he could not. There might be left for them no foes more dire than windmills and fulling mills, than currency and tariff, consumer and manufacturer; but in this veteran knight was an undying flame which made him charge upon shadows in his path, cast by ogres of more or less reality. But the warrior zeal was genuine and the sense of duty unfailing.

XXIII

LAST YEARS AND LABOURS

(1877–1884)

THE unflinching justice and courage with which Phillips could meet an occasion complicated by the differences between his friends was illustrated by his eulogy of Sumner, and, incidentally, of Motley, after the death of the latter in 1877, both of whom he considered had been treated unfairly by Grant, for whom in turn he had great respect. But on this occasion he could arraign the President and Secretary Fish for stooping to a meanness, quoting Sumner's own plain words to the Secretary of State. "Sir, you are a tool of the President for base purposes; and this removal [of Motley from the British mission] is out of spite"; adding, "And it is true. The testimony is on the files of the diplomatic service itself."

In the fall of this year Phillips was again approached with a proposal regarding a nomination for the Governor's office, which he declined to consider, as he did a nomination to Congress the next year. His friends wished to show him how widely his labours and character were appreciated; but he decided to continue his service to good causes in the way that a lifetime of practice had made familiar. The public platform, trammeled by no party direction or policy, where speech was restrained by nothing more powerful than hisses and missiles, was to him more inviting than legislative halls and government offices where an agent of a party must keep within regimental lines.

Instead, he still preferred to be an independent scout, discovering where a foe to humanity was lurking, and to be the first to warn, to attack, and to summon the laggard host.[1] Just at this time his sleepless vigilance encountered sundry attempts to put persons undesirable to their relatives in insane asylums; and as he himself was once in similar danger from his family in early abolition days, he checked the present movement by calling a public meeting and making a speech, which resulted in memorializing the Legislature to pass laws for the better protection of persons charged with the malady about which there was no recourse to the customary process of law, and to secure for inmates of retreats the right of frequent and fair examinations and timely release.

The death of his co-worker, Garrison, in New York City, May 24, 1879, was the occasion of another eulogy, such as he might be expected to pronounce on the life, labours, and character of the elder partner in long years of service together in a common cause. "The hour is for the utterance of a lesson, to contemplate an example, a rich inheritance, a noble life worthily ended, and to emphasize what it teaches. The remarkable elements in his career were his consecration to a great idea; the earnestness and vigour of his carrying it out; the sagacity of his discernment of hidden forces; the loftiness of his motives; his grasp on

---

[1]That congressional life had its attractions for him, and was one of the prospects which he surrendered for an independent career, I am assured by one of his friends, who writes: "That which really attracted him was public life and not the bar, and nothing attracted him more. His dream would have been a life in the United States Senate, as he himself told me."

American character; his courage in facing obstacles; his
few mistakes; his happy life; his unflagging hope and
serene faith; a leader, brave, tireless, unselfish; 'the blessing
of him that was ready to perish' is his eternal great reward." The cause in which they had laboured together
was still demanding the watchfulness and advocacy of the
survivor. Oppressed by white domination, thousands of
the subject race were fleeing the Southern states until their
former masters, fearing a scarcity of labourers, attempted
to turn back the exodus from their own tyranny. To
help the fugitives, a meeting was held in June to protest
against interference with freemen's right to emigrate, and
to raise funds to help them. Phillips was foremost in the
movement and spoke with his old-time interest and power.
The Administration heard the protest and took some action;
but it was not possible to head off the stampede or stop it
so long as the white over-lords could make conditions
uncomfortable for the blacks.

When the Radical Club of ultra-liberal Unitarians drew
the radical reformer into their meetings at the house of his
life-long friend, Rev. John T. Sargent, and into theological
discussion, they found that his reformatory spirit did not
extend to the faith of his fathers. His religious belief was
consistent with all his efforts at bettering human society,
and did not need to be improved to match amendments of
any kind in the social fabric. Therefore, whether the
traditional conception of the Christian religion, its Founder,
or Edwards, its greatest New England exponent, were
attacked, they all found a defender in the agitator and
political reformer, the man who attacked everything else.
He drew the limiting line of destructive criticism and recon-

structive at the portal of orthodoxy, while he often lamented that its members and ministers did not see how comprehensive its principles of benevolence and charity were, and how all-persuasive its benign and reformatory activities ought to be. It was his open criticism of such shortcomings that brought upon him the charge of disloyalty to religion, whereas he was its reproving prophet for righteousness' sake.

An instance of this occurred in January, 1880, in a famous controversy with the liberal clergy of Boston on the liquor question, after he had addressed a committee at the State House on the license system, in which he pleaded for closing rum shops and scored the city authorities and the police for complicity with the trade. When Dr. Bartol apologized for some sorts of drinkers, he cited the example of Mr. Pierpont, who was driven from his pulpit for agitating the temperance question, and was ostracized by his professional brethren. Dr. Crosby, in 1881, fared no better after his notable lecture against total abstinence. "His own city, with license laws, is yet so ruled and plundered by rum that timid statesmen advise giving up Republicanism, and borrowing a leaf from Bismarck to help us." The entire reply, given by request of certain clergy of Boston before a large audience, is to be found in the second volume of his speeches.

A crisis in Irish affairs led him to speak on this topic at a Land League meeting in February, in which he made the startling statement that separation from England was the only solution of a problem which English and Irish statesmanship had been trying to solve for more than a century. He proposed to cut the knot that bound the two islands together, so great are the difficulties in the way of their union. He did not attempt to predict what would become of a state of only ten millions of people among the powers of Europe. Not long after, he was invited to advocate their cause in Ireland itself, but was obliged to refuse on account of declining health.

In June, of his seventieth year, he delivered what may be considered his valedictory oration, on the hundredth anniversary of the Phi Beta Kappa of Harvard College. His *alma mater* had contemplated his radical career with cool reserve, but after Boston had begun to appreciate the nation's recognition of her citizen, Harvard ventured to permit him to speak for himself — not without risk, some must have thought who recalled Emerson's famous oration of 1837, and no one had become literary bondsman for Phillips on this occasion, as when he addressed the public schools of Boston. There was much curiosity and some apprehension as to how he would use the academic opportunity of his life, although he had spoken on similar occasions at Williams, Dartmouth, and Yale. Nevertheless, he was loyal to the traditions of elegant and scholarly address, although colloquial and seemingly extemporaneous; but he was also faithful to his own convictions of what the Scholar in a Republic should be and to his sense of what scholarship in American colleges actually is — " cowardly, timid, and selfish." A few sentences will explain the surprise that the whole caused.

History is, for the most part, an idle amusement, the daydream of pedants and triflers. Journals [diaries] are the magnets that get near the chronometer of history and make all its records worthless. Of what value are its minutiæ? Law has no atom of strength only so far as public opinion endorses it. We live under a government of men and newspapers — not of law. The first attempt to storm dominant opinions will reveal this to you. Education is not book learning. New England learned more from sundry discussions and events than from a hundred colleges, more from Frémont's campaign and Harper's Ferry than from a thousand academic chairs. Timid scholarship shrinks from these agitations or denounces them. Distrust of the people pervades the book-educated class, which shrinks from that free speech which is God's school for educating men. Trust the people and you educate the race. Therefore all attempts against universal suffrage are bad. If the interests of the best are endangered let the worst be educated to see their mistake. College bred men should be agitators to tear a question open and riddle it with light and to educate the moral sense of the masses. Intemperance is making universal suffrage a failure and a curse in every city, and scholars have given it nothing but a sneer. So in the law's non-recognition of woman, and in the rule of Ireland through fear of it, scholarship stood afar off. No government is rightful unless resting on the consent of the people, and one which assumes to lead in asserting the rights of humanity. At last that disgraceful seal of slave complicity is broken. Let us inaugurate a new departure. We must be better than our fathers. Prohibit temptation if it rots great cities. Intrench labour against that wealth which wrecked the Grecian and Roman states. Sit not, like the figure on our silver coin, looking ever backward. New occasions teach new duties.

Anyone who will read the entire oration in the second series of his speeches will see that only here and there a line has been taken to show the drift of his address, which was, in a way, a thought here and a sentence there from the discourses of a lifetime as fearless, uncompromising, and

consistent on the Commencement stage as in Faneuil Hall
or the lyceum platform of a country town. As usual, he
presented an aggressive front and measured men by their
approach to his advanced outpost. His friends said that
he remembered only the lapses of scholarship and forgot
Sumner and Lowell, Channing and Emerson, Parker and
Palfrey, Adams and Quincy. It was his lifelong way to
let good men's deeds stand as their eulogies, while he was
Cato the censor for the shortcomings of his friends and
the great accuser of all who opposed the largest liberty
of speech or of life under the laws. His admirers — and
they were many — felt that he himself was the living refu-
tation of his charge against the cowardice of scholarship;
but not many could say that they themselves had been
so courageous or so valiant in a long strife as he had been.
Later, they saw more clearly what he endured and how
great his achievements were. To comments at the time
he replied: "Well, I suppose they wanted me to bring
myself." When was he ever known to bring any other
man's opinion or manner of speech?

It was a custom of Greek orators to continue a little
while after the climax of discourse and descend to a close
approaching the level of their opening paragraphs. Without intention Phillips's last years had a similar movement.
He believed that they could be but few after the threescore
and ten; and although he was strong in mind and body,
and was in undiminished demand by the public, there was
a note of grim endurance in his "working hard and battling
with snow-storms and drifts as I used to ten years ago,
and hoped I should n't now,"—in the December after the
June day at Harvard. Then, in the next spring, came the

necessity of removing from the house he had occupied for more than forty years, to make room for widening Harrison Avenue; and although the old home was reproduced as far as possible at No. 37 Common Street, near by, it was not the same for the two who had been peculiarly at home at No. 26 Essex Street. This breaking up was for Phillips the beginning of the end. "It is no matter," he remarked as he stood looking upon the vacant corner lot where his house had stood. "I am almost through with it all." He kept on, however, lecturing here and there as far as Philadelphia in the winter of 1882–83 on Labour and Capital, but felt obliged toward the end of the latter year to decline attending the fiftieth anniversary of the American Anti-slavery Society in Philadelphia. In his reply to the invitation, he spoke of the completion and triumph of a movement which in its progress touched all the great questions of the age — and now that its first purpose was accomplished it seemed wasteful that the skill and experience got from such labour and agitation should be lost. Freedmen would need the protection of a vigilant public opinion for a generation. "Labour and finance claim our aid in the name of humanity and justice. Let it not be said that the old abolitionist stopped with the Negro and was never able to see that the same principles he had advocated applied to every claim of downtrodden humanity." This broad philanthropy, which he was always practising, ought to have been a constant rebuke to the charge of fanaticism and narrow sympathies.

Five days before the close of the year 1883 Phillips spoke in the Old South Church at the unveiling of the statue of Harriet Martineau. It was his last public utterance. The same essential breadth characterized it that underlay all his discourse.

In moral questions, I say, there are no nations. We should endorse this memorial because the service of Harriet Martineau transcends nationality, a woman who has the great honour of having always seen the truth one generation ahead. She saw here, in 1834, the grandeur of the great movement just opened, whose proportions and results will be seen in time to come. We want our children to see the statue of this woman who came to observe and remained to work, and having put her hand to the plough persevered until she was allowed to live where the pæan of the emancipated four millions went up to heaven, showing the attainment of her great desire.

If his hearers had been told that this tribute was to be his last public utterance, they would have said that the spirit of it was as true of himself as of the reformer he was eulogizing. The last half of the final sentence might, with the change of person, be placed beneath his own statue; but to it could be added an expression of the philanthropy which embraces every race and every man, and of the heroism that shrinks from no sacrifice and counts nothing as a reward except the triumph of right over wrong.

During the month of January, 1884, he was kept at home by the serious illness of Mrs. Phillips. On the 26th he was suddenly seized with the form of heart trouble known as angina pectoris, whose first attack is premonitory of death. To a friend asking him about his faith, he spoke of Christ as the centre and solution of the history of humanity; of his more than human nature, and of his spirit as enabling him to do and suffer; and of the future life as sure as to-morrow. With returns of paroxysms and agony he lingered through the week, until on Saturday evening, February 2d, after a day of comparative rest, he fell into the sleep whose waking is in the next stage of life.

The death of a man of national and international fame was an affliction to his friends and a calamity to the city, state, and nation, which all made no delay in recognizing. In hearts and homes, in halls and churches, in city councils and state Legislature, in the West, and even in the South, there were tributes of affection for a kindly heart, of admiration for surpassing ability, and of respect for a courageous life. Mention of him was made in pulpits on Sunday; the press recorded its estimates the next day. On Wednesday the funeral service at the Hollis Street Church was followed by the gathering of a vast throng, and by a continuous procession through Faneuil Hall where the body lay in state, thousands doing homage to a name which had been canonized by death. Thousands more followed the guard of honour to the grave in the old Granary Burying Ground, where in the family tomb was laid the form of him whose familiar places should know him no more, but whose works should follow him.[1]

On the Saturday evening following the funeral a commemorative meeting was held in Faneuil Hall by friends and admirers of the departed, at which tributes of affection and honour were pronounced by one and another. And on the 18th of April, under the auspices of the city government of Boston, memorial services were held in Tremont Temple, where George William Curtis delivered a eulogy that was worthy of the subject of it. No survivor of that

---

[1] On the death of Mrs. Phillips a little more than two years later both were buried in Milton, where they had frequently passed the summer.

group which had made the mid-century a famous period
in the history of eloquence could have rendered a more
sympathetic and faithful tribute to the life and character
of Wendell Phillips. Both had laboured together in the
same cause, often in the same way, and with a marked
similarity in their experience with audiences, and to some
degree in their manner of address. Boston could not
have better honoured its illustrious orator and reformer,
atoning for its tardiness in recognizing, or at least in acknowledging, the loftiness of his aim, the sincerity of his
purpose, and his faith in an instructed public conscience.

Ten years later the city placed a tablet on the outer
wall of the building which stands on the site of the Phillips
homestead on Essex Street, bearing the following inscription:

HERE

WENDELL PHILLIPS RESIDED DURING FORTY YEARS,
DEVOTED BY HIM TO EFFORTS TO SECURE
THE ABOLITION OF AFRICAN SLAVERY IN THIS COUNTRY.

THE CHARMS OF HOME, THE ENJOYMENT OF WEALTH AND LEARNING,
EVEN THE KINDLY RECOGNITION OF HIS FELLOW-CITIZENS,
WERE BY HIM ACCOUNTED AS NAUGHT COMPARED WITH DUTY.

HE LIVED TO SEE JUSTICE TRIUMPHANT, FREEDOM UNIVERSAL,
AND TO RECEIVE THE TARDY PRAISES OF HIS OPPONENTS.
THE BLESSINGS OF THE POOR, THE FRIENDLESS,
AND THE OPPRESSED ENRICHED HIM.

IN BOSTON

HE WAS BORN 29TH NOVEMBER, 1811, AND DIED 2D FEBRUARY, 1884.

THIS TABLET WAS ERECTED IN 1894, BY ORDER OF THE
CITY COUNCIL OF BOSTON.

THE SUBSTANCE OF PHILLIPS'S ORATORY

IN THE brief extracts from Phillips's speeches and the condensations that have been given the main purpose has been to show what his sentiments were upon the issues paramount. Incidentally, also, is often seen the intensity of his convictions and the fearless earnestness of his expression. Moreover, where the quotation has been direct and continuous, even of a fragment, much can be learned of his sentence and paragraph construction, his vocabulary, his figures of speech and thought, his illustrating anecdotes and historical allusions, his mastery of irony and invective, with his perfect control of himself and his audience, two powers that are not always found together. Furthermore, the variety of citations made will be found to exemplify a wide range of rhetorical principles and oratorical precepts.

But beyond these qualities that may be illustrated by such brief citations as the limits of this volume permit, there are characteristics which belong to the framework of entire discourses and to the class to which they must be assigned. It is in this last particular that the great orator's versatility, variety, and adaptation to the subject and the occasion are exhibited, and in which it is conspicuously evident that he was much more than the mere abolition lecturer of tradition and men's memories. To illustrate his constructive ability adequately nothing less than entire speeches should be read and analyzed. The two volumes of these fortunately permit such study,[1] but even one example cannot be examined in the space assigned to the substance of the speaker's oratory, as distinguished from its form, treated in another chapter. It will therefore be necessary to illustrate a few classes of his discourse by reference to eminent instances of each, and to note his management of a few important rhetorical divisions, which have grown out of a long experience of speaking men with listeners.

First in the order of time — and he would have said in other respects — Phillips was a lecturer, with instruction as his main purpose. Not in the academic sense of a reader of formal discourse on themes of greater or less profundity and interest — sometimes associated with dulness on the part of the reader and the hearer likewise. Instead, his topics were not difficult to understand, and he was never commonplace nor his hearers sleepy. The continuous call for one of his earliest popular lectures, that on The Lost Arts, throughout his lifetime, shows that he remained a lecturer upon occasion to the end. Delivered from hastily assembled notes at first, to meet sudden summons, it met also a certain thirst for the curious until it had been repeated — according to the editor of the second volume of Addresses — over two thousand times. Mention of this lecture has been made already in Chapter VII, in connection with his entrance upon the platform. Another popular lecture, on Street Life in Europe, was of great interest when foreign travel was less common than it now is. In the first period of his career Phillips often

[1] "Speeches, Lectures and Addresses," two volumes, Boston, Lee and Shepard, 1902.

spoke upon subjects taken from the domain of science, invention, and discovery; but as it was not his habit to read a manuscript, no reports of these early discourses remain.

Soon, however, Phillips's lectures began to have a purpose beyond popular information in science, art, and travel. With reforms in his mind it was not always certain whether his utterances could be called lectures, addresses, or speeches. Strictly speaking, the instructive element prevails in a lecture, and with it is associated the thought of premeditation and preparation; and as Phillips himself should be the best authority it is fair to accept his classification in the volume which was prepared in his lifetime — the first.[1] In it the following are called lectures: Idols, Harper's Ferry, Lincoln's Election, Disunion, The War for the Union, Toussaint l'Ouverture. In the second volume, compiled after his decease, only one title — The Lost Arts — heads what is termed a lecture. Like this one, the others mentioned were delivered in courses of lectures or upon special invitation, sometimes in different places, and bear the marks of orderly and careful thought and as if with the local character of an audience in mind. Such was the Fraternity Lecture delivered in Boston, largely a review of the city's "Idol" — Webster — and of his eminent eulogists, as also was that on Harper's Ferry, with his own eulogy of John Brown and his arraignment of Virginia and its governor, closing with the lines he loved so well — "Right forever on the scaffold, wrong forever on the throne." Disunion and

---

[1] To the publisher of this volume Phillips wrote:
"Four or five of them ('Idols,' 'The Election,' 'Mobs and Education,' 'Disunion,' 'Progress') were delivered in such circumstances as made it proper I should set down beforehand, substantially, what I had to say. The preservation of the rest you owe to phonography."

The War for the Union are two remaining lectures, which ought to be read on the same day, delivered as they were in the same memorable year of 1861, before and after the opening of the war, the one indicating what he meant by disunion and the other his position with regard to war as an arbiter of the sectional dispute.

As an example, however, of that kind of lecture which he oftenest delivered after the early period of scientific information, the half biographical, half political one on Idols is a good illustration. The opening paragraph is as informal as the first sentences of a skilled after-dinner speaker who takes his cue from the toastmaster, as Phillips himself evidently did from the presiding officer, or from some preliminary speaker.

Mr. President and Ladies and Gentlemen: I feel half inclined to borrow a little wit from an article in a late number of the *Atlantic Monthly* — "My Double, and How He Undid Me" — and say, "I agree entirely with the gentleman who has just taken his seat. So much has been said, and so well said, that there is no need of my occupying your attention." But then I should lose the hearty satisfaction it gives me to say with what delight I stand upon this platform, and how sincerely I appreciate the honour you do me, Mr. Chairman, by allowing me to aid in opening this course of lectures.

While the topic of exordium is being considered it should be said that Phillips was always a gentleman on the platform and off, and knew how to conciliate an audience from the start, as in this instance. But he did by no means always follow this cardinal precept of the rhetoricians. If he was reasonably sure of their agreement with him at the close of his discourse, he cared very little for their favour at its beginning. Indeed, their hostility was as inspiring to him as a refractory steed was to his friend Rarey, the horse-trainer. Sometimes, if his hearers lacked this inspiriting opposition, he provoked it immediately. In this lecture, after two gracious and appreciative paragraphs, he might have felt that acquiescence was not stimulating enough, for he began the third in this way:

There are men who prate about "nationality," and the "empire," and "manifest destiny"—using brave words, when their minds rise no higher than some petty mass of white states making money out of cotton and corn. My idea of American nationality makes it the last, best growth of the thoughtful mind of the century, treading under foot sex and race, caste and condition, and collecting on the broad bosom of what deserves the name of an empire, under the shelter of noble, just, and equal laws all races, all customs, all religions, all languages, all literature, and all ideas. I remember, a year or two ago, they told me of a mob at Milwaukee that forced a man to bring out the body of his wife, born in Asia—which, according to the custom of her forefathers, he was about to burn—and compelled him to submit to American funeral rites, which his soul abhorred. The sheriff led the mob, and the press of the state vindicated the act. This is not my idea of American civilization. . . . They will show you at Rome the stately column of the Emperor Trajan. Carved on its outer surface is the triumphal march of the Emperor, when he came back to Rome, leading all nations, all tongues, all customs, all races, in the retinue of his conquest; and they traced it on the eternal marble, circling the pillar from base to capital. Just such is my idea of the empire, broad enough and brave enough to admit both sexes, all creeds, and all tongues in the triumphal procession of this great daughter of the West of the Atlantic.

This single paragraph might stand as an epitome of the substance and form of the orator's discourse. His comprehensive political and humanitarian creed is here; a hint of his wide information; and an example of his apt use of a noble figure in illustrating a lofty sentiment, combined with outspoken, if unwelcome, truth at first, which was received with "loud applause" as he closed a paragraph classic in its construction. But, as a rule, the first sentences which he uttered were such as to secure silence and a hearing, and accorded with the general sentiment on the introductory topic, which did not always relate to the line of remark to follow. As in this lecture, when he made the lyceum one of the four sources of education, and woman's influence upon society and literature was asserted, there was a pleased assent and the audience went with the speaker, and even applauded when he said that "New England, with toleration written all over her statute-book, has a pope in every village; and the first thing that tests a boy's courage is to dare to differ from his father." When, however, he presently remarked of Webster that he was the bankrupt chief of a broken and ruined party and added sundry other uncomplimentary statements, hisses began to be heard; which was always the sure sign that Phillips was getting into the body of his discourse.

On this occasion — in Boston, 1859 — he was intending to speak to its citizens about one of its "idols." He had laid a foundation for his remarks by dealing broadly with good literature and government, but as he drifted from these into personal criticism of "the opposition," it is better to look for a more representative example of what is called "the argument."

One can be found in his Boston and New York lecture on The War for the Union in which was answered the question as to his position after hostilities began.

I will not speak of war in itself — I have no time; I will not say, with Napoleon, that it is the practice of barbarians; I will not say that it is good. It is better than the past, but there is not an element of good in it. I mean, there is nothing in it which we might not have gotten better, fuller, and more perfectly in other ways. And yet it is better than the craven past, infinitely better than a peace which had pride for its father and subserviency for its mother. . . .

Some men say they would view this war as white men. I condescend to no such narrowness. I view it as an American citizen, proud to be the citizen of an empire that knows neither black nor white, neither Saxon nor Indian, but holds an equal sceptre over all. If I am to love my country, it must be lovable; if I am to honour it, it must be worthy of respect. What is the function God gives us — what the breadth of responsibility he lays upon us? An empire, the home of every race, every creed, every tongue, to whose citizens is committed the grandest system of free government. Tocqueville tells us that all nations and all ages tend with inevitable certainty to this result; but he points out, as history does, this land as the normal school of the nations, set by God to try the experiment of popular education and popular government. . . .

The war power of Congress is not an unconstitutional power, but the moment it comes into play it rises beyond the limit of constitutional checks. I know it is a grave power, this trusting the Government with despotism. But what is the use of Government, except to help us in critical times? All the checks and ingenuity of our institutions are arranged to secure for us men wise and able enough to be trusted with grave powers —bold enough to use them when the times require. Lancets and knives are dangerous instruments. The use of surgeons is, that, when lancets are needed, somebody may know how to use them and save life. One great merit of democratic institutions is that, resting as they must on educated masses, the Government may safely be trusted, in a great emergency, with despotic power, without fear of harm or of wrecking the state. No other form of government can venture such confidence without risk of national ruin. . . .

Now this Government, which abolishes my right of *habeas corpus* — which strikes down, because it is necessary, every Saxon bulwark of liberty — which proclaims martial law, and holds every dollar and every man at the will of the Cabinet — do you turn round and tell me that this same Government has no rightful power to break the cob-web—it is but a cobweb—which binds the slave to his master — to stretch its hands across the Potomac, and root up the evil, which, for seventy years, has troubled its peace, and now culminates in rebellion? I maintain, therefore, the power of the Government to inaugurate such a policy; and say, in order to save the Union, do justice to the black.

I would claim of Congress — in the exact language of Adams — of the *"Government"* — a solemn act abolishing slavery throughout the Union, securing compensation to loyal slave-holders. As the Constitution forbids the states to make and allow nobles, I would now, by equal authority, forbid them to make slaves or allow slave-holders.

This has been the usual course at such times. Nations, convulsed and broken by too powerful elements or institutions have used the first moment of assured power — the first moment that they clearly saw and fully appreciated the evil — to cut up the dangerous tree by the roots. So France expelled the Jesuits, and the Middle Ages the Templars. So England, in her great rebellion, abolished the nobility and the Established Church; and the French Revolution did the same, and, finally, gave to each child an equal share in his deceased father's lands. For the same purpose, England, in 1745, abolished clanship in Scotland,

the root of the Stuart faction; and we, in '76, abolished
nobles and all tenure of estates savouring of privileged
classes. . . .

We grapple the Union together with hooks of steel —
make it as lasting as the granite which underlies the continent. . . .

I would have the Government announce to the world
that we understand the evil which has troubled our peace
for seventy years, thwarting the natural tendency of our
institutions, sending ruin along our wharves and through
our workshops every ten years, poisoning the national
conscience. We know well its character. But Democracy,
unlike other governments, is strong enough to let evils work
out their own death — strong enough to face them when
they reveal their proportions. It was in this sublime
consciousness of strength, not of weakness, that our fathers
submitted to the well-known evil of slavery, and tolerated
it until the viper we thought we could safely tread on, at
the touch of disappointment, starts up a fiend whose
stature reaches the sky. But our cheeks do not blanch.
Democracy accepts the struggle. After this forbearance
of three generations, confident that she has yet power to
execute her will, she sends her proclamation down to the
Gulf — Freedom to every man beneath the Stars, and
death to every institution that disturbs our peace or
threatens the future of the Republic.

In this lecture Phillips was instructing a popular assembly
on the nature and powers of a republican government. It
was a critical time, demanding unusual measures, which
must be justified before the people, the source of all authority.
In two cities, centres of opinion and influence, he argued
the cause of the Government in its hour of extremity when
the Union was imperilled. He did this in plain words,
from admitted premises, supported by historical examples.

His conclusion was that to which the Government came not long after, thus giving the highest sanction to his discourse. In its entirety it stands as a fair sample of his method in the principal occupation of many years — educating the people in that civic righteousness which exalts a nation. Information and instruction, education of the mind and of the conscience, was the "burden" of this prophet in his independence, personality, and wide-reaching influence. At the time this lecture was delivered he saw a growing political party taking up his work and Congress beginning to adopt his sentiments.

When it is said that Phillips was primarily a lecturer, it should be understood that this statement does not rest upon the few discourses that are entitled Lectures. The term itself is inclusive and broad. So is the designation of another class called Addresses. Nor is it always easy to find the distinction between the lecture and the address, the same quality of instruction pervading examples of each. Indeed, one cannot read far in the two volumes of his speeches without concluding that the designation of his discourses does not always rest upon peculiar characteristics. The occasion and the place of their delivery seem to have determined their classification. In a place of worship before a congregation it is a discourse or an address; before a legislature, a plea or an argument; in a convention or mass meeting, a speech. It will be a better principle of division to observe his work — under the general form of lecture or address — as expository, argumentative, eulogistic; or, once more, to regard the speaker as a citizen, an abolitionist, a lawyer, a reformer, a censor, a eulogist.

An example of his expository ability has been given in the foregoing citations from his lecture on The War for the Union. In it is also revealed the high plane which the speaker occupied as the citizen of his country, above a party, beyond the bounds of his state and province, advocating no narrow measures of relief, abandoning the cherished holding of twenty years when the reason of it had passed away. As a citizen of his own city he proclaimed his love for it and for its good name when he made the eloquent appeal that helped to save the Old South Church from being sacrificed to Mammon. The basis of it was historical and patriotic, for the perpetuation of memories that make a people better, a city self-respecting.

Naturally in our streets and neighbourhood came the earliest collision between England and the Colonies. Here Sam Adams, the ablest and ripest statesman God gave to the epoch, forecast those measures which welded thirteen colonies into one thunderbolt, and launched it at George III. Here Otis magnetized every boy into a desperate rebel. Here fit successors of Knox and Hugh Peters consecrated their pulpits to the defence of that doctrine which the State borrowed so directly from the Christian Church. The towers of North Church rallied the farmers to the Lexington and Concord fights; and these old walls echoed the people's shout, when Adams brought them word that Governor Hutchinson surrendered and withdrew the red-coats. . . .

On Bunker Hill let somebody point out to you the church-tower whose lantern told that Middlesex was to be invaded. Search till your eye rests on the tiny spire which trembled once when the mock Indian whoops bade England defiance. There is the elm where Washington first drew his sword. Here Winter Hill, whose cannon-ball struck Brattle Street Church. At your feet the sod is greener for the blood of Warren, which settled it forever that no more laws were

to be made for us in London. . . . We cannot afford
to close any school which teaches such lessons. . . .

But these walls received a real consecration when Adams
and Otis dedicated them to liberty. We do not come
here because there went hence to heaven the prayers of
Sewall and Prince and the early saints of the colony. We
come to save walls that heard and stirred the eloquence
of Quincy. These arches will speak to us, as long as they
stand, of the sublime and sturdy religious enthusiasm of
Adams; of Otis's passionate eloquence and single-hearted
devotion; of Warren in his young genius and enthusiasm;
of a plain, unaffected, but high-souled people who ventured
all for a principle, and to transmit to us unimpaired, the
free lips and self-government which they inherited. Above
and around us unseen hands have written, "This is the
cradle of Civil Liberty, child of earnest, religious faith."
I will not say it is a nobler consecration; I will not say that
it is a better use. I only say we come here to save what our
fathers consecrated to the memories of the most successful
struggle the race has ever made for the liberties of man.
. . . Think twice before you touch these walls. We
are only the world's trustees. The Old South no more
belongs to us than Luther's, or Hampden's, or Brutus's
name does to Germany, England, or Rome. Each and all
are held in trust as torchlight guides and inspiration for
any man struggling for justice, and ready to die for the
truth.

It is a natural sequence to consider the professional work
of a man after his efforts as a citizen. Although Phillips
abandoned his law practice in the courts, he did not lose his
knowledge of legal principles nor his skill in presenting
them before legislators. His achievements on several
occasions are proofs of the ability which he might have
brought to the bar, and which he did bring to committees
of the Massachusetts Legislature and to that body itself.

They are also examples of his versatility, showing that he could address a small number of hard-headed men as effectively as a multitude, swayed by its varying impulses. The Argument for the Removal of Judge Loring from Office is an instance. It is in as marked contrast to his speeches before vast audiences as these were to the Committee on Federal Relations before which it was delivered.

The people of Massachusetts have always chosen to keep their judges, in some measure, dependent on the popular will. It is a Colonial trait, and the sovereign state has preserved it. Under the King, though he appointed judges, the people jealously preserved their hold on the bench, by keeping salaries year by year dependent on the vote of the popular branch of the Legislature. This control was often exercised. When Judge Oliver took pay of the King, they impeached him. [See Washburn's Judicial History of Massachusetts.] When the Constitution was framed the people chose to keep the same sovereignty in their own hands. Independence of judges, therefore, in Massachusetts, gentlemen, means, in the words of Governor Childs, "the fullest independence consistent with their responsibility."

The opinions I have read you [Hallam, the Report of Constitutional Convention Committee of 1829, Chief Justice Shaw, Prescott, Davis, and other recognized authorities] derive additional weight from the fact that all the speakers were aware of the grave nature of the power, and some painted in glowing colours how liable to abuse it was. Still, not one proposed to take it from you. . . .

You may think, gentlemen, that I have occupied too much time in proving the unlimited extent of your power. But it seemed necessary, since the press which defends the remonstrant, and he also, though they do not in words deny your unlimited authority, do so in effect. They claim that you destroy the independence of the bench, and *abuse* your power, if you exercise it in any case but a clear violation of the law. In words said to have been used by Rufus Choate in a recent case, "A judicial officer may be removed if found intellectually incapable, or if he has been left to commit some great enormity, so as to show himself morally deranged." Has, then, a proper case occurred for the exercise of this power? In other words, ought you now to exercise it? The petitioners think you ought for the following reasons.

Enough has been given to indicate the judicial tone of Phillips's argument when the law itself was to be justified. He could be as exact in citing authorities, and the constitutional history of a state as a judge on the bench, and could state clearly and calmly his own conclusions. And in his final appeal for the removal of the judge he observes a restraint which the importance of the case and the dignity of the occasion imposed.

In his plea before another committee of the Massachusetts Legislature for the abolition of capital punishment Phillips displayed a similar wealth of learning and skill in presenting his arguments under the questions of the right, the obligation, and the necessity of taking human life. As there was no person, private or official, involved in this case it is probably the best example of calm and cogent reasoning in all his public speaking. Scriptural command, and civil precedent are carefully weighed; also the supposed restraint from crime by open or private execution. The most passionate appeal in it is the suggestion of coming down one more step in the series that has abolished the rack, tearing with wild horses and red-hot pincers, the faggot and stake.

You cannot tolerate these things now. Society has been forced, by the instinct of humanity, against its logic, to put away these cruel penalties. Men have been crying out continually against this instinct of mercy which sought to make the dungeon less terrible; they feared to remove a cobweb from that dungeon's cruelty, lest the world should go to pieces. Yet the world swept it down, and is safer to-day than ever before.

Now we ask you to abolish the gallows. It is only one step further in the same direction. Massachusetts has thrown it away for almost all offences; she only retains it for one or two. We ask you to take one more step in the same direction. Take it, because the civilized world is taking it in many quarters! Take it, because the circumstances of the time prove you may take it safely! Take it, because it is well to try experiments for humanity, and this is a favourable community to try them in. These are the arguments, gentlemen of the committee, on which we ask you to abolish the punishment of death in this commonwealth.

In his character as a lawyer and as an advocate of civil and social reforms might be included his pleas for woman, temperance, labour, and education; but the most of these topics did not require the careful statement, citation of authorities, nor the restraint of speech and reserve in personal criticism demanded by legal argument. While he did not chafe under the professional curb, he was not, of necessity, so interesting as on the untrammeled platform and before a free popular assembly. Still, there is a moderation in discussing these minor causes which often disappears when the insistent claims of abolition as the most needful of all reforms press upon him.

Of his spirited eloquence at such times so many fragments have been given in preceding chapters that the tone of his discourse on the subject nearest his heart cannot be mistaken. In many respects one of these speeches resembles the majority of them; but there were as many sides to the one question as facets to the Kohinoor. One which was always presenting itself to critics was the violence of abolition speakers as a hindrance to their cause. The answer to this charge is made in more than one address; but in the Philosophy of the Abolition Movement Phillips appears as the apologist of his coterie with special reference to strictures made in England and published in the London *Leader*. As a defender of denunciatory methods he is careful not to employ these in his justification of them — on the ground that a crying evil demands corresponding outcry against it. But in this apology for their use his language is temperate and free from the personality which he deemed necessary when men became synonymous with bad measures.

What is the denunciation with which we are charged? It is endeavouring, in our faltering human speech, to declare the enormity of the sin of making merchandise of man — of separating husband and wife — taking the infant from the mother, and selling the daughter to prostitution, — of a professedly Christian nation denying, by statute, the Bible to every sixth man and woman of its population, and making it illegal for "two or three" to meet together, except a white man be present! What is this harsh criticism of motives with which we are charged? It is simply holding the intelligent and deliberate actor responsible for the character and consequences of his acts. Is there anything inherently wrong in such denunciation or such criticism? This we may claim, — we have never judged a man but out of his own mouth. We have seldom, if ever, held him to account, except for acts of which he and his own friends were proud. All that we ask the world and thoughtful men to note are the principles and deeds on which the American pulpit and American public men plume themselves. We always allow our opponents to paint their own pictures. Our humble duty is to stand by and assure the spectators that what they would take for a knave or a hypocrite is really, in American estimation, a doctor of divinity or secretary of state.

After an enumeration of the evils incident to human bondage he adds:

Prove to me now that harsh rebuke, indignant denunciation, scathing sarcasm, and pitiless ridicule are wholly and always unjustifiable; else we dare not, in so desperate a case, throw away any weapon which ever broke up the crust of an ignorant prejudice, roused a slumbering conscience, shamed a proud sinner, or changed, in any way, the conduct of a human being. Our aim is to alter public opinion. To change public opinion we use the very tools by which it was formed. That is, all such as an honest man may touch.
Have we not also addressed ourselves to that other duty of arguing our question thoroughly? — of using due discretion and fair sagacity in endeavouring to promote our cause? Yes, we have. No one step has ever been gained but by the most laborious research and the most exhausting argument. Of that research and that argument, of the whole of it, the old-fashioned, crazy Garrisonian anti-slavery movement has been the author. From this band of men has proceeded every important argument or idea which has been broached on the anti-slavery question from 1830 to the present time [1853]. . . .

Much has been said about Phillips's sharpness of tongue. It is not easy to find more of it than in any earnest reformer's discourse when a giant wrong is assailed. In the above instance a concrete form of it was presented on the occasion of the hasty and perfunctory forms of justice to one whose death was a foregone conclusion; being to the speaker a pioneer and doomed martyr, whose captors and slayers inspired his friend's execration. Even here, however, he preserves a Ciceronian dignity of sentence and phrase, or even better, since he is arraigning a nation and its press rather than a single conspirator. And in the entire "lecture" there prevails a tone of moderation that dignifies and justifies its character.

From Phillips on the defensive it is natural to turn to him in an aggressive mood — a more common one when engaged in controversy. It is best to note his invective in the thick of battle as the strongest expression of his aggressiveness.

We have been carrying on this insurrection of thought for thirty years. When we commenced the anti-slavery agitation, the papers talked about slavery, bondage, boldly, frankly, and bluntly. In a few years it sounded hard; it had a grating effect, as they spoke of the "patriarchal institution," then of the "domestic institution," and then of the peculiar institution and in a year or two of "economic subordination," and baptized it by statute and warranteeism. The Methodists advised their bishop, a slave-holder, to get rid of his "impediment," and Rufus Choate phrased it "a different type of industry." And so men have banished slavery into pet phrases and fancy flash-words. This is one evidence of progress. . . .

You will remember, all of you, citizens of the United States, that there was not a Virginia gun fired at John Brown. Hundreds of well-armed Maryland and Virginia troops rushed to Harper's Ferry, and — went away! *You* shot him!

Sixteen marines, to whom you pay eight dollars a month

— your own representatives! When the disturbed state could not stand on her own legs for trembling, you went there and strengthened the feeble knees, and held up the palsied hands. Sixteen men, with the vulture of the Union above them, your representatives! . . . Soldiers and civilians — both alike — only a mob fancying itself a government! They do not begin to have the faintest conception of what a government is. Here is a man arraigned before a jury or about to be. The Chief Executive, bound to keep his mind impartial as to the guilt of any person arraigned, hastens down to Richmond, and proclaims to the assembled Commonwealth, "This man is a murderer, and ought to be hung." In the theory of English law, it was not possible to impanel an impartial jury in Virginia. If Jeffries could speak, he would thank God that at last his name might be taken down from the gibbet of History since the Virginia bench has made his worst act white, set against the blackness of this modern infamy. And yet the New York press daily prints the accounts of the *trial*. Trial! In the names of Holt and Somers, of Hale and Erskine, of Parsons, Marshall, and Jay, I protest against the name. No decent form observed, and the essence of fair trial wholly wanting, our history and law alike protest against degrading the honoured name of *Jury Trial* by lending it to such an outrage as this. The Inquisition was heaven-robed innocence compared with the trial, or what the New York press called so, that has been going on in crazed and maddened Charlestown.

A nearer approach to the Roman orator in personal invective is his upbraiding of Kossuth's inconsistency in pleading for his oppressed Hungary with never a word for the enslaved here.

What, then, is the shadowy line by which, while he claims our sympathy and aid for Hungary, he separated the slave from his own? Can he plead for liberty with such

bated breath and whispered humbleness that to serve his
purpose he can always remember to forget the self-evident
rights which God gave — to which the slave has as much
right as the noblest Magyar of them all? More than this,
can he find it in his heart to strengthen by his silence, by
his example, and his name the hands of the ruthless violator
of those rights; cry "glorious" and "amen," while the black
is robbed of his hard toil, of the Bible, of chastity, wife,
husband, and child — only to persuade slave-holders to
aid in securing for the Magyar peasant the right to vote,
and for the "Magyar noble the right to legislate." The
world thought his lips had been touched by a coal from the
altar of the living God — and lo! he has bargained away
his very utterance and presents himself before us thus
cheaply bought and gagged!

Just as was Phillips's view and merited as was the censure
of Kossuth's expedient blindness, it is remarkable that his
censor did not condescend to more scathing terms on this
single occasion when his temper is said to have come near
getting the mastery of him. There were times when he
could use epithets and comparisons that held sundry contemporaries up to ridicule and scorn, but he was provoked
rather than indignant, and amused his audience rather
than roused their resentment. From all this and every
form of his warfare, however, it is pleasant to turn to another
aspect of his eloquence and note him as a eulogist.

Brief "Tributes" to Theodore Parker, Francis Jackson,
Abraham Lincoln, Helen Eliza Garrison, William Lloyd
Garrison, and Harriet Martineau exhibit such a knowledge of character and appreciation of different qualities
as belong to a loving and yet discriminating commemorator
of noble lives; and if he had left nothing more in this direction than these reminiscent remarks at memorial services

and the like, he would have added another feature to his versatility. But there are three or four examples of extended eulogy which establish his reputation as one of the greatest masters of commemorative oratory.

The earliest of these memorial tributes is that pronounced at the funeral of John Brown before the family and a few neighbours gathered to pay respect to his memory at the farm house on the border of a wilderness in a December day of 1859. The simplicity and tenderness of his remarks accord with the lowly surroundings, with the loving reverence and sublime confidence that was paid the man who was counted a martyr by his friends. The speaker's fitting words reveal the felicity with which he could adapt himself to an unwonted occasion and to hearthstone sorrows.

How feeble words seem here! How can I hope to utter what your hearts are full of ? I fear to disturb the harmony which his life breathes round this home. How our admiring, loving wonder has grown, day by day, as he has unfolded trait after trait of earnest, brave, tender, Christian life! . . .

What lesson shall these lips teach us ? Before that still, calm brow let us take a new baptism. . . . Men said, "Would that he had died in arms!" God ordered better, and granted to him and the slave those noble prison hours — that single hour of death; the echoes of his rifles have died away in the hills — a million hearts guard his words. God bless this roof — make it bless us! God make us all worthier of him whose dust we lay among these hills he loved. He sleeps in the blessings of the crushed and poor, and men believe more firmly in virtue, now that such a man has lived.

Standing here, let us thank God for a firmer faith and fuller hope.

Daniel O'Connell was a man after Phillips's own heart. He had met him and corresponded with him and was in full sympathy with his efforts for Irish liberty, as the statesman was with the American agitator's purposes for the slave here. Therefore, when on August 6, 1875, the hundredth anniversary of O'Connell's birth was celebrated in Boston, Phillips was naturally the orator of the occasion.

In a swift review of recent Irish history he places his hero among British statesmen as one who lifted the Island to a fixed and permanent place in English affairs, putting its independence beyond peril and making it the pivot of British politics. He outlines his work, delineates the sterling nobility of his character, and at the close passes to his oratorical power.

Broadly considered, his eloquence has never been equalled in modern times; certainly not in English speech. Do you think that I am partial? I will vouch John Randolph, of Roanoke, the Virginia slave-holder, who hated an Irishman almost as much as he hated a Yankee, himself an orator of no mean level. Hearing O'Connell, he exclaimed, "This is the man, these are the lips, the most eloquent that speak English in my day." I think he was right. I remember the solemnity of Webster, the grace of Everett, the rhetoric of Choate; I know the eloquence that lay hid in the iron logic of Calhoun; I have melted beneath the magnetism of Sergeant S. Prentiss, of Mississippi, who wielded a power few men ever had. It has been my fortune to sit at the feet of the great speakers of the English tongue on the other side of the ocean. But I think all of them together never surpassed, and no one of them ever equalled O'Connell. Nature intended him for our Demosthenes. Never since the great Greek, has she sent forth anyone so lavishly gifted for his work as a tribune of the people. In the first place, he had a magnificent presence, impressive in bearing, massive like that of Jupiter. Webster himself hardly outdid him in the majesty of his proportions. . . . There was something majestic in his presence before he spoke; and he added to it what Webster had not, what Clay might have lent — infinite grace, that magnetism that melts all hearts into one. I saw him at over sixty-six years of age, every attitude was beautiful, every gesture grace. He had a voice that covered the gamut. The majesty of his indignation, fitly uttered in tones of superhuman power, made him able to "indict" a nation, in spite of Burke's protest. I heard him once say, "I send my voice across the Atlantic, careering like a thunder-storm against the breeze, to tell the slave-holder of the Carolinas that God's thunder-bolts are hot, and to remind the bondman that the dawn of his redemption is already breaking." You seemed to hear the tones come echoing back to London from the Rocky Mountains. Then, with the slightest possible Irish brogue, he would tell a story, while all Exeter Hall shook with laughter. The next moment, tears in his voice like a Scotch song, five thousand men wept. And all the while no effort. He seemed only breathing. . . .

We used to say of Webster, "This is a great effort"; of Everett, "It is a beautiful effort"; but you never used the word "effort" in speaking of O'Connell. And this wonderful power, it was not a thunderstorm: he flanked you with his wit, he surprised you out of yourself; you were conquered before you knew it.

One cannot read this characterization of the great Irish agitator's eloquence without applying much of it to his American admirer, who was yet no imitator.

"Toussaint l'Ouverture" was called by its author a sketch, and a short biography, and an historical argument in a lecture which was in frequent demand in the war years. Essentially it was a eulogy, as truly as was Everett's famous oration upon Washington. For the hour the black man was

white through the magic of Phillips's citation of history and a
comparison of his hero with the great ones of the earth.
It was a marshalling of facts in a story that was eloquent
in its simplicity, and interesting to most of his hearers
through its novelty. The argument was comparative, to
the great advantage of L'Ouverture when placed side by
side with the honoured in history.

I would call him Napoleon, but Napoleon made his way
to empire over broken oaths and through a sea of blood.
This man never broke his word. . . . I would call him
Cromwell, but Cromwell was only a soldier, and the state
he founded went down with him into his grave. I would
call him Washington, but the great Virginian held slaves.
This man risked his empire rather than permit the slave
trade in the humblest village of his dominions.
You think me a fanatic to-night, for you read history,
not with your eyes, but with your prejudices. But fifty
years hence, when Truth gets a hearing, the muse of History
will put Phocion for the Greek, and Brutus for the Roman,
Hampden for England, Fayette for France, choose
Washington for the bright, consummate flower of our
earlier civilization, and John Brown for our noonday; then
dipping her pen in the sunlight, will write in the clear blue,
above them all, the name of the soldier, the statesman, the
martyr — Toussaint l'Ouverture.

As this final paragraph may be taken as perhaps the best
example of his perorations, so it may also represent the
acme of his eulogistic compositions. Its effect upon
audiences was overwhelming.

If one looks for the climax of his achievements during
the whole of his career, the Phi Beta Kappa oration at
Harvard on the society's hundredth anniversary may be
taken as occupying that position. In his seventieth year,

in 1881, his *alma mater* had at last come to honour the chief orator of the nation with an invitation to address its principal literary society; not without misgivings as to what he might say. Williams, Dartmouth, Yale, and Brown had risked listening to his discourse during the 'fifties, and the great controversy now being fifteen years past it was concluded to make the venture.

It turned out to be an onslaught on the timid conservatism of academic habits, until roused by a catastrophe, and an appeal to trust, and therefore to educate, the entire people, and by means of agitation of great questions to inform minds and quicken consciences until the nation should rule itself wisely and righteously. But there were passages in this bold address that made the dry bones of mere book learning rattle and the ghosts of tradition squeak and gibber. Twenty years later the essential wisdom of this advanced thinker was admitted with better grace.

The oration itself was not remarkable for its scholarly form nor for its periodic flow. Its words were not academic; its quotations were from the literature of protest. It was rather a shrill call to duty amidst the perils that beset a republic, that the scholar share with the citizen the burden of shaping a nation. It was the final legacy of a veteran instructor of the people at large as contrasted with the cloistered teaching of a university. He had his own message to his college, and he delivered it with the unsparing fidelity that marked his discourse throughout half a century. More than most of his utterances it should be read in its entirety, since it was one which was written before it was spoken, of which, however, there was no hint in the delivery.

In this the dramatic element appeared once more. The

old man eloquent and valiant afield so long, had returned
to the arena of youthful contention in his collegiate years.
Unlike his fellows, he had not been a frequent participator
in class reunions and fraternity festivals. *Alma mater*
herself had no benignant smile of welcome for him during
five stormy decades, and no thought of crowning him with
academic honours who had won the highest distinction
in the art of arts, and had taught half a continent to do
justly and love mercy. With hesitation and doubt, curiosity
and fear, she at last permitted him, like Paul before Festus,
to speak for himself. The venerable crusader had fought
too many battles afar to play soldier at home, and he looked
for the vulnerable spot in the scholastic body which made
it indifferent and valueless in reforming eras, and pierced
it with Apollo's shaft. There was the customary writhing
and the usual protest; but also the perplexed wonder at
the dissent and unbounded admiration for the grace and
efficiency of his entrancing eloquence, and for his undaunted
courage of convictions. As faithful to these before university dignitaries as before the commonalty, he stood for
what was high and heroic to the end: a censor of wrong,
an advocate of right; a defender of the oppressed, and a
prophet of a better future.

Such, in brief, was the substance of Phillips's oratory.
Whether it be called a lecture, address, speech, oration
or discourse, it was always adapted to the occasion, the subject, and the audience with its varying moods. In this
versatility of adaptation lay much of his power. People did
not listen to an oratorical performance on some high theme,
but to a personal argument or discourse of interest addressed
to their understanding as directly as in the conversation

of one man with another, in the manner of one with a group of listeners, and broadened and elevated as the group swells to a crowd. But the speaker himself did not change essentially, as the actor must. He produced his effects without the artifices which belong to the stage, and always with simplicity because with the utmost sincerity, yet with certain characteristics which may be noted as belonging to the form of his discourse as distinguished from its substance. Some of these are of personal interest.

XXV

THE FORM OF HIS ORATORY

IN THE foregoing account of the life and labours of
Wendell Phillips sundry characteristics of the orator,
the agitator, and the man have revealed themselves. It remains to gather these into the unity which belongs to a personality and gives it distinction.

He was known to most people chiefly as a public speaker.
For one person who saw him in Boston there were thousands
who had heard him for an hour on some platform. If alive
now they would recall him as he appeared in the winter
evenings of the old lyceum lecture years, when expectant
audiences watched the dial for the moment when the presiding officer should usher in the lecturer and introduce
him to an impatient house. It was a thankless task to this
prior functionary, and if overdone was trying to the assembly, eager to hear from the chief speaker. Meanwhile
the lecturer had ample time to lay aside the well-known
gray overcoat and felt hat, and to classify the throng before
him with the accuracy with which a geologist makes note
of a stony field. The speaker on a thousand platforms
had learned to pick out boulders of the glacial period and
rocks of the carboniferous age, and could distinguish sand-
stone from granite at a glance. Moreover, he was quick
to discern fossil formations and to discover if there were a

living organism among them. All this he readily saw and more, and pitched the keynote of his discourse accordingly.

What the audience first noticed as he sat waiting was a head of classic mould, with clear-cut profile and assured mien, slightly severe in its serenity, a person not to be easily confused, suggesting defensive and aggressive qualities not to be trifled with. Steady blue eyes, a blond complexion of ruddy cast, and tawny hair betokened a sanguine temperament of good hope and great courage. The regulation introduction over, a tall, well-proportioned man, with broad shoulders and deep chest, stepped to the front of the platform with patrician grace and self-possession, having no manuscript or notes in hand, and needing no support of desk or table. In a forehead broad and high, a commanding presence, and a far-carrying voice lay the resources of his art. The first impression was pleasing rather than overwhelming, that of an accomplished gentleman, entirely at home on the stage, who had something of serious importance that he wished to say to his listeners. These he seemed to address as individuals, and as if there were a dozen of them instead of hundreds. Yet no one of a thousand but believed that he himself was one of the addressed. Largely, this impression came from the tones of voice with which the speaker began his remarks.

It is easier to recall than to portray that voice. Technically, it has been described as of no great range or volume, and thin in the higher register, but rich in the lower notes, a baritone whose distinction was in its quality or timbre and the absolute purity and vibratory resonance which sent it to the end of the largest halls. It has also been likened to the penetrating mellowness of the flute and violin rather than the blast of a bugle. Its chief value, however, aside from its reaching and finding power, lay in its flexibility and modulation to every shade of meaning, as in conversation. In the middle notes of ordinary speech he would give a new significance, distinction, and discrimination to a word or phrase without raising his voice, running the entire scale of emotion in colloquial tones, with neither scream nor bellow, whisper nor shout. If he knew his limitations, he also knew how to indemnify himself. To do this required the perfection of understanding and taste to suit the tone to the thought, which belongs only to the highest art or the profoundest feeling. With this man every note was true because natural, and natural because sincere and out of the depths of profound conviction. From first to last he was terribly in earnest, and the burden of his speech was on that lower level which men naturally use when they mean what they say.

Furthermore, this naturalness of sincere speech in moderate tones was greatly helped in its audibility by a distinct but unaffected enunciation and a deliberateness of utterance which never lagged into slowness. Intensity in many great speakers of his time ran into a rapid and sometimes boisterous flow of words, with hardly perceptible separation between the drops of the stream; his words were as distinct as those of a printed page, and every vocal vowel and consonant as clear, securing the first requisite of speech as of composition — intelligibility. There was no wearying strain of the listener to catch every word, as there was also none to understand what he meant. Therefore he did not tire his hearers, but kept them in a restful mood so far as exertion on their part was concerned. Moreover, there was no appearance of bodily fatigue or mental effort on the speaker's part to induce a sympathetic feeling in the sensitive listener; as in the instance of certain eloquent but laborious preachers in New England and Old in the last generation, whom our ancestors would have called "painful." Rarely, and after much speaking, he used to say that his throat would not allow him to continue longer, and it is on record that at such times his voice occasionally broke; otherwise the listener might well have believed that public speaking was as naturally pleasant to him as singing to the public singer.

His delivery was as natural as the tones of his voice. With graceful attitude, so poised as to turn easily to right and left, yet seldom changing position or walking the stage, he could readily adapt action to sentiments. His gestures were so in harmony with the thought and its moderate tones of expression that they seemed fewer than they were; and because his strong words were so forceful they did not need emphasizing by violent gesticulating, which often enfeebles more than it reënforces speech. The referential or antithetic movement of a hand, or the placing of one upon the palm of the other in asserting a proposition or establishing a conclusion, all far inside the windmill sweep of the primæval American orator, were only such as are used in animated conversation — outside Romance peoples. But, whatever they might be, they were symbols of the sentiment uttered and, like the needle of the compass, significant of polar direction without reaching clear to the poles. Yet there was no hint of the awkward constraint which self-consciousness imposes on the unaccustomed speaker. It was reserved action, itself the pledge of unemployed power. In the hearer's certainty that there was such a store of unused force lay a large part of Phillips's subtle attraction. Would he exhibit all his strength in some supreme passage? Or would he go on in his level discourse, moulding hearts and wills with an action of mind and voice, of thought and speech, as quiet and sure as the polished engine whose work seems its play? What storage of electric power unconsumed lay at the radiating point of the wireless communication which was flowing from him to his hearers? And while they waited expectant the hour flew by, the speaker closed as quietly as he began, and the throng reluctantly moved away, pleased but hungering still; delighted, but unable to tell why; convinced, but against their convictions; persuaded, but contrary to their will.

This contrariety of will and opinion, when the slavery question was his theme, often made the temper of his hearers far more unquiet than his own. Indeed, he was sometimes the only unmoved person in the house, while a part of the audience stormed with resentful rage, and the rest of it was wrathful against the disturbers of the assembly. Occasionally these pro-slavery and anti-slavery sentiments would surge together like the Gulf and Arctic currents by the Cape of the Pilgrims. In the early days forces of madness and hate drove hissing and foaming against him alone. Then he would stand unmoved as a sea-girt tower until the storm was over; or with a flash of scornful wit or a word of wisdom would calm the tempest as with a "Peace, be still." Few were the turbulent and malicious crowds that he could not tame into quietude enough to hear what he had to say, however they might receive it or act upon it afterward. Sometimes it would have been safer for him if he had not compelled them to listen. When the

spell was broken forty men were needed more than once
to protect him from the violence his speech had provoked,
but which his magnetic presence had controlled so long
as he was before the audience. This often became a mob
in the street, as it would have been in the hall had he not
subdued it. Such triumphs belong to few speakers in
twenty-five centuries of recorded eloquence. Many men
have won applause from concurrent hearers, and some
from divided houses; as Webster, for instance, in his reply
to Hayne; but only one American orator in our history
has been able to master hostile assemblies year after year
in one state after another until the tide of opposition ebbed.
It is one thing to ride with a storm and upon it; another
to stem and to quell it. Therefore the primacy must be
accorded to this speaker, not only for the outer graces of
oratory before a courteous assembly, but for supremacy
over such antagonism as never was met by the advocate
of any other cause for a long period.

Next after the exterior qualities of presence, voice, and
action, with the charm called magnetism, must be considered certain elements which belong to the mental contingent in the compound product of oratory. The most
obvious of these is the language which the speaker uses.
The style of this, like his manner, was free from pretence;
simple, sincere, and therefore intelligible. Often it was
colloquial, bordering on the familiar and conversational;
but always in accord with the precept he sometimes gave
to young aspirants: "Never use a word in conversation that
you would not use in public speech." Consequently, his
own diction was pure without being stilted, and free from
any approach to slang, which is the special temptation of

extemporaneous speakers when thoughts outrun words. So elevated was his taste that when he sometimes clipped a final g, it seemed in him like the little negligences of dress or manner that often distinguish the self-assured from the careful gentleman. If he occasionally pronounced either and philosophy with a long i, it was not because he did not know the better usage, nor because some Englishman did so; and if he frequently used can't, was n't, should n't, and similar colloquial forms, it was because he was talking to that representative person, or a dozen of him in the audience, whom the old Greeks called *tis* — a certain man. But to his common words, addressed to the common sense of the multitude before him, he could give an inflection, a movement, an emphasis, and a force that clothed them with a new significance, If there was one element he lacked it was the pathetic. Full of compassion as he was, and tender hearted, he did not greatly affect pathos or move an audience to tears. Perhaps his prevailing moods, defensive and aggressive, did not much favour pathos.

His career had called for the opposite quality of invective. In this he was masterful. Irony, sarcasm, ridicule, were so many arrows from a full quiver, shot without rant or scream, in a voice quiet and steady, but finding their mark with unerring precision. And the man or measure or policy that was struck seemed to wither into immediate contempt. It is doubtful if any milder treatment would have served his purpose so well in those stormy years of hand-to-hand warfare against a giant wrong. The drawback to it was an undiscriminating stroke now and then which slashed some friend who had ventured out over the circle which the reformer in his intensity had drawn with a short radius around himself and his own companions. Outside this circle all were aliens, and they as much as any who within it were not far away but yet not close to the central standard. For them he had severe reserves of criticism. Still, however violent these were, he was seldom known to be thrown off his balance. When Kossuth came here to plead for his oppressed countrymen, but had no word of sympathy for Southern slaves, knowing that this would interfere with his success, Phillips's scorn for the Hungarian's restricted philanthropy transcended its customary restraints. Doubtless the national encouragement that the advocate of foreign freedom received here magnified the essential inconsistency of his plea, and Phillips, in upbraiding a partial vision of universal liberty, intended to score Kossuth's supporters as well. They were so many, both North and South, that the aggregation ran away with the agitator's temper for once, and he overdid the onset, as most men do oftener than he upon equal provocation. It was in these scornful moods, however, that he was most brilliant, and was at his best when the audience treated him worst. No man of them could spring a surprise on him to which he did not send back a ready retort that made the interrupter wish he had held his tongue. The laugh he had unwisely sent rippling toward the speaker came back with a roar as of the sea which engulfed Pharaoh and the Egyptians. The rash wight was overwhelmed by the shouting of his fellows, who could not resist the sudden turn of wit that the accomplished orator had made. Those who had once felt its sting learned not to venture within its reach a second time.

No enumeration of the great orator's qualities would be

complete without mention of his versatility. This was apparent in the ease with which he could turn from one theme to another, sometimes in the same hour; but it was still more evident in the almost infinite variety which he gave to the chief topics of thirty years' discussion. To speak a hundred times in a year upon the same subject, and to have verbatim reports of these speeches printed, and keep the seeming freshness of new utterance was a feat which few of the orators of the lecture period accomplished as they made the circuit of the states with two or three well-worn manuscripts, which, like casks of water on a long voyage, had a period when they nauseated the lecturer at least. But this agitator could draw off-hand a dozen unlike draughts from the same source, albeit the basis was the same acid, cleansing and caustic, but so tempered to each occasion and taste that the Scriptural question concerning sweet water and bitter from the same fountain seemed to be answered affirmatively. He would go from city to city and by some sleight of hand produce from one repertory addresses on the single lesson of the hour, differing as widely as the names of those cities differ, and adapted to the diverse moods of their people. Moreover, one might compare the reports of successive speeches and find that their similarity was chiefly in their common theme and general tone. Occasionally an illustrative anecdote, always a good one, told in an inimitable manner, would be repeated, and sometimes a favourite comparison used more than once; but the places were few in which the same sentence and paragraph occurred, while the tone of discourse always varied with degrees of longitude. The secret of this diversity lay in the speaker's quick apprehension of his audience and his knowledge of public sentiment in the region. Any one might guess the difference between Worcester and Philadelphia on abolition; but a keener perception would be required to discriminate between the cities along the lines from Boston to Chicago and further westward. A traveller once heard on three successive evenings three differing speeches on the same subject between and including New York and Springfield which were adapted to the temper and temperament of as many audiences. Such performance, so far as it can be explained, must be charged to a mind full of knowledge about the general theme, and which had brooded over it in its hundred phases, until any one of them was replete with prolific interest. Like a dweller in the city of a hundred gates this man saw from any one of them roads radiating wide and far, leading into territory unknown and unsuspected by the home-staying and sordid. Therefore the reach of his vision and speech embraced every place and interest and policy that a great and central wrong might corrupt by malarial winds blowing to every point of the horizon. For him to turn from one aspect or prospect to another was as easy as to address the right or left, front or rear of an assembly; which, however, did not always recognize the essential unity of his subject in the diversity of his manifold exposition.

There was another and rarer but most impressive feature which has sometimes been overlooked in traditional accounts of his prevailing colloquial address — that is, the beauty and sublime impressiveness of his closing paragraphs when the subject required it. Occasionally the same perfection of rhythmic speech marked the end of some division of an address. The example that will first occur to most readers is the close of the lecture on Toussaint l'Ouverture, since it is now one of the oftenest declaimed in schools. Those who were so fortunate as to hear him will never forget the great orator delivering in clear and quiet tones the lines beginning, "You think me a fanatic to-night, for you read history, not with your eyes, but your prejudices." And they will recall through the years the ascending steps up which he led his hero past the brave and the good of all time, and then wrote "in the clear blue above them all the name of the soldier, the statesman, and the martyr." It was a climax of biographic and historical argument to which not one in a hundred of his hearers expected to assent at the start, but at the close found themselves assisting at the apotheosis of a "St. Domingo chief, an unmixed Negro, with no drop of white blood in his veins," as the speaker defined him at the start, and he was apt to make the strongest statement of his proposition first, get hissed, and then prove its truth. At the close, L'Ouverture appeared to outshine all the stars in the bright constellation of renown. Especially noteworthy also are the perorations of the addresses entitled "Under the Flag" and "War for the Union," "The State of the Country" and "Lincoln's Election," "Christianity a Battle," "The Education of the People," "The Scholar in a Republic," "Daniel O'Connell," and "William Lloyd Garrison." The last two, with other tributes, show that when he chose he could rival the "classic eulogies of brave old men and martyrs," which he used to say he had by heart.

It is natural to ask how far education contributed to the sum total of his excellence as a public speaker. No amount of training would alone have made him eminent; nor would merely natural gifts if unimproved. But to his princely endowment of these he added more labour and pains than is commonly known. At an early day he had excellent opportunities to study audiences of every grade and size, from the groups in country schoolhouses and dozens in town houses to the city throngs in Faneuil Hall, and others in Boston, New York, and elsewhere. His immediate success in these gave him confidence; but there were things to be learned from hard-headed countrymen about themselves and himself and the Cause, which he was not slow to catch to his profit and improvement. By near contact with the crowd he found the need and cultivated the practice of debate between himself and them — a most necessary equipment in his unpopular crusade. So the frequent repetition of such a lecture as The Lost Arts enabled him to learn what was best liked, until at the thousandth delivery it was as near perfection as such a popular discourse could be made. In a less degree some of his abolition speeches got emendations or alterations which frequent repetition suggested, at the same time preventing stereotyped versions. He had enough of ordinary human nature to profit by mistakes, and possibly to humour the unaccountable adoration of bosh which hearers often display to the discredit of their understanding and taste. But his general effort was to lift them to a higher grade intellectually, morally, and politically. If he had to descend to the level of the average comprehension in words and thoughts, he never sunk below it; and crediting the common people with uncommon sense, lifted them up with the progress of his discourse, and led them on year after year with the growth of national sentiment for freedom. Thus he grew in his own methods as a leader of thought and action by personal discussion and effort in the great movement of the republic, without allying himself with politics or party, creating and moulding the opinion and belief which underlies all political action and eventual legislation, until that which was at first called heretical and fanatical became in the end sane and constitutional.

There were other qualities which contributed to the versatility of his eloquence that may be enumerated by recalling the illustrious Ten of Attica, who together made oratory the first of arts. It is too much to say that a modern speaker could appropriate them all and retain his personality; but some of his hearers might have thought that he learned from Pericles directness of address and disregard of popular favour, attended by restrained and majestic diction when occasion demanded; or at another time the simplicity and vividness of Lycias and his quick discernment of opportunities; or most often the intense earnestness of Isæus, passing to closing passages suggesting the melodious cadences of Isocrates when he took oratory into the service of good citizenship in a republic. And always in his extemporaneous speech there was the spontaneity attributed to Æschines and his seeming freedom from laborious preparation, aided by a colloquial manner that placed the hearer on friendly terms, while its dignity ensured his respect. To all this was added a restful variety which Demosthenes valued so much for securing the hearers' attention, ranging from conversational vivacity to severe solemnity, with a fusing current of emotion throughout, itself controlled and intensified by masterful restraint, the secret of supreme command. For the invective, which was so marked a feature of his discourse at times, he had provocation frequent and strong; also eminent predecessors and fine examples from Cicero and his Philippics, Tertullian and his bold censure of the Carthaginians, Ambrose and his charges against the evils rife at Milan, and many another brave spirit who dared to raise his protest against the wrongs of his age. Or, nearer his own, Phillips could find Fox's famous diatribe, and Patrick Henry's speech on the stamp act, and John Randolph's defence of slavery. Many of these, however, had an undertone of bitter resentment in which this orator did not indulge. He expected personal abuse and took it as an incident of his mission, sparing his irony for those who through greed or in fear or for political advancement stood in the way of what they knew was just and right. For such there were no words of a common scold, but such as turned deftly against them a tide of opinion and even accusing consciences within. It was a part of the orator's system — to enlist mightier forces than his own single-handed effort, and a part of his philosophy that "one on the right side is a majority."

This favourite saying of his suggests the epigrammatic element which abounds in his discourse. After figures of speech and thought or apt anecdotes, nothing fastens the gist of a paragraph in the hearer's memory like barbed epigrams, which are not necessarily poisoned arrows. Ecclesiastes, the Preacher, had their staying quality in mind when he spoke of the "words which are as nails well fastened by the masters of assemblies"—or "collectors of sentences," according to the later version. Phillips had a condensing invention which could mass the weighty discourse of an hour into a single sentence, point it as with steel, and drive it through triple-plated armour of prejudice, greed, or wrong. A long list of epigrams might be compiled, of which the following are examples:

There is no republican road to safety but constant distrust.

They have put wickedness into the statute book, and its destruction is just as certain as if they had put gunpowder under the Capitol.

Power is ever shifting from the many to the few.

The race is rich enough without the greatest intellects God ever let the devil buy.

Popular agitation is the life of a republic.

Whether in chains or in laurels, Liberty knows nothing but victories.

Never look for an age when the people can be quiet—and safe.

On God's side, one is a majority.

As an agitator his hope rested on this principle. He believed that the people would eventually side with righteousness when they saw it clearly. Therefore his labour began with them wherever any would listen; in a country schoolhouse, town hall, or vestry in his native state, speaking to a dozen sympathizers and a hundred opposers. After years of patient struggle with prejudice his audiences swelled to two or three thousand, with only enough opposition to stir him to his best achievement. To leaders and legislators he did not pay much attention. Politicians represented the average sentiment of the people and parties, mixing with the masses instead of leading them. His idea of leadership was to be so far in advance of the host that few could see the outpost they were expected to reach. He took this

extreme position from the first, called to the sons of men
to come up to it, never went back toward them to offer
any less stringent measure or to make a single compromise
in an age and country of compromises. Abolish slavery,
make citizens of the Negroes as you are making them out
of the dregs of every nation dumped on our shores. To
colonize men of all shades in Africa was to send mixed
American blood there; to pay their owners for them was
to repay them for their fathers' piracy and for their own
improvement of a stolen inheritance. This was high and
unpopular ground to take in the 'thirties, and even in the
'fifties, but in the next decade the North and the civilized
world came to a moral state and a conviction about universal
freedom that made the further existence of slavery impossible. Phillips did not ask for himself more than the
average of public opinion is now ready to accord him —
there will always be differences of view; but none can
deny that his work was done, not like many who received
their full meed of praise for an eleventh hour of labour,
but as one of the few who bore the burden and heat of
the day, when there was only scorn and hatred for the
same words and deeds which later won praise and honour
for other men. Therefore, whatever opinion is handed
down by tradition or gathered from contemporary records,
to be stereotyped as history, with regard to occasional mistakes such as all men make, those of this man may, like
some of his sharp words, be considered incident to the
intense earnestness of one who saw a great wrong early
in the day of its power and laboured until nightfall for its
removal, surrendering all other ambitions to a single purpose, which the majority now are ready to call good or high

or noble. It is the old story of the prophets — the children are garnishing the sepulchres of those whom the fathers stoned. It will not be strange, then, as the account of a great episode of American history is written and rewritten, if this agitator take his place with reformers who came to their own after the dust of strife was laid, and their work and motives appeared in the perspective that time and disinterestedness bring. This millennial year will not arrive for him until the day of present estrangement is over, a heritage from the last generation; but it will eventually come, as the day of deliverance came from a national evil through a conflict of which the present reminiscence is only as the clouds vanishing after a storm.

As Phillips's public record will be that of an orator and agitator, so his traits that will be best known are those which belong to an advocate of reform; aggressive, uncompromising, insistent, incessant, perceptive, sagacious, undaunted. Those who heard of his methods or read his speeches were surprised when they met the man in social converse. Apart from the arena with its severities of attack and defence, he met his fellow-men with a warm-heartedness and gentle friendliness which lasted through all the years of animosity that might have embittered a smaller soul. Confident, as he had reason to be, of the wisdom of his matured conclusions, he was patient with those who had well-considered views of their own ; and in the narrowed circle of intimate friends the testimony of one of them, in a letter to Mrs. Phillips, would have been generally endorsed in other instances besides this one:

The preëminent magnanimity of your dear husband in the affair so interests me that I cannot withhold from you the expression of my admiration of it. It is so entirely in unison with the whole tenour of his beautiful life and conduct. The dignified forbearance which he, so wisely, sees fit to exercise in these issues will doubtless speak even more eloquently than the article which we all know he might have written, had he seen fit. . . . After all, there is no foresight like his, whether in his silence or utterance or in the entire beautiful harmony of his life.

It would be possible to trace the ramifications of these two prominent traits of courage for righteousness and goodwill toward mankind. Of the former, instances were necessarily more public than those of the latter, which were frequently in the direction of unmentioned deeds of charity. His executor found a private memorandum of gifts to needy causes and persons amounting to $64,000; and in settling the joint estate discovered that Mr. and Mrs. Phillips had spent nearly all their considerable property in charities and reforms. It was then known, beyond what had been believed, that the principles which had been proclaimed abroad had been practised at home. Besides, there were fireside virtues in the observance of which conspicuous persons often drop to ordinary levels, and home becomes a place of reactions from public strain. To many, a house hushed for invalidism, with needful seclusion from much companionship, might have its depression as the months and years wore on, even if the lover period were prolonged and the sympathies of young hearts were unfading, as, according to unvarying testimony, they were in the two who lived in retirement, without loneliness or gloom, and with never a thought but for the health of the one and the happiness of the other. Every sacrifice did not procure the first one's health: the making them seemed to be that other's life-long joy. Perhaps, too, the ostracism attending those who encountered political and commercial prejudices made the hearthstone more precious; but there must have been a sense of solitude in the midst of a populous town and of aversion on its streets which would grate on an honest and kindly heart. Only a rare manliness could withstand the atmospheric pressure of disapproval, relentless through half a century, without growing morose. To keep a cheerful temper, a genial heart, and an open hand, to forgive misunderstanding and malice, to hold fast one's faith in the essential rightness of human consciences, to rise above untruth, misrepresentation, slander, and the unspoken thought of evil requires the truest and most heroic manliness that is given to men, or kept with all diligence amid adverse conditions. Orators and reformers have sometimes performed brilliant and worthy tasks without these homelier and inconspicuous virtues, and have gone down in history as illustrious benefactors of the race: this man added unostentatious qualities to the conspicuous; and because he did, under untoward circumstances, it is well that the generations that follow him should know how good a man he was, as well as how complete an orator and how sincere a reformer. It is moderate praise to say that he was a shining example of Cato the Censor's definition of an orator — "A good man skilled in speaking."

XXVI

REMAINDERS

IN THE account of any life worth commemorating there is the frequent opportunity to insert trivial matters that have an interest of their own, but do not belong to the higher plane along which the narrative should move, like a planet in its orbit. Yet often the intervening face of the sky with its clouds and storms, and even the nearer earth with its sunshine and shadow are of more interest than wheeling worlds in the sidereal heavens. So in an exalted career there are always minor features that appeal to our curiosity because they reveal human elements on a level with the humdrum existence which the majority lead. They exhibit the phases and the routine of living which differ among men no more than their occupations.

The life which has been sketched in its professional aspect was no exception to this law of the common lot. Like other lives it had to be maintained by the ordinary means, although there was no necessity for other labour by one with an income of from $10,000 to $15,000 a year and more when lecturing. It was largely life in a New England city and in the neighbouring countryside, or on the highways and byways of travel near and far. Though preëminently a home life, it was also among throngs of busy men, among the needy, the unfortunate, the poor, and fugitives from bondage. Like his neighbour and relative, Dr. Holmes, he loved the very streets of Boston, he used to say, as Mammon loved the golden pavements of heaven. The Common was his boyhood's playground and the park where he walked daily for threescore years, and where, strolling with Edmund Quincy once, an Englishman remarked of them to Ticknor that they were the only men he had seen there who looked like gentlemen. In his modern Athens he was a peripatetic philosopher, not so abstracted that anything worth noting escaped him, and not so absent-minded as to forget on his homeward way to get the choicest delicacies for the invalid wife who was waiting to hear the latest news and to be read the newest book by one whose reading charmed all who were fortunate enough to hear him.

Nor was the domestic life absolutely secluded. It was shared occasionally by a few friends rather than by a wide circle of acquaintances; by children often when adults could not be welcomed. In the modest brick house inherited from her father by Mrs. Phillips there was a dining-room on the ground floor where French was the language of the table at the half-past seven breakfast, the two o'clock dinner, and the half-past six supper, where no product of the sugar cane was used, nor any cotton fabric produced by slave labour, in all the house. Of the double parlours above, one is said to have been used as a depository for the newspapers accumulated on lecture trips and for many additional journals of all shades which he subscribed to and carefully read. It was also a library containing 2,500 volumes, stocked largely with books of the historical and essay type and many pamphlets. If he had a favourite author it was De Tocqueville, and his "Democracy in

America" is quoted by the orator oftener than any other book. In this room he would sometimes shut himself for days when an important occasion called for special preparation; meditating upon his subject in an easy chair or on a lounge, since his nature was inclined to indolence — if his wife's remark in a letter to a friend that "Wendell is as lazy and easy as ever" means anything. His own saying that "writing is a slavery — a man chained to an inkpot," and the evidence of a few surviving notes to neighbours show how sincere was his aversion to a pen. But there was either intense mental labour or immense talent behind the continuous discourse of a lifetime, indicating the genius of a great public speaker which could be independent of desk and pen. He held, moreover, that few men could be both good writers and effective speakers; nor did he count himself as an exception. With the Hebrew poet he might have said, "My tongue is the pen of a ready writer."

He was also an omniverous reader. Newspapers, pamphlets, magazines, and books furnished incidents, anecdotes, facts and principles which were stored in a tenacious and reproductive memory, to be summoned by association, fitness, or contrast whenever needed. Therefore he was always prepared to speak. When committees asked him if he happened to have this or that lecture with him he replied, "I carry all my lectures with me," meaning in his head. Sometimes he ran two together for the thrifty who wished to be sure of their money's worth, without their discovery of the dividing line. He took pay for the literary or scientific half only, if the other was anti-slavery. Yet his income from some of the former was large: $150,000 from the repetition of The Lost Arts alone, it is said.

Considering the length of his career, he was on the road more than any other speaker in the country; and what would be remarkable in these days, without a serious accident in fifty years. Against stationary perils of cold rooms and damp sheets he guarded himself by the blanket shawl, which was every man's companion and multiform friend in the 'fifties and later; while to avoid the uncertainties of so-called tea he carried his own favourite brand of breakfast tea which he frequently prepared to his taste, particularly the three cups which with three raw eggs were his bracer for an evening's speaking. It would not be safe to conclude that this prescription will make an orator of every speaker.

More to the purpose is his answer to a student's inquiry for helpful suggestions: "Practice is the best of teachers. Think out your subject, and read all you can about it. Fill your mind; and then talk simply and naturally. Forget that you are to make a speech, or are making one. You are to carry a purpose, effect an object; then having forgotten yourself, you will be likelier to do your best. Talk up to an audience, not down to it. The commonest audience can relish the best thing you can say if you say it properly. Be simple; be earnest." This advice was exemplified by himself, and is good for any speaker as far as it goes, but an unmentioned element is necessary to such success as his. He was too modest to name it, or perhaps could not define it.

Ready as he was to speak on almost any topic, he was not at the beck of every occasion that was to be enlivened by speeches, especially public dinners, where under the dulling influence of solids and fluids, alcoholic fumes and tobacco smoke, orotund commonplaces often pass for wisdom and facetiousness for wit. Wine he did not drink, nor, according to Sir Walter Raleigh's phrase, did he "drink tobacco." Modern table-talk, which unlike its historic predecessor is postponed till all have fed, did not appeal to him. He relished more keenly such conversation as was heard from diners in the days of Hazlitt and Coleridge and Wilson, or in his own time at the dinners of the Atlantic Club. Ordinarily he was a better listener than talker, learning something from everyone, although the charm of his conversation was delightful in congenial company. His mood was reflective and his thoughts too constantly upon serious matters which concerned public welfare in the last century to favour the lighter conversational habit which sparkles and breaks like foam over the deep currents of life, public and private. These he was quick to discern and was not silent then; as, for example, when one morning he was sitting by a Southern woman, a niece of Jefferson Davis, who was returning from a lecture trip not so well paid as himself, with whom he insisted upon sharing his own profits of the evening before. As she did not know what these were, she could not know that he gave her all he had received, as he did to a poor student now and then. His benefactions for a period of thirty years have already been mentioned.

If he was not a great talker it was for no lack of ideas or readiness. For instance: a minister in Ohio returning from a convention in a car full of clerical brethren, felt called upon to stand up and ask him in the stillness of a stopping place:

"Are you Mr. Phillips?"

"I am, sir."

"Are you trying to free the niggers?"

"Yes, sir; I am an abolitionist."

"Well, why do you preach your doctrines up here? Why don't you go over into Kentucky?"

"Excuse me, are you a preacher?"

"I am, sir."

"Are you trying to save souls from hell?"

"Yes, sir; that is my business."

"Well, why don't you go there?"

The assailant hurried into the smoker amidst a roar of unsanctified laughter.

It may be superfluous to ask in closing what Phillips's position would be on this and that question of the present day. Several of them he anticipated in his outlook beyond his own generation, generally on the line of subsequent march, sometimes on one which was not followed, just as population has not always followed the predictions of shrewd city prospectors in the West. In the present strife between labour and capital his course could be divined from his alliance with the working man thirty years ago, and he certainly would have no sympathy with the centralization of wealth, against which he warned the nation in his later years. On the ever-present but never settled temperance question he would see his prohibition policy obtaining favour in sections where he least expected legislative aid, and might redouble his efforts with individuals, as his own manner was from the beginning. To foreign immigrants he would fling the doors wide open, even if the assimilative powers of the country should be severely taxed, believing that all children born here become American, whatever their fathers may have been. And after, if not before, hospitality to wanderers from Europe, Asia, and the Orient he might be urging better protection for our dumb but steadfast friends, especially in chambers of torture known as places of scientific research. On disputed issues of tariff and currency he might still be not infallible, as many experts have shown themselves not to be. On the race question he would have a great deal to say. After all, it may be doubted if he would find any problem to call out his best effort as in his own day, whose stirring issues were a part of the forces which made him the power that he was. Moreover, he would not now find a group of speakers comparable to that constellation which surrounded him then, and not without its influence upon him and one another, making the age one to be taken account of in the history of public speech. It is not necessary, however, to suppose that this art has perished forever because it is in the hollow of a wave whose crests appear at wide intervals along the course of twenty-four centuries. Its sweep is long, but it is sure to rise again in some future period when deep shall call unto deep, and when one man shall sway a thousand because his heart is true, his vision clear, his gifts great, and raised to their highest power by the stress of the times. If such an age is reformatory, as those which have produced the best oratory have always been, it is beyond question that among examples in the past the one which will be earliest studied, because of its own excellence and its latest position, will be whatever survives of the eloquence of Wendell Phillips.

INDEX

INDEX

A

Abolition of slavery, 1, 126
  aggressive and educational, 180, 186
  immediate, 129
  in District of Columbia, 235
"Abolition movement, Philosophy of the," 146.
Abolition speeches, 332
Abolitionism, growth of, 77
  in Boston, 101, 141, 142
  shades of, 186
Abolitionists, 22
  British, 22, 131, 140
  criticism of one another, 167
Adam, Professor, 80, 81
Adams, Charles Francis, 122
Adams, John, 197
Adams, John Quincy, 40, 124, 127
Adams, Samuel, 63, 139
Addresses of Wendell Phillips, 327
Address to the nation, 119
Advanced positions, 37, 120
Aggressiveness, 361
Agitation, abolition, 74, 211
  in Congress, 128, 156
  preliminary to political, 191
Alcott, Bronson, 253
Allies, zealous, 152
Alton riot, 51
  meeting in Faneuil Hall, 214
Amalgamation, 28, 249
Anderson, Mayor, 254
Andersonville, 274, 277
Andrew, John A., 124
Anti-slavery cause, 19
Anti-slavery societies, 20, 63
  American, 79,
  disbanded, 289

Anti-slavery societies—*continued*
  Boston, 67
  British and foreign, 81
  New England, 22
Anti-slavery sentiment, 20, 217
  growth of, 133
  in the North, 211
Antony's speech to the populace, 61
Appleton, Thomas, 6
Argument, 324
Arguments, legal, of W. P., 330, 331
Athletics in the 'thirties, 12, 16
Attucks, Crispus, 193
Austin, James T. 54

B

Bailey, Gamaliel, 50
Balance of power, 135, 176
Ballots vs. bullets, 221
Banks, N. P., 186
Beecher, Henry Ward, 92, 141, 154
  Lyman, Dr., 13
Benevolence of Phillips, 362
Bowditch, W. I., viii
Birney, J. G., 49, 80, 81
Blagden, Mrs. J. G., viii, 20
  MSS., 87, 206, 233, 264
Books and reading, Phillips's, 36
Boston, 151
  in 1810, 3
  subserviency of, 146
Boston Latin School, 6
  massacre anniversary, 193
  mobs, 23, 100, 214, 216
Bowring, Sir John, 80
Bright, John, 249
Brooks, Preston S., 174
  assault on Sumner, 175
  commended for, 176

371

Phillips, Wendell—*continued*
cellaneous reading, 16; admitted to the bar, 17; business in office and courts, 18; prospects, 19; early abolitionism, 31; witness of Garrison mob, 31; how far an abolitionist before this time, 32; influence of Ann Terry Greene, 33; engagement and marriage, 34; meets Garrison, 35; contrast of conditions, 36; his idealism, 37; announces his position in a resolution and a speech, 38, 39; second speech, 40; tribute to John Quincy Adams, 41; defence of the right of petition, 42; endorsement of Adams, 43; fundamental principles first advocated, 44; inconspicuous at first, 45; Fourth of July address at Salem, 46; desertion of friends, 46; other sacrifices, 46; the call, 47; renunciation, 48; in Faneuil Hall, 54; speech on the murder of Lovejoy, 55; its importance, 57; recognition, 57; commendation and detraction by contemporaries, 58, 59; the dramatic element, 60, 61, 62; labours afield, 63; Marlboro' Chapel speech, 64; argument before the Mass. Legislature, 65; on annexation of Texas, 66; detail work, 67; president of Boston Anti-slavery Society, 67; on slavery in District of Columbia, 69; speech in Faneuil Hall, 70; work of instruction and organizing, 71; general agent of the Massachusetts Anti-slavery Society, 72; uncongenial allies, 73; agitation his method, 74; work interrupted by European travel,

Phillips, Wendell—*continued*
76; commendation, 77; in Europe, 78; delegate to London convention, 78; the disturbing woman question, 79; a stormy debate, 80; Phillips's protesting position, 81; addresses the British India Society, 82; continental travel and letters, 83; returns home, 84; housekeeping, 86; family letters, 87; dislike of writing, 89; mental composition, 89; on the lecture platform, 90; its educational value, 91; Phillips's early lectures, 92; on the "Lost Arts," 92; characterized, 93; its popularity, 94; an abolition lecture, 95; character of audiences, 96; on Irish Appeal to Americans, 97; abstract of speech, 98; fundamental issues before abolition, 99; a fugitive slave in Boston, 100; speech in Faneuil Hall on arrest of Latimer, 101; attacks constitution, 102; provocation, 103; an orator's struggle, 104; invective, 105; opposition to political alliances, 108; will not vote, 108; clerical antagonism, 109; his orthodoxy, 110; speaks on adverse influence of church, 110; note by Neal on his oratory, 111; recognition and leadership, 112; address to President Tyler, 112; pamphlets and lectures, 113; resents treatment of Mr. Hoar by South Carolina, 114; on second Irish address, 115; admiration of O'Connell, 116; protest against politics, 117; holds to his original methods, 118; on annexation of Texas, 119; total abolition, 120; peaceable withdrawal, 121;

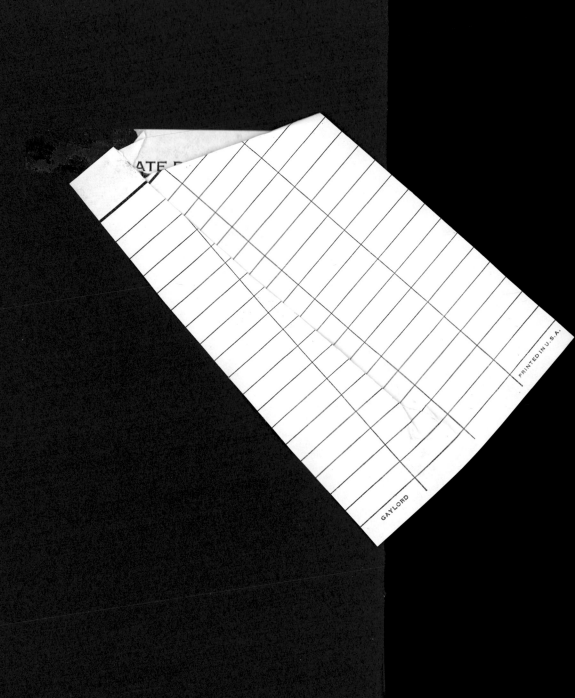

ATE D

PRINTED IN U. S. A.

GAYLORD